THE BALLAD OF
Sir Aldingar

THE BALLAD OF

Sir Aldingar

ITS ORIGIN AND ANALOGUES

BY

PAUL CHRISTOPHERSEN

OXFORD
AT THE CLARENDON PRESS
1952

Oxford University Press, Amen House, London E.C.4

GLASGOW NEW YORK TORONTO MELBOURNE WELLINGTON
BOMBAY CALCUTTA MADRAS KARACHI CAPE TOWN IBADAN

Geoffrey Cumberlege, Publisher to the University

PREFACE

THE draft of this book in its successive stages has accompanied me in my peregrinations during the past few years. It was begun in England, continued in Denmark, and completed here in Nigeria, where a distance of several thousand miles lends not only enchantment to the view but also a better perspective.

There is always a risk that between the writing and the printing of a book fresh literature on the subject will appear. I understand that a paper on 'The Lineage and Birth of Sir Aldingar' by Donald S. Taylor is about to be published in the *Journal of American Folklore*. For the sake of completeness I should perhaps also mention two articles on the historical basis of the Constance story which I have only recently seen: by R. M. Smith in the *JEGP* for October 1948 and by Margaret Schlauch in the *Philological Quarterly* for October 1950. They add nothing to my general conclusions.

A word of explanation about the ballad translations in the Appendix may not be inapposite. They are meant chiefly for readers whose knowledge of Scandinavian languages—if they have any—is insufficient to guide them through the intricacies of dialects. The English versions therefore follow the originals line for line without any attempt at rhyme. But the modern idiom would have been too glaringly inappropriate as a medium, and so an endeavour has been made, while preserving the closeness of the rendering, to give the language a ballad flavour.

I am obliged to Dr. C. Matras and Dr. Harry Andersen, both of the University of Copenhagen, for giving me their opinions on some troublesome passages in the Faroese and Icelandic versions, and to Mr. L. Pink, of the University Library, Cambridge, for help with the palaeographical analysis mentioned on p. 27.

I cannot conclude without recording my gratitude to the late Professor H. M. Chadwick and to Mrs. N. K. Chadwick for friendly encouragement. The interest in ballads that they inspired has been to me a source of abiding pleasure.

P. C.

UNIVERSITY COLLEGE, IBADAN
March 1952

CONTENTS

ABBREVIATIONS

Archiv	*Archiv für das Studium der neueren Sprachen und Literaturen.*
Arw.	A. I. Arwidsson, *Svenska Fornsånger.*
AS.	Anglo-Saxon.
DgF	*Danmarks gamle Folkeviser*, by S. Grundtvig, A. Olrik, and H. Grüner Nielsen.—Roman numerals after *DgF* indicate volumes, Arabic numerals individual ballads.
EETS	Early English Text Society.
ESt	*Englische Studien.*
JEGP	*Journal of English and Germanic Philology.*
ME.	Middle English.
MHG.	Middle High German.
Migne	J. P. Migne (ed.), *Patrologiæ Cursus Completus.*
Mon. Germ. Hist.	Monumenta Germaniæ Historica, ed. G. H. Pertz, &c.
NAGG	*Neues Archiv der Gesellschaft für ältere deutsche Geschichtskunde.*
NED	*New English Dictionary*, by Murray and others.
OHG.	Old High German.
ON.	Old Norse.
PMLA	*Publications of the Modern Language Association of America.*
SATF	Société des Anciens Textes Français.
ZfdA	*Zeitschrift für deutsches Altertum.*
ZfdPh	*Zeitschrift für deutsche Philologie.*
ZfrPh	*Zeitschrift für romanische Philologie.*

I

INTRODUCTION

§ 1. *Scope and Purpose of this Study*

THE ballad that has been selected for study in this book, Child's
Sir Aldingar and Grundtvig's *Ravengaard og Memering*, is in
none of its versions, on either side of the North Sea, an out-
standing example of the art of balladry. It is not a noble, stirring
poem. Far better ballads could have been chosen to exemplify
the highest peaks of literary achievement in the art—if that were
our aim, which it is not. The ballad has been chosen because of
its wide ramifications in Britain and Scandinavia. The history
of this ballad throws light not only on the origins of the genre
but, even more, on the vexed question of the relationship between British and Scandinavian ballads and on the equally vexed
question of the debt that balladry owes to romance.

A special occasion for bringing out just now a fresh study on
this already much-debated subject has been provided by a recent
controversy between Sir Edmund Chambers[1] and Professor
W. J. Entwistle.[2] Sir Edmund thinks it a 'gratuitous' assumption that the story of Gunhild as told by William of Malmesbury
should represent an early form of the ballad as we know it from
the Percy MS. The fallacy of this view has been well demonstrated by Professor Entwistle, and this book can sometimes do
little more than underline his argument. Nevertheless, another
gleaning of the field has here and there produced a few ears
of corn, as in the case of the names *Memering* and *Mimecan*,
where fresh evidence is added here to show the debt of the
Scandinavian versions to the early British ballad. The book itself
owes a great deal to predecessors in the field, especially to
Grundtvig and Child, without whose pioneer work it could not
have been written. It is also, to some extent, modelled on a series

---

[1] See his *English Literature at the Close of the Middle Ages*, p. 154.
[2] See his 'Sir Aldingar and the Date of English Ballads'.

of similar analyses of individual ballads and their origins,[1] whose findings it serves on the whole to corroborate.

§ 2. *Ballad Literature in General*

It is useful to begin by defining what one is talking about. The word *ballad* has a number of different meanings; it is sometimes employed loosely almost as a synonym for *song*, especially a song of a sentimental kind. In this essay its use is restricted to the meaning that is common among folk-ballad scholars. One could define a ballad, as Professor Gerould has done, simply by saying that it is 'a folk-song that tells a story'. *Folk-song* itself is a term of wider application, covering not only narrative songs but others that tell no story, in fact any song habitually sung by the people and preserved chiefly by oral tradition—whether or not it was originally composed by 'one of the people'. This latter consideration does not enter into the definition of a ballad or folk-song; it is linked with the question of origins, on which some light will perhaps be shed in the course of this study. Some scholars would include anonymity in the definition of a ballad. This, too, seems unnecessary. A long course of oral transmission will in most cases mean not only that the original author is forgotten, but that his product is so altered that it can hardly be called his any longer; it belongs to the people. It is the oral transmission and not the authorship itself that makes it a ballad.

A definition is not much use unless it is accompanied by examples. Much has indeed been written about the distinguishing characteristics of ballads, their impersonality and terseness, their preference for stock formulae, and so on; but the best way of illustrating their nature is no doubt Professor Ker's in his paper 'On the History of the Ballads': 'In spite of Socrates and his logic we may venture to say, in answer to the question "What is a ballad?"—"A ballad is *The Milldams of Binnorie* and *Sir Patrick Spens* and *The Douglas Tragedy* and *Lord Randal* and *Child Maurice*, and things of that sort".'

[1] Olrik, 'Riboldsvisen'; Liestøl, 'Dei tvo Systar'; and Taylor, '*Edward*' and '*Sven i Rosengård*'.

Ballads in this sense are not an isolated phenomenon. They exist, or are known to have existed, all over Europe and in parts of Asia and America.[1] The unity or kinship of ballads from this vast area is established by the recurrence of the same or similar subjects, the same sort of situations, the same way of handling a theme, the same habit of repetition and fondness for stock phrases. Besides these obvious similarities there are also important differences. Lyrical qualities enter into many ballads, but in proportions varying from country to country. 'There are some, such as Lithuania, which have no purely narrative ballads, but a shading of lyric into narrative as subtle as the spectrum; in other countries, such as Spain and Portugal, the ballad is formally marked off from the lyric' (Entwistle, p. 18). There are also differences as regards metrical form; in many countries, for example in Spain, ballads are not divided into stanzas, but run on continuously from beginning to end. According to Professor Entwistle (pp. 21 ff.), it is possible, chiefly on the basis of metre and technique, to distinguish several ballad areas in Europe. In the north-west there is a Teutonic region, consisting of Britain, Scandinavia, and Germany, and distinguished, among other things, by the stanzaic form of the ballads.[2] France, although primarily a member of the Romance group in the south-west, shares certain characteristics, to some extent the metrical form, with the Teutonic group. The other European ballad areas, in the south-east and in Russia, will not concern us in this study.

§ 3. *Ballad History*

The 'communal' theory of ballad origins—the theory which, in its extreme form, would explain ballads as due not to individual authors but to the whole community at festive gatherings, 'the dancing throng'—should undoubtedly be taken with

---

[1] See Entwistle, *European Balladry, passim.*

[2] There are two main types of ballad stanza; one is a four-beat rhymed (assonated) distich and the other a quatrain rhyming (assonating) *abcb.* See, for example, Gerould, *The Ballad of Tradition*, pp. 117–30. A fuller account is given in Hendren, *A Study of Ballad Rhythm*, chs. 4–7.

many grains of salt.[1] Nevertheless, the theory has at least served
to emphasize what is unquestionably a fact: ballads are in large
measure due to social conditions; they are the result of a certain
type of civilization—whatever the origin of each particular
ballad. This explains why ballads do not coincide in time in all
countries, why in some parts of Europe ballad-making is a dead
or dying art, while in other countries it is still a living habit. The
theory also makes it plain that there need be no direct connexion
between the various regional groups of ballads; they may have
arisen independently. But such is not the case within each
region. The similarity of metrical form between, for example,
the ballads of Britain and Scandinavia cannot be a mere coincidence; nor can it have come about through any similarity in
the social structure of the two countries. Ballads, like other
forms of art, are subject to external influences, and just as
themes often wander from country to country, so on occasion do
metrical forms.

The origin of ballads everywhere and at all times is a vast and
complicated problem and has not been made clearer by those
communalists who have talked, in the same breath, of the rise of
ballads and the origin of poetry, as if the two were necessarily
one and the same thing. We are on safer ground if we confine
our attention to one concrete type of ballad of a fairly well-
defined structure, as for example the Teutonic type. Here the
rise seems to have taken place within historical times, and we
may hope to throw light on it by the ordinary methods of historical and philological research.

The problem can be approached in two different ways. Either
one can attempt to find early evidence for the genre as such, first
of all for the rise of the ballad metre, or one can examine the
origin and development of individual ballads which go back to
a relatively remote antiquity. It is the latter method that has
been adopted in the present study, which is concerned mainly

[1] The latest discussion of the issue between communalists and indi-
vidualists is in Hodgart, *The Ballads*, pp. 152–63, and Wells, *The Ballad
Tree*, pp. 193–205.

with the history of one particular ballad as far back as it can be traced. Nevertheless, before taking up our special investigation, it may be wise to look for a moment at what is known about the early history of ballads in north-west Europe. Very little in point of fact, is established beyond a doubt. The evidence has been marshalled and discussed by others[1] and will not be rehearsed here in detail, but one or two points deserve mention.

We know that the four-beat rhymed couplet was in use in England in the twelfth century and perhaps as early as the eleventh: this is testified by a fragment of four lines quoted in the *Liber Eliensis* and attributed by the chronicler to King Canute.[2] It is doubtful if the verse form goes farther back than that in England, although attempts have been made to prove it to be indigenous.[3] In Scandinavia the ballad couplet is evidenced from *c.* 1200 onwards, and the four-lined stanza a little later;[4] in Germany no early examples have survived.[5]

The existence of the ballad stanza at an early date does not, of course, in itself constitute proof that narrative ballads in our sense of the word were in existence. Although the Canute song has been hailed as a genuine ballad, the few lines that have been preserved contain no indication of what the rest of the song was like, and we have no right to conclude that it was narrative.

Many scholars have sought the origin of the Teutonic type of ballad in France. There is no extant early poetry in France of which we can say with certainty that it is folk-poetry; in all the texts that have come down to us we feel the influence of courtly literature. Nearest to our ballads are the so-called *chansons d'histoire*, short narrative songs with refrains; but in spite of

---

[1] For British ballads see Bryant, *A History of Balladry*, ch. ii; and esp. Gerould, op. cit., ch. viii. For Scandinavian ballads see Steenstrup, 'De danske Folkevisers ældste Tid', and Larsen, *Fire danske Viser*. On the problem in general see Verrier, *Le Vers français*, vol. iii, chs. 38 and 48, and the same author's 'Den firliniede Folkevisestrofe'.

[2] See Bryant, pp. 50–55, and Gerould, pp. 195–6.

[3] Especially by J. W. Rankin, *PMLA*, vol. xxxvi (1921), pp. 401 ff. Cf. Gerould, pp. 218 ff.

[4] See Steenstrup, pp. 233 ff.; and Verrier, *Vers*, p. 215, and 'Den f. F.', pp. 4 ff.

[5] Verrier, *Vers*, pp. 73–74.

striking similarities these *chansons* seem too polished and sophisticated to have served as models for popular ballads. Although,
however, no genuine French folk-poetry has survived, we seem
to see it reflected in the courtly songs that have come down to us.
The ballad cannot be descended from the *chanson d'histoire* itself, but it may go back to the primitive folk-song on which the
chanson appears to rest. There is ground for believing that the
folk-ballad as we know it from Britain and Scandinavia took its
rise in an early French dance song, the *carole*,[1] which made its
way from France to the neighbouring countries and was there
fitted to texts of a more narrative kind. France, for centuries the
cradle of European modes and manners, appears to have also
bequeathed this new dance fashion to her neighbours. In the
north the *carole* was introduced in the twelfth century by Scan-
dinavians who had studied in France; to England it was presumably brought by the Normans, before or after the Conquest.
Though French, and perhaps also Anglo-Norman, society soon
substituted more polished songs, the primitive *carole* continued
its existence among Scandinavian gentry and in Saxon circles in
England. In the latter country the song seems in large measure
to have lost its connexion with dancing, as witness the absence of
refrains with the greater part of the extant British ballads.

One piece of evidence has received several different interpreta-
tions since its discovery. It is the story of the Cursed Dancers,
one of the most widely circulated legends of the Middle Ages,[2]
relating an event which is supposed to have happened at
Kölbigk, in the Duchy of Anhalt north of Saxony, early in the
eleventh century. Certain revellers outside a church were cursed
by the priest and as a result had to go on dancing round the
church for a whole year. In one of the early versions of this story,
purporting to be the account of one of the dancers named Theodoric, we find a few lines which he and his companions are said

---

[1] This view has been expressed, for example, by Jeanroy, *Origines de la
poésie lyrique en France*; by Ker, 'On the Danish Ballads'; and by Verrier,
'Bele Aiglentine et Petite Christine'.
[2] A detailed account of its ramifications is given by E. Schröder, 'Die
Tänzer von Kölbigk'. See also G. Paris, 'Les Danseurs maudits'.

to have sung whilst dancing. Unfortunately the author of the account, which is in Latin, turns the lines into Latin verse. Telling the story in the first person, he says:

Ductor furoris nostri alludens fatale carmen orditur Gerlevus:
Equitabat Bovo per silvam frondosam,
Ducebat sibi Merswinden formosam.
Quid stamus? Cur non imus?

The last line is of course the refrain. The author very aptly remarks, a little later in the account,

Semper vero insultabat nostre pene cantilene regressus:
Quid stamus? Cur non imus?
qui nec restare nec circulum nostrum mutare potuimus.

Now these lines are strikingly like the beginning of a folk-ballad. It is precisely this sort of opening that a ballad would use, jumping into the middle of a situation without any explanation. The metre, too, reminds one of a common folk-ballad type, the two-lined four-beat stanza followed by a refrain. Although we do not know how the story went on, we have reason to believe that the complete song was like the folk-ballads that have come down to us in the vernacular.

The importance of this snatch lies in the fact that it seems to go farther back than any other known ballad, and the discussion that it has provoked is due to our ignorance regarding the language in which the song was originally composed. It seems that there are three possibilities. It may have been Old Saxon. At first sight that would appear the natural view to take, seeing that the dancers were Saxons and, according to the account, sang the song themselves. On the other hand, the version of the story in which the song appears is not of German origin. It is fairly certain that it was at least revised by a Frenchman, and there is also some evidence for a later revision in England. The possibility therefore remains that the song may have been inserted during one of these revisions.

The evidence for a Saxon or English provenance of the song

has been carefully examined by Verrier,[1] who arrives at the result that the song could not have been composed in either of those languages. If his argument, which is too long and detailed to be summarized here, is correct, only the third possibility remains: the song must be of French origin. Moreover, Verrier produces evidence to show that the song was probably inserted during a revision that the story underwent in France in the twelfth century. The oldest manuscript that we possess of this version of the Cursed Dancers is in the handwriting of Orderic Vitalis, the well-known monk of St. Évroul, whose literary activity falls within the years 1124–42. His handiwork is noticeable in the highly elaborate style in which the account is couched, and the song seems to have been inserted by him to heighten the rhetorical effect. It was no doubt an ordinary dance song which Orderic happened to have heard; we know that he was interested in popular traditions.[2]

Unlike the two other countries in question, England and Saxony, France is able to produce a close analogy to the song of the Cursed Dancers. In an early-thirteenth-century romance, *Guillaume de Dole* by Jean Renart, a large number of songs and refrains are woven into the tale, put into the mouths of the characters. One of these songs is strikingly like the one we have been discussing:

> ll. 2380–2: Renaus et s'amie chevauche par un pré;
> Tote nuit chevauche jusqu'au jor cler.
> Ja n'avrai mès joie de vos amer.

It is the same kind of metrical pattern and very much the same sort of opening. Here, too, unfortunately, only one stanza is

---

[1] Verrier, 'La Plus Vieille Citation de Carole'. See also the same author's *Le Vers français*, vol. iii, pp. 75 ff.

[2] Verrier's theory has been contested by Schröder, 'Das Tanzlied von Kölbigk', and by Meier, 'Das Tanzlied der Tänzer von Kölbigk'. I do not consider that the arguments of either of these scholars militate against a French origin of the song. To argue from the form of the names (*Mersint* or *Merswind*, &c.) is to beg the question, since we cannot be sure that they were originally part of the song. One or both of the characters may have been rechristened when the song was adapted to suit the situation and the names in the Kölbigk legend.

quoted, and the song is not known from elsewhere. It must go back at least to the latter half of the twelfth century.

It seems, then, if Verrier is right, that in both these songs, in 'Renaus et s'amie' and in 'Equitabat Bovo', we have examples of that early type of French song which has almost vanished in the mother country, but which has been perpetuated in the ballads of Britain and Scandinavia.

II

ACCOUNT OF THE VERSIONS

§ 4. *The British Versions*[1]

OUR ballad, Child's No. 59 (*Sir Aldingar*), is extant in three British versions, which Child calls A, B, and C. Version A is English, and B is Scottish. C, which is also Scottish, is only a fragment and so mutilated that it is of no use to us here.

Version A goes back to the Percy MS., which is in a hand of about 1650. The story is as follows: Sir Aldingar, King Harry's steward, after a vain attempt to seduce Queen Elinor, planned to take revenge. When one day a blind and lame leper came to the king's gate, Sir Aldingar laid him in the queen's bed and fetched the king to see this alleged proof of the queen's infidelity. The king went forthwith to see the queen, and she, on hearing the accusation, asked for a knight to fight on her behalf against Sir Aldingar. The king granted her request: if at the end of forty days she had not found a champion, she was to be burnt. The queen sent a messenger to the south, but he met with no success. She then sent a messenger to the east, and one day he came upon a little child, who told him to return to the queen and remind her of a dream she had had in which a griffin had tried to carry off first her crown and kirtle of gold and then herself, and would have succeeded but for a little hawk which killed the griffin. The messenger rode back and told the queen the glad tidings, and she rewarded him richly. Forty days went by, but no champion appeared. Arrangements had already been made for the execution, and the queen had been put in a tun which was to be set alight, when they spied a little man who came riding from the east. He rode up to the queen and offered himself as her champion. Sir Aldingar thought but little of his opponent, and the two exchanged some contemptuous remarks. The fight began, and with a single blow the dwarf severed Sir Aldingar's

[1] For the texts see the Appendix. No tunes have been recorded.

legs at the knee. Aldingar straightway called for a priest to shrive
him before he should die, and he confessed that the accusation
was false and asked the queen's forgiveness. The king and queen
were reunited, and the leper was made steward instead of Sir
Aldingar.

The Scottish version is found in Scott's Minstrelsy under the
title *Sir Hugh le Blond*.[1] It was written down, says Scott, from
the recitation of an old woman, long in the service of the Arbuthnot family. Neither the king's nor the queen's name is
mentioned: the steward is called Rodingham. The ballad opens
with an interview between him and the queen, in which he tries
to seduce her but is repulsed. In revenge he takes a leper whom
he finds by the roadside, gets him intoxicated, and lays him in
the queen's bed. He then fetches the king, who after seeing the
leper tells the queen that she is to be burnt at the stake; he may
withdraw his words, however, if she can find a Christian man to
fight as her champion against Rodingham. 'Alas,' she says, 'there
is not a man in all Scotland will fight with him for me.' She
sends out messengers to south, east, and west, but without avail.
She then sends messengers to the north, and there they meet
Sir Hugh le Blond, who offers to fight for the queen. The day
appointed for the combat comes, but there is no sign of her
champion. The fire is already lit, and the queen has given up all
hope, when Sir Hugh suddenly arrives. He wins the battle by
stabbing his opponent to the heart. Before Rodingham dies,
Sir Hugh makes him confess his treachery. The queen is taken
into favour again, and Sir Hugh is rewarded by rich gifts of
land: 'If Arbattle is not enough, To it we'll Fordoun join.'

---

[1] Another copy of *Sir Hugh le Blond* was printed in *Twentieth* (!) *Century
Verse*, June–July 1937. Apart from *ye* for *you* in st. 5, l. 3, this copy is
word for word and stanza for stanza the same as Scott's; even differences in
spelling are negligible. One of the editors, Mr. F. S. Beecroft, informs me
that he can no longer recall with certainty where he found the ballad, but he
believes that he saw it written on the fly-leaf of a late-eighteenth-century
chap-book in the British Museum. There is a possibility, therefore, that the
Scottish tradition was not entirely oral; the almost complete identity between
the two copies points to a literary prototype. As we shall see later (p. 158),
there is some reason for assuming a partially independent Scottish tradition.

§ 5. *The Scandinavian Versions*[1]

The Scandinavian ballad, Grundtvig's No. 13 (*Ravengaard og Memering*), exists in nine complete Danish versions and two fragments, all from Jutland, and in two Faroese and one Icelandic version. We have evidence, also, of the former existence of a Norwegian version; it is now lost, but we possess a fairly detailed summary of the action. I follow Grundtvig's system of denoting the versions: A, B, C, G, H, I, K, L, M being the Danish versions, D and E the Faroese, and F the Icelandic version. The two Danish fragments are termed N and O, and the Norwegian version I call P.

Version A is the earliest recorded Scandinavian version. It goes back to the Karen Brahe Folio, which dates from about 1550. The action is as follows: Lady Gunder dwells at Spire, and the greatest men from all corners of the earth sue for her hand, but she gives it to Duke Henrik of Slesvig and Brunswick. When, one day, he has to go to the wars, he enjoins Ravengaard to keep good watch over his lands, but above all to take care of Gunder. As soon as the duke is away, Ravengaard goes to 'the queen', as the ballad calls her, and demands the sword Adelring, which is in her keeping. She refuses, and in retaliation he threatens to slander her to the duke when he comes home. Ravengaard is the first to receive the duke on his return, and when Henrik inquires about his lands and his wife, Ravengaard replies that all is well, save that Gunder has behaved amiss. Henrik refuses to believe it, but Ravengaard asserts that he has seen with his own eyes the archbishop lying with Gunder. Henrik beats her, and nobody dares to intercede except two ladies-in-waiting; on their entreaty he promises her a trial by battle. She goes to the hall where the warriors sit drinking. They all arise when she enters; but when she asks, 'Is anyone willing to fight for a woman?' everybody remains silent save Memering, who says, 'For fifteen years I served in your father's court, but never did I see you so woe-

---

[1] For the texts see the Appendix. Seven tunes have been recorded in Denmark within the last hundred years (see *DgF* xi), but they cannot be utilized for this study owing to the lack of tunes elsewhere.

begone. Your father gave many costly gifts, but to Ravengaard
he gave most of all; yet he has forsaken you first of all. My
place was always at the end where no good gifts came; I will
fight for you now if you will give me the sword Adelring.' She
promises him that. The account of the combat is somewhat confused, but in the end Memering strikes off Ravengaard's head.
Gunder asks Henrik, 'Will you now believe that Ravengaard's
accusation was false?' He strokes her cheek in answer and asks
her forgiveness. Memering comes staggering home with bloody
limbs, but Gunder promises to heal his wounds and clothe him
in scarlet all his days.

  The remaining eight Danish versions, which are all modern,
have many features in common, while they differ from A in
certain essential points. The names of the characters are the
same except for minor variations (see ch. vi), but the reason for
Ravengaard's treachery is rejected love, and Henrik and Gunhild are not reconciled. Memering and Gunhild ride away together, except in H, where Gunhild wishes to stay and revenge
herself on Henrik. Memering and Ravengaard are mentioned in
several of the versions[1] as the little and the big one, respectively.

  Our knowledge of the Norwegian version is derived from some
remarks by a late-eighteenth-century writer, Hans Strøm, who
mentions the ballad as still in existence, although dying out, on
the island of Rundø, and he then proceeds to summarize it. It
appears that the beginning was missing: the ballad opens with
Gunhild's going to the hall to ask if any warrior dares to fight
for a woman against a big champion named Ronnegaar. Everyone is silent except little Mimmer-Tand. Gunhild says contemptuously that he had better stay at home and tend his sheep,
but that does not deter him. He wins the battle, cuts off Ronnegaar's head, ties it to his saddle-bow and brings it home in
triumph. The ballad ends with a reference to a marriage at Spire.

  [1] B 22, C 31–32, and I 22. In G 21 the line has become corrupted; cf.
B 22 and I 22. There may also be a reference to the difference in size between the two opponents in the obscure and obviously corrupt line 'Nu har
jeg vunden hende baade liden og stor' (G 23, I 24). Memering's smallness
is also mentioned in H 20, K 32, M 21, D 27–28, E 25, and P.

The Icelandic version of the ballad, Grundtvig's F, dates from a seventeenth-century manuscript. It differs in several respects from the story as known from the British and Danish versions. Rögnvald, the steward, makes love to Queen Gunhild, is rebuffed, and takes revenge by impugning her virtue to King Theodoric (Þiðrik) on his return. The king beats her; and nobody dares to plead for her save his two children, who ask him to let Gunhild carry iron and tread on steel to test her virtue. Her innocence is proved, and Rögnvald goes to hell while Gunhild ascends to heaven.

Both the Faroese versions were written down in the early part of last century. One of them, D, is partly in Danish, some of the stanzas being in that language and some in Faroese (see the Appendix): even in the latter stanzas one notices a strong Danish influence on the style. The Faroese tradition seems altogether of a mixed nature. Both versions agree with the Icelandic version in having an ordeal instead of a trial by battle. Yet Memering occurs, in D with absolutely no purpose at all, while in E he is given the task of helping Gunhild to carry out the ordeal. That the figure is due to Danish influence is shown by the fact that the stanzas in D in which he appears are in Danish (cf. § 29). Gunhild's husband is King Theodoric (Tiðrik), as in the Icelandic version; her accuser is called Roysning or Roysningur.

§ 6. *Preliminary Classification*

British Versions:	A	c. 1650	English
	B	c. 1800	Scottish
	C (fragment)	19th c.	
Scandinavian:	A	c. 1550	
	B	19th c.	Danish (Jutland)
	C	,,	
	D	,,	Faroese
	E	,,	
	F	17th c.	Icelandic

G	19th c.	
H	,,	
I	,,	
K	,,	Danish (Jutland)
L	,,	
M	,,	
N (fragment)	,,	
O ,,	,,	
P	18th c.	Norwegian

Our ballad versions can be grouped in various ways. The Faroese-Icelandic versions stand apart by having an ordeal instead of a single combat. Other evidence of a separate Faroese-Icelandic tradition is the name of Gunhild's husband, which is Theodoric (Tiðrik, Þiðrik) as opposed to Danish Henrik and English Harry. We may have further proof of a separate tradition in the Faroese and Icelandic names for the accuser, Roysning(ur) and Rögnvald, which differ considerably from the Norwegian and Danish forms (cf. § 34). Finally, the Faroese and Icelandic versions alone have the incident of the king's two children interceding for Gunhild, though there may be a reminiscence of that in Danish A, where we are told that two ladies-in-waiting plead for mercy on Gunhild's behalf.

In the 'trial by battle' group the Scottish version alone has a fight between two normal-sized human beings. In all other versions in this group the fight is between a dwarf and a giant. It is true that in Danish A and L there is no specific mention of size (cf. p. 13 n.); but Gunhild's champion is in all the Danish versions known as Memering, a character who, as we shall see later (§ 29), figures elsewhere in Danish balladry as a person of puny physique. In the English version, Gunhild's champion is without doubt a supernatural being; his name is not mentioned.

Where the accusation against Gunhild is concerned, the line of division is a different one. The English and Scottish versions form a group apart by having the trait of the leper in the bed, which is found in no Scandinavian version. Danish A and C mention an archbishop as Gunhild's lover; the same feature occurs in D and F, while E says that he is 'the bishop's brother'. E and F say that there are also other lovers. The rest of the Danish versions—apart from H, which merely calls Gunhild a 'whore'—talk of her as 'sparing neither monk nor priest'.

A few more points may be noted. The place-name Spire occurs in all the main divisions of Scandinavian versions: Danish, Norwegian, Faroese, and Icelandic (cf. § 20). British A mentions no place-name, while in B the action is set in Scotland. The name Gunhild in varying forms is found in all the Scandinavian versions, but in no British. Henrik's beating of his wife is peculiar to Scandinavia, as is also the feature that Henrik departs for the war at the beginning of the ballad.

III

THE BRITISH TRADITION

§ 7. *Percy's and Scott's Evidence*

THOUGH infidelity stories are extremely common in medieval literature, we do not find many traces of the story of Gunhild's accusation and trial outside the ballads just mentioned. It will be our task in this chapter to examine such traces as there are in Britain and to discuss their relation to the ballad.

Bishop Percy says in the introduction to his edition of *Sir Aldingar*:[1] 'It has been suggested to the Editor that the author of this poem seems to have had in his eye the story of Gunhilda, who is sometimes called Eleanor, and was married to the Emperor (here called King) Henry.' I have not found elsewhere that Gunhild, wife of King (later the Emperor) Henry III, was ever called Eleanor. Whoever introduced the name Eleanor into our ballad (for it is almost certainly a later addition) is more likely to have been thinking of one of the English queens of that name, presumably Eleanor of Aquitaine, Henry II's wife, who figures elsewhere in English balladry (Child No. 156) as a woman of doubtful virtue. It is interesting, however, that the name Gunhild should have been suggested to Percy at all: one would like to know how and by whom, since the name does not occur in either of the British versions of the ballad. Many hundred years earlier, in the twelfth, thirteenth, and fourteenth centuries, we have evidence of a widely known story about Queen[2] Gunhild, which in many ways tallies with what our ballads say. Was this story still a living tradition in the eighteenth century? Or was the suggestion based only on an antiquarian knowledge of the past?

Sir Walter Scott, who believed *Sir Hugh le Blond* to be the original of the English ballad, tried in vain to find a Scottish queen to whom the story might apply. He tells us that the

[1] *Reliques of Ancient English Poetry*, Ser. II, bk. i, No. 9.
[2] Henry III did not succeed to the imperial throne till after Gunhild's death; cf. p. 95.

tradition upon which the ballad is founded was still universally current in his day in the Mearns,[1] but what exactly he means by that I do not know, since he does not amplify the statement. He also refers to a tradition (or is it the same one?) in the Arbuthnot family, which claimed descent from Sir Hugh le Blond, and in whose possession a sword, supposed to have been Sir Hugh's, was kept for a long time. The ballad, according to Scott, was taken down from the recitation of an old woman in the service of that family,[2] and the place-names in the last stanza support this tradition: 'Arbattle is the ancient name of the barony of Arbuthnot. Fordun has long been the patrimony of the same family' (Scott, p. 366). There was actually a Sir Hugh of Arbuthnot in the thirteenth century, and Scott points out that about the year 1242 Mary, wife of Alexander II, was 'somewhat implicated in a dark story concerning the murder of Patrick, Earl of Athole'. Scott thinks it 'not impossible that some share taken in it by this Sir Hugh de Arbuthnot may have given a slight foundation for the tradition of the country'. All this, however, is extremely slender and doubtful evidence. Moreover, even if we could prove for certain that Sir Hugh was mixed up in the affair, that event could never have been the origin of more than the specific Scottish tradition, for the story as such can be traced much farther back elsewhere. Scott also believes that he has seen both the name (i.e. *Aldingar* or *Rodingham*) and the story in an ancient prose chronicle; unfortunately he is unable to give any reference in support of his belief, but the chronicle may very well have been one of those mentioned in the following pages.

§ 8. *William of Malmesbury and Matthew Paris*

The earliest English reference to our story that I know is in William of Malmesbury's *De Gestis Regum Anglorum*. He says:[3]

For the rest, as I began to say, Hardicanute gave his sister Gunhild, Canute's daughter by Emma, a girl of extraordinary beauty, for whom

[1] *Minstrelsy of the Scottish Border*, p. 359.
[2] Cf., however, p. 11 n.
[3] Vol. i, pp. 229–30 (as far as I can see, no date is given; but William says that Hardicanute ruled from 1040 to 1042, so the event must have happened

in her father's lifetime many wooers had sighed in vain, to Henry, the German Emperor, in marriage. The wedding procession was splendid, and is even in the present century the theme of a popular song, when this greatly renowned maiden was conducted to the ship. All the great men of England were there, and contributed to the expense all that the public purse and the royal treasury contained. Arriving at her husband's residence, she lived with him for a long time as his wife. Finally, charged with adultery, and all her other retainers having fled, seized with fear, she appointed as her champion against the accuser, who was a man of gigantic stature, a small boy, the keeper of her starling,[1] whom she had brought with her from England. And then, when the duel had begun, by a miracle of God the defamer was hamstrung. Rejoicing at this unexpected victory, Gunhild separated from her husband; nor could she ever afterwards by threats or blandishments be induced to share his bed, but taking the veil she passed the rest of her life peacefully in the service of God.

William of Malmesbury's account has been frequently used by later historians. It is quoted, for example, by Vincent of

some time within that period): 'Ceterum, ut dicere coeperam, Hardecnutus Gunhildam sororem suam, Cnutonis ex Emma filiam, spectatissimae speciei puellam, a multis procis tempore patris suspiratam nec impetratam, Henrico imperatori Alemannorum nuptum misit. Celebris illa pompa nuptialis fuit, et nostro adhuc seculo etiam in triviis cantitata, dum tanti nominis virgo ad navem duceretur; stipantibus omnibus Angliae proceribus, et in expensas conferentibus quicquid absconderat vel marsupium publicum vel aerarium regium. Ita ad sponsum perveniens, multo tempore foedus conjugale fovit: postremo, adulterii accusata, puerulum quendam sturni sui alumpnum, quem secum ex Anglia duxerat, delatori, giganteae molis homini, ad mono-machiam apposuit, ceteris clientibus inerti timore refugientibus. Itaque, conserto duello, per miraculum Dei insimulator succiso poplite enervatur. Gunnildis, insperato triumpho tripudians, viro repudium dedit; nec ultra minis aut delinimentis adduci potuit ut thalamo illius consentiret, sed velum sanctimonialium suscipiens, in Dei servitio placido consenuit otio.'

[1] The Latin phrase *sturni sui alumpnum* has given rise to some speculation. Later chroniclers, basing their accounts on William of Malmesbury's, have often hesitated at this phrase. Henry of Silegrave has 'puerum suum quem aluerat et ex Anglia duxerat'. Matthew Paris's interpretation is very similar. Ralph Niger on the other hand, keeps the original wording: 'puerculum quendam sturni sui alumnum'. Savile, the sixteenth-century scholar and editor, reads *fratris* for *sturni*, but how two such entirely different words could have come to be confused I cannot see. As the phrase stands, it can only have one meaning. Stubbs suggests that Gunhild may have had a pet starling, of which the boy was the keeper. Tame starlings were not uncommon in the Middle Ages; see, for example, the story of Branwen in *The Mabinogion*, vol. i, p. 58, where Branwen rears a starling and teaches it to speak.

Beauvais in his *Speculum Historiale*, bk. 25, ch. 17. Others, such as Ralph Niger, Henry of Silegrave, and John Brompton (see § 10), reproduce the account in a slightly changed form as their own work. The story is also found, with various additions, in Matthew Paris's *Chronica Majora*:[1]

At the same time, Hardicanute, King of the English, gave his sister Gunnild, King Canute and Queen Emma's daughter, a girl of remarkable beauty, to Henry, the Roman Emperor, in marriage. In Canute's time, however, this girl, because of her incomparable charm, had been sought in marriage by many of the nobility, but in vain. The wedding procession was so splendid, because the king, her brother, and nearly all the inhabitants of the realm lavished treasures of gold and silver, and mantles and precious stones and costly horses to such a degree that even today, at banquets and in inns, minstrels and harpists are hardly able to extol this wedding festival adequately in play and song. They lived long together in marriage, but at last

---

[1] Vol. i, pp. 514–15 (the first three words refer to the preceding paragraph, which is headed: Anno gratiae MXLI): 'Per idem tempus rex Anglorum Hardecnutus, Gunnildam, sororem suam ex Cnutone rege et Emma regina generatam, ingentis pulchritudinis puellam, Henrico imperatori Romano destinavit matrimonio copulandam. Erat autem haec virgo temporibus Cnutonis regis propter ejus incomparabilem decorem a multis viris nobilibus petita, sed non impetrata. Unde nunc adeo celebris fuit illa nuptialis pompa, quod rex frater ejus et omnes fere habitatores regni thesauros auri et argenti cum palliis, gemmis, et equis pretiosis ita effuderunt, quod usque in hodiernum diem in conviviis et tabernis histriones et fidicines instrumentis et canticis hanc pompam digne efferre non sufficiunt nuptialem. Stetit autem inter eos multo tempore foedus conjugale. Sed novissime a discordiae animatoribus Gunnilda est apud imperatorem de crimine adulterii accusata. Oportebat ergo juxta consuetudinem regionis, ut Gunnilda per duellum contra accusatorem, giganteae immensitatis hominem, famam suae puritatis redimeret. Sed ex omnibus militibus vel ministris nec unus fuit inventus, qui cum illa ab Anglia venerant, qui auderet cum *bellatore* (a) congredi, propter horrendam corporis ejus deformitatem *et immensitatem* (b). Cumque Gunnildae angustiae essent undique, puer quidam, quem ab Anglia secum adduxerat, et in ejus thalamo educatus fuerat, qui nanus erat et propter corporis parvitatem Mimecan dicebatur, duellum pro domina, quam per mendacium noverat accusatam, suscepit; et conserto proelio cum gigante, per miraculum Dei succiso delatoris poplite, ipsum enervavit. Quo ruente in terram, Mimecanus caput ejus praescidit, et illud suae dominae praesentavit. Tunc imperatrix, ex insperato gaudens effecta triumpho, imperatori repudium fecit, nec ultra minis aut blanditiis vinci potuit, ut thorum ejus ascendere consentiret.' (a) Later correction in the Corpus MS. for orig. *delatore*; (b) addition in the Corpus MS. Both these entries are presumably in Matthew Paris's own hand; see below.

scandal-mongers hinted to the emperor that Gunnild was guilty of adultery. According to the custom of the country, Gunnild had to redeem her reputation by a duel with the accuser, a man of gigantic bulk. But of all the soldiers and servants who had come with her from England not one could be found who dared to meet the warrior in the lists, because of the dreadful deformity and bulk of his body. But just when Gunnild found herself in this extreme distress, a certain boy, who had come with her from England and had grown up in her bower, and who was a dwarf and was called Mimecan because of the smallness of his body, undertook to fight for his mistress, whom he knew to be falsely accused. And when the combat with the giant had begun, he managed by a miracle of God to hamstring the defamer and thus to paralyse him. When he tumbled to the ground, Mimecan cut off his head and presented it to his mistress. Happy at this unexpected victory, the empress repudiated the emperor and could not be persuaded by threats or blandishments to share his bed.

Several other chronicles, for example Roger of Wendover's *Flores Historiarum* and Richard of Cirencester's *Speculum Historiale*, contain the story of Gunhild in almost the identical form in which Matthew Paris has it. This is due to the fact that all these accounts, including Matthew Paris's, go back to a common source, a chronicle compiled in the monastery of St. Albans, which in its turn must have borrowed the Gunhild story from William of Malmesbury. We cannot here enter into the complicated question of the authorship of this original compilation, on which Roger of Wendover and Matthew Paris based their chronicles.[1] Dr. Luard believes the author to have been a certain John de Cella, who was abbot of St. Albans from 1195 to 1214. John's work, extending to 1188, was taken up by Roger of Wendover, who enlarged and altered it and carried it down to 1235. Matthew Paris had the original chronicle as well as Wendover's continuation copied out, correcting it with his own hand and introducing alterations and additional matter.[2] In Dr.

---

[1] Richard of Cirencester's version of the Gunhild story appears to have been transcribed from Roger of Wendover, except for the last sentence, which has been taken from William of Malmesbury.

[2] Two such corrections have been noted on p. 20 n. They occur neither in Roger of Wendover nor in Richard of Cirencester.

Luard's view, our passage must have formed part of John de
Cella's compilation, which was probably written during his
abbacy, but Professor Jenkins[1] tentatively advances the theory
that only the part from 1154 to 1188 is due to John de Cella,
while the preceding portions are of earlier date. The part in which
our particular passage occurs he would assign to the abbacy of
Geoffrey (1119–46) or to that of Ralph (1146–51).

It is obvious that the St. Albans account is based principally on
William of Malmesbury's. Not only is the general outline of the
story the same, but entire sentences have been taken over almost
word for word. The main difference resides in the fact that the
St. Albans story is somewhat fuller. One of the reasons for this
is that its style is less terse. It is significant that when the St.
Albans author takes over a whole sentence from William he
usually puts in a little extra padding. Although some of the
differences in matter may go back to a hypothetical extra source,
others may be explained as products of the author's own imagination. Thus, William talks of the riches lavished on the
wedding festivities: the St. Albans author amplifies this and talks
of *palliis, gemmis, et equis pretiosis*. Similarly, William's remark
that the splendour of the wedding was still being sung in the
streets has become: 'usque in hodiernum diem in conviviis et
tabernis histriones et fidicines instrumentis et canticis hanc
pompam digne efferre non sufficiunt nuptialem'. Further, the
St. Albans author inserts the remark that the duel was to take
place *juxta consuetudinem regionis*: but this may very well be an
observation of his own.[2]

There are two additions, however, which we can conclude
must have been taken from some source other than William of
Malmesbury. First the name Mimecan. This name is found in
two other English chronicles, Ralph de Diceto's and John
Brompton's (see §§ 9 and 10), but both of these appear to be in-

---

[1] *The Monastic Chronicler and the Early School of St. Albans.*

[2] It is uncertain whether trial by battle was known in Britain before
1066; see G. Neilson, *Trial by Combat* (Glasgow, 1890), pt. ii. The above
remark would seem to indicate that the author regarded it as something
rare and strange. Cf. also pp. 115–16.

dependent of the St. Albans chronicle. The name cannot, therefore, have been invented by the St. Albans chronicler; it must
have come from some other source, ultimately the same as that
from which Ralph de Diceto and John Brompton derived their
knowledge. Another new feature is the information that Mimecan, after having stretched his opponent to the ground, cut off
his head and presented it to the queen. This is a common feature
in combats of this kind as narrated in popular literature. It is
found in the Scandinavian versions C and P of our ballad and in
the Middle English romances of *Octavian* (see § 17) and *Libeaus
Desconus* (cf. p. 52, n. 3); in the folk-tale of *Jack the Giant-Killer*
it is combined with the feature of cutting off the legs at the knee
(see p. 52). The passage in question can therefore scarcely be a
mere invention of the St. Albans author.

It is unfortunate that we know nothing about the source or
sources of these additions. The whole question becomes even
more involved when we consider a peculiarity in the Corpus
MS. of Matthew Paris's chronicle. In the margin opposite our
passage there is a drawing of the combat scene. It is only a rude
sketch;[1] its interest lies in the fact that the names of both the
opponents are given in explanation of the picture: *Mimekan
nanus* and *Rodogan gigas*. The text itself, it will be recalled,
mentions only Mimecan. The fact that the giant's name occurs
here has passed unnoticed by previous writers on the subject.
Few people, indeed, seem to have noticed the existence of the
drawing. Luard mentions it in a footnote, but says nothing about
the explanation that accompanies it.

It was once generally held that the first literary work to men-
tion the giant's name was a French metrical Life of Edward the
Confessor.[2] That honour must now be ceded to Ralph de Diceto's
Abbreviationes (see § 9). The occurrence in the Life can only

---

[1] It is reproduced in James, *The Drawings of Matthew Paris*, Pl. II.
The drawing and the accompanying caption are mentioned in the same
author's *Descriptive Catalogue of the Manuscripts in the Library of Corpus
Christi College, Cambridge*, vol. i, p. 52 (p. 165 of the MS.).

[2] Ed. Luard, *Lives of Edward the Confessor*; and James, *La Estoire de
Seint Aedward le Rei* (facsimile). The MS. contains a picture of the fight and
a description in verse of the illustration.

claim second place; moreover, it should be realized that there is a direct connexion between that occurrence and the one in Matthew Paris's chronicle, and that the dates of the two cannot differ greatly. The similarity between them is striking. In both instances we have a text giving the story of Gunhild and including Mimecan's name, but not the giant's. We have a picture of the fight, and an explanation of the picture in which both names occur. Moreover, the form *Rodegan* (*Rodogan*) is peculiar to these two instances; elsewhere in English records the giant is known as Rodingar, a form which comes closer to the ballad names Aldingar and Rodingham and also to the name as we find it in Scandinavian tradition (cf. ch. vi). There is a strong presumption, therefore, that the form of the name was deliberately changed by the author of the Life of St. Edward to suit the rhyme:

S'en cumbat le neims Mimecan
Au très grant sesne Rodegan (Luard, p. 3; p. 8 of the MS.).

Who was this author? A number of different hypotheses have been put forward. Luard thinks that the author was connected with Westminster, because he enlarges on everything concerning that locality and gives a full description of the abbey church. This view is echoed by Fritz,[1] who thinks that the author was a monk of Westminster. Montagu James[2] is of the opinion that the book is the work of Matthew Paris, carried out at St. Albans Abbey under his supervision, but not by his own hand. Most recently[3] J. G. Noppen has advanced the view that the Life is the work of one Master Henry, *versificator regis*, who in 1245, the date agreed on by all as the probable year of composition, received a large sum of money from the king 'for his services in writing the lives of St. Edward and St. George'.

This is a very attractive and probable theory. It should be borne in mind, however, that we also have to account for the close connexion between the Life of St. Edward and Matthew Paris's

---

[1] *Ueber Verfasser und Quellen der altfranzösischen Estoire de Seint Aedward le Rei.* [2] *La Estoire,* &c., p. 17.
[3] In *The Times Literary Supplement,* 4 May 1946, p. 211.

chronicle. It seems that their authors must in some way have collaborated.[1] It is clear that the drawing in the chronicle was suggested by the picture in the Life and must have been carried out after the Life had been completed, or the giant's name would not have had the form that it has. It may be regarded as certain, therefore, that Matthew Paris knew the picture in the Life; he very likely had it before him when he made the drawing in the chronicle. As the Life of St. Edward seems to have been composed in 1245, the drawing in the Corpus MS. must be placed somewhere between that date and Matthew Paris's death in 1259. But it seems also very probable that the Life was influenced by the chronicle or, alternatively, that it drew on the same source that was utilized in compiling the chronicle. The former seems the more likely possibility,[2] and the sequence of events may then be imagined as follows: the original St. Albans chronicle contained the name Mimecan; the Life of St. Edward borrowed the story of Gunhild from that chronicle, adding the name Rodegan; Matthew Paris entered this addition in the chronicle.

[1] Noppen suggests that Matthew Paris may have been responsible for the pictures in the Life, but from ll. 3961–6 it appears that the illustrations were executed by the author's own hand. This, perhaps, is the reason why the two pictures that we are discussing show practically no resemblance in their design and execution. The St. Edward one is very carefully executed; the emperor is seated on the left; by his feet lies Rodegan; on the right Mimecan is severing his ankles with a sword, and behind him Gunhild is kneeling. On the extreme right is a group of spectators. The picture in the chronicle is in Matthew Paris's shorthand: a rough sketch of two figures, a dwarf and a giant, both standing, the dwarf on the giant's left. The dwarf is cutting off the giant's legs at the knee.

[2] The Life purports to have been translated from the Latin and is obviously in the main a translation of Ailred of Rievaulx's Latin prose life of St. Edward; but the story of Gunhild does not occur in Ailred. A reference is found, at the end of the story, to some written source: 'Cum la estoire, k'est escrite, Le dit' (ll. 528–9); in my theory, the author is here thinking of the St. Albans chronicle. Besides the inclusion of Mimecan's name but not the giant's, there are other little points of resemblance between the account in the chronicle and in the Life, for example, the remark that 'Sulum custume de l'empire Purger se cuvint d'avutire Par bataile' (ll. 516–18; Luard has *da untire*, but this is a mistake: see R. Atkinson in *Hermathena*, vol. i (1874), pp. 24–25); the chronicle has: 'Oportebat ergo juxta consuetudinem regionis, ut Gunnilda per duellum . . . famam suae puritatis redimeret'. See also Fritz, op. cit., p. 34.

But this has brought us no nearer to explaining where the original chronicle got the name Mimecan and where the Life of St. Edward borrowed that of Rodegan. We know that the original St. Albans chronicler used another source besides William of Malmesbury; whether written or oral we cannot say, but considering William's remark *in triviis cantitata*, it is not improbable that some version of this song, possibly a different one from that known to William himself (see also p. 31), supplied the name Mimecan. If the source was written, it was no doubt preserved at St. Albans Abbey, where it may have been seen by the author of the Life of St. Edward. It is possible, at least theoretically, that the St. Albans chronicler read the source very carelessly and overlooked the giant's name, which was later noticed by the author of the Life; but this explanation is somewhat far-fetched. The theory of an oral source explains the facts much better; for instance, it makes it easier to understand the liberty that the author of the Life took with the form of the giant's name.

My theory, then, is that the author of the Life, who probably received help from Matthew Paris and read the story of Gunhild as told in the St. Albans chronicle, also knew a version of the song which gave the names of both the combatants. Perhaps this song did not come to his notice till after he had already completed the poem itself, for the account given there seems based entirely on the chronicle; but in his brief rhyme describing the picture of the combat scene he included the giant's name. Matthew Paris read the poem after its completion, and on seeing the picture he decided to add a similar illustration in the margin of his chronicle. In copying the name of the giant he made the slight mistake of putting *Rodogan* for *Rodegan*.

§ 9. *Ralph de Diceto*

The passage in Ralph de Diceto's *Abbreviationes Chronicorum* in which Gunhild is mentioned is taken almost word for word from Henry of Huntingdon. Talking of Canute, Ralph says (under A.D. 1027):

Erat autem dux totius Daciae, totius Angliae, totius Norwagiae, simul et Scotiae. Extra numerum vero bellorum quibus maxime splenduit, tria gessit eleganter. Primum quod filiam suam imperatori Romano cum ineffabilibus divitiis maritavit. Secundum . . .

The rest of the passage does not concern us here; nor is the reference to Canute's daughter of much interest in itself, since it was copied from Henry of Huntingdon. Of decided interest, however, are two marginal notes in one of the manuscripts, Lambeth Palace MS. 8. Here we find, first, the name *Gunnil-dam* with a mark to indicate insertion after *filiam suam*, and, secondly, a longer note to be inserted after *maritavit*:

quam Rodingarus Alemannicus impetivit de adulterio, sed Mime-kinus eam defendit et Rodingarum interfecit.

The manuscript that contains these additions[1] was, according to Stubbs,[2] without doubt an original possession of the author's. It seems to have been begun in 1188. It has received a large body of later additions and emendations, made either by Ralph himself or under his immediate direction; it was apparently his personal copy. The sister manuscript, Cotton Claudius E. III, was left unaltered. Most of the corrections and additions in the Lambeth MS. have been incorporated in a transcript made a few years later for the abbey of St. Albans, Royal MS. 13 E. VI, but the notes that we are concerned with here occur only in the Lambeth MS. They appear to have been inserted after the transcript was made. There can be no doubt, however, that they were inserted, if not by the hand that wrote the rest of the manuscript, at least by a hand of the same period and penmanship. They must be among the last entries made by Ralph, dating probably from about the year 1200. The second note has the distinction of containing the earliest known mention of the name *Rodingar*.

[1] It has proved necessary to consult several of the MSS. Stubbs, the editor, prints *Gunnildam* as part of the text, thus implying that it occurs also in the other MSS. He mentions the occurrence of the second note, but says nothing about its probable age.

[2] Cf. also James and Jenkins, *Descriptive Catalogue of the Manuscripts in the Library of Lambeth Palace.*

Where did Ralph get his information from? We can point to
no literary source: if he had one, it appears to be no longer extant.
But his source may have been oral; it may have been a version
of the song that William of Malmesbury earlier in the century
spoke of as sung *in triviis*.

§ 10. *John Brompton*

John Brompton's version of the story of Gunhild is as follows:[1]

[Anno *Hardeknouti* regis secundo . . .] eodemque anno iste *Harde-
knoutus* misit *Gunnildam* sororem suam *Henrico* imperatori filio
Conradi, per regem *Kanutum* patrem suum antea sibi nuptam; quæ
ad sponsum veniens multo tempore foedus conjugale fovit. Postremo
super adulterio accusata, mirabili duello cujusdam juvenis nomine
Municon, quem secum ab Anglia duxerat, contra hominem giganti
similem nomine *Roddyngar*, sicut Deus per miraculum voluit, se
purgavit; unde ipsa de triumpho insperato gaudens, repudianti viro
repudium dedit, & nunquam imposterum voluit ejus consortio con-
sentire, sed velum sanctimonialium suscipiens vitam castam in Dei
servicio terminavit.

John Brompton, or whoever the author was,[2] seems to have
based his story mainly on William of Malmesbury, several of
whose sentences occur unaltered. He may not have taken the
story direct from William, however; certain phrases remind one
of Ralph Niger's version. Be that as it may, the most important
passage, the one containing the names of the two opponents,
occurs neither in Ralph nor in William. Once more we are at a
loss to discover the source of the information.

The forms of the names require comment. *Muni-* for *Mimi-*
(or *Mime-*) in the name of Gunhild's champion is clearly due to
a misreading of some literary source, but at what stage the mistake occurred we cannot say. At any rate, the blame cannot be
laid at the door of the editor, Roger Twysden; he seems to have

---

[1] Ed. Twysden, *Historiæ Anglicanæ Scriptores X*, vol. i, col. 933.
[2] On the question of authorship see Sir T. D. Hardy's *Catalogue of
Materials*, vol. ii (Rolls, 1865), p. 540 n.; and James, *A Descriptive Catalogue of the Manuscripts in the Library of Corpus Christi College, Cambridge*,
vol. i, p. 184.

based his edition mainly on the Corpus MS. (No. 96), which clearly has *Muni-*. The Cotton MS.,[1] apparently the only other known manuscript, is less clear, and it is impossible to tell whether the name, as written there, represents *Mimicon* or *Municon*. Both the manuscripts, which date from the fifteenth century, appear to be transcripts of an earlier one, and the mistake may have occurred either during the transcription or through the use of a literary source by the compiler of the chronicle. For all we can tell, the mistake may go farther back still, to the source of this source. The second part of the name, the ending *-con*, as compared with Matthew Paris's *-can* and Ralph de Diceto's *-kin*, is best explained by assuming an oral link somewhere in the transmission. The name of Gunhild's accuser, *Roddyngar* or, as the Cotton MS. spells it, *Roddynggar*, is also strange. The double *d* to denote a preceding short *o* is un-Latin. It seems to point to a vernacular source and possibly, though we cannot be sure, to an oral one.

§ 11. *More than one Ballad?*

If we insist on a connexion between the various occurrences of the names Mimecan and Rodingar (and a connexion, surely, there must be, however remote or involved), the simplest way is to assume an oral tradition.[2] Direct proof of this assumption is difficult. We have already seen various evidence rendering it extremely probable: are there any further pointers in that direction?

William of Malmesbury says that in his day people still sang in the streets about the splendour of Gunhild's wedding; but he does not say whether their song also related the story of Gun-

---

[1] Tiberius C. XIII and not, as Hardy gives it (*Catalogue*, &c., vol. ii, p. 539), C. XVI.

[2] By oral tradition I mean first of all ballads. Wright, *The Cultivation of Saga in Anglo-Saxon England*, pp. 30–31, thinks, though he produces no direct evidence to prove it, that there was originally a prose tale about Gunhild. With the advent of new fashions of dance and song, he says, this and similar sagas were metamorphosed into songs of the new type. It is not improbable that there may have existed for a time, side by side, a prose tale and a ballad about Gunhild.

hild's accusation. Grundtvig takes this for granted: 'Although, to be sure, it is nowhere said so expressly, yet we cannot doubt that the same ballad also treated her later romantic story, or, in other words, that the ballad which is still extant in English . . . was sung in England seven hundred years ago.'[1] In my opinion this conclusion, as Grundtvig formulates it, is not warranted. We have other evidence that the memory of Gunhild's beauty and magnificent wedding lived on independently of the story of her accusation and trial. Henry of Huntingdon, William of Malmesbury's contemporary, says that Canute married his daughter to the Roman emperor *cum ineffabilibus divitiis* (cf. p. 27), but he evidently knows nothing of the accusation brought against her. It is a well-known fact that Henry derived much of his information from oral tradition, perhaps from current songs.[2] There is reason to believe, therefore, that the passage in question is based on the song mentioned by William of Malmesbury. The very words *cum ineffabilibus divitiis* remind one of the St. Albans chronicle: 'minstrels and harpists are hardly able to extol this wedding festival adequately in play and song'. Furthermore, evidence has come down to us that as late as the fourteenth century some people still knew about Gunhild's wedding, though apparently the story of her trial was unknown to them. In some historical entries in the Consuetudinarium of the Abbey of Bury St. Edmunds (Harl. MS. 3977), a volume of the fourteenth century, there occurs the following note:[3] 'Anno gratiae MXL Hardecnutus filius Cnuti et Emmae Reginae frater Sancti Edwardi qui regnavit annis tribus. Huic erat soror, nomine Gunnilda, pulcherrima feminarum, quam Henricus Romanorum imperator duxit uxorem. De qua celebris fama usque ad presens habetur.' These words must be understood to mean that there was an oral tradition, and most likely it had the form of a song.

[1] *DgF* i, p. 183. These words were written nearly a century ago; it is now over 800 years since William of Malmesbury finished his chronicle.

[2] Cf. Arnold's introduction to the Rolls edition, pp. lx–lxi. See also Wilson, *Lost Literature in Old and Middle English*, pp. 21 ff.

[3] See Ellis, *General Introduction to Domesday Book*, vol. ii, pp. 137–8.

On the other hand, there is good ground for supposing that the names of the two opponents in the Gunhild story were preserved by word of mouth. That would account for the inconsistencies in the appearance of the names as explained in previous sections. Considering that in later times there was a ballad on the subject of Gunhild's trial,[1] we may assume with some justification that that ballad in an earlier form was the source from which the chroniclers drew their information.

The conclusion to which we are led is that there were two ballads, one about Gunhild's memorable wedding and another about her accusation and trial. This result is borne out by the fact that the extant British Gunhild ballads know nothing of her wedding. On the other hand, echoes of the wedding scene are found in several of the Scandinavian Gunhild ballads (for example, in A; cf. p. 93), which are certainly first of all about her trial. It seems probable, therefore, that there was also a ballad, such as Grundtvig presupposed, combining the stories of her wedding and trial.

§ 12. *The Chroniclers' Debt to the Ballad*

It must be presumed, then, that William of Malmesbury knew the song about Gunhild's trial and summarized it in his chronicle. One may wonder why he did not give the names of the two opponents. He may not have known them, of course; the version with which he was familiar may not have contained them. Or, what is more probable, he may have left them out when summarizing the ballad. His account is very brief and relates only the most important points.

Although the St. Albans author no doubt based his story on William of Malmesbury's rendering, the two additions mentioned on p. 22 show that he knew also the ballad itself. Why, in that case, did he only include Mimecan's name? The simplest

---

[1] Always supposing, of course, that we are right in taking the name Eleanor to be a later addition (cf. p. 17). The occurrence of the names Aldingar (from Rodingar) and Harry (= Henry) speaks for the identity of the two stories.

solution is that his version contained only that name. That could be explained either as due to a later loss or by assuming that the name Rodingar was not added till the story reached England and then not in all the versions (cf. p. 64). The name Mimecan, as will be demonstrated later, was imported with the story from the Continent.

With Ralph de Diceto and John Brompton we are on less safe ground; but considering in particular the varying forms of the names, an oral transmission is the best explanation. We must assume, then, that after the completion of his *Abbreviationes* Ralph de Diceto, having heard the ballad, inserted a marginal note giving Gunhild's name, and another note about her accusation and trial in which he quoted the names of both the opponents. John Brompton, too, or his source, drew the names from oral tradition, but he worked them into the text itself.

IV

ENGLISH ROMANCES
ON RELATED THEMES

§ 13. *Queen Emma*

BESIDES the Gunhild tradition there were other stories of the same kind current in England in the Middle Ages. One of them, strangely enough, was about Gunhild's own mother, Queen Emma. At the instance of Robert of Jumièges, a Norman whom Edward the Confessor had made Archbishop of Canterbury, and who exercised a great and far from beneficial influence over the king, Emma was accused of having a bishop for her lover. At her own request, she was submitted to the ordeal of walking barefoot over red-hot ploughshares. The trial took place in Winchester Cathedral. The spectators were all weeping 'intolerably' and crying, 'St. Swithin, help her!' But the queen said calmly, 'O God, who didst deliver Susanna from the wicked elders, save me, by the merits of St. Swithin, from the fire prepared for me.' She then walked over the ploughshares unhurt. When the king saw that, he fell to her feet, saying, 'Mother, I have sinned against heaven and in thy sight, and I am no more worthy to be called thy son.'

The above description is taken from the Annals of Winchester.[1] The story of Emma is found under the date 1043. It seems to be ultimately derived from an account written by Richard of Devizes, a monk of St. Swithin's. At any rate, it was certainly written by a Winchester monk of the time of Richard (end of the twelfth century). Where the author took the story from we do not know; there can be no doubt that it has no foundation in fact.[2] It is worth noting that the tale bears a certain resemblance to the Scandinavian versions of the Gunhild story: the bishop as a lover and the ordeal are also met with in the Icelandic and

---

[1] Ed. Luard, *Annales Monastici*, vol. ii, pp. 20–25.
[2] See Freeman, *Norman Conquest*, vol. ii, pp. 569 ff.

D

Faroese versions. The story shows an even closer resemblance to
some stories once current in Germany about the Empresses
Richardis and Cunegund. Indeed, the resemblance is so close
that there is reason to suspect a borrowing, and in view of the
priority of the German tradition, we must suppose that the
story wandered from the Continent to England (see p. 100).

The account in the Winchester Annals has served as a basis
for later versions such as those by Robert of Gloucester (c. 1300)
and Ranulph Higden (first half of the fourteenth century).[1]
Higden's account, in its turn, was copied by several later fourteenth-century chroniclers: Richard of Cirencester, Henry
Knighton, John Brompton, &c. Based on the Winchester
Annals themselves is the version given in the *Historia Major
Wintoniensis* (1454) by Thomas Rudborne,[2] himself a monk of
St. Swithin's. Here, for example, the actual words of the queen's
prayer are quoted, while the other versions content themselves
with a bare mention and thus leave out the reference to Susanna.

The Emma tradition was not confined to written literature.
The Register of the Priory of St. Swithin's, Winchester, tells
us that when Adam de Orleton, bishop of Winchester, in 1338
visited the prior, Alexander de Herriard, musical entertainment
was provided for the guest: 'cantabat joculator quidam Here-
bertus nomine canticum Colbrondi, necnon Gestum Emme
regine a judicio ignis liberate, in aula prioris'.[3] Child (vol. ii,
p. 38) takes this passage to mean that there existed a ballad on
Queen Emma's trial. In support of his view he quotes *Piers
Plowman*, where the idle dykers and delvers are said to 'drive
forth the long day with *Dieu vous saue, Dame Emme*';[4] Child
thinks that this may be the same or another ballad on the subject. That the reference in *Piers Plowman* is to Queen Emma's

---

[1] The history of the Emma tradition in England is told by Hibbard,
'*Athelston*, A Westminster Legend', pp. 235 ff., where further references
will be found.

[2] Ed. Wharton, *Anglia Sacra*, vol. i, pp. 233–5.

[3] Quoted by T. Warton, *History of English Poetry* (ed. W. C. Hazlitt,
London, 1871), vol. ii, p. 97. The register, so far as I know, is still unpublished.

[4] Skeat's edition, A-text, Prol. 103; B, Prol. 224; C, Passus I, 225.

trial can hardly be doubted. It also seems certain that the quotation is a snatch of a song;[1] but was it a ballad in our sense of the
word? At any rate, it cannot have been an English ballad; the
words, as Langland quotes them, are in French. As the event
described happened in England, a ballad of continental origin
on this subject seems out of the question; but there is scarcely
sufficient evidence for supposing the existence of a French
popular ballad of English growth.[2] It is indeed strange that the
dykers should be singing in French, and it seems safe to assume
that what they sang had not the form of a popular ballad. The
same applies to the song or poem that Herbert recited in the
prior's hall: failing other evidence, it is more likely to have been
a romance. At any rate, we have no evidence that it conformed to
the particular type of song that we associate with the word
ballad. The other song with which Herbert is reported to have
entertained his audience, the one about 'Colbrond', was undoubtedly some version of *Guy of Warwick*, since in that romance
the hero vanquishes a gigantic Danish champion called Colbrond. It is perhaps significant that the earliest extant versions
of *Guy of Warwick* are in French and that the Middle English
versions appear to have been translated from the French.[3] Very
probably, both of the songs or poems recited by Herbert were in
French.

With regard to the source of the two songs about Emma, the
minstrel's and the dykers' (or were they one and the same?),
there is no certain evidence of an unbroken oral tradition since
the time of the first occurrence of the story. As the entertainment took place at Winchester, the scene of Emma's trial, the
minstrel could have had access to some written source.[4] On the

---

[1] Cf. Skeat's note on the passage.

[2] There remains the possibility that it was a bilingual, macaronic ballad
with perhaps only the refrain in French. There are other examples of the
refrain of a ballad being in a foreign language, for example Child No. 19,
King Orfeo, or version D of the Scandinavian Gunhild ballad.

[3] See Hibbard, *Mediæval Romance in England*, p. 128.

[4] In the same way, and at roughly the same time, the romance *Athelston*
was composed by an unknown minstrel, from material drawn from some
written description of Emma's trial. See Hibbard, op. cit., pp. 144 ff.

other hand, we cannot overlook the possibility that there may have been a local tradition in the town about this strange event, possibly in the form of a prose tale. We know that the memory of Guy's fight with Colbrond, which also belongs to Winchester tradition, was kept alive by word of mouth for centuries.[1]

§ 14. 'Olif'

A romance on a theme like Queen Emma's trial would be nothing unique. There existed at one time a number of English romances on similar themes. These do not concern us directly at the present stage of our investigation, since the stories they tell are not versions of the Gunhild story as such, but variants of the motif in general. Nevertheless, it is expedient to summarize them now, while we are dealing with the English tradition. Their place in the history of the motif will be dealt with in ch. viii.

One of these romances is no longer extant, but has been preserved in a Norse prose translation.[2] In the first chapter of the Norwegian romantic saga *Af Frú Olif ok Landres Syni Hennar* (*Karlamagnús Saga*, pt. ii) we read that

Lord Bjarni Erlingsson of Bjarkey found this saga written and told in the English language while staying in Scotland the winter after King Alexander's death. After him Margaret took the kingdom, daughter of the gracious Lord Erik, king of Norway, son of King Magnus; and the said Margaret was Alexander's granddaughter. The reason that Lord Bjarni was sent out west was to secure and make firm the realm under the maiden. And in order that this saga might be the better understood, and that men might get the more profit and pleasure from it, Lord Bjarni had it turned from English into Norse.

---

[1] John Leland tells us in his *Itinerary* (*c.* 1540; ed. L. T. Smith, London, 1907, pt. iii, p. 272) that 'On the south side of Hyde Abbay betwixt it and the waulle is a medow caullid Denmark, wher the fame is that Guido Erle of Warwik killid great Colebrande the Dane *singulari certamine*'.

[2] A modern English retranslation from the Norse is found in H. M. Smyser and F. P. Magoun, *Survivals in Old Norwegian* (Baltimore, 1941), pp. 3–27.

We happen to know of this Lord Bjarni from other sources; he was an important figure in Norwegian political life towards the end of the thirteenth century.[1] He went on frequent diplomatic missions to Britain, and in 1281 he was among those who negotiated the marriage of young King Erik, nicknamed Priesthater, to Margaret, daughter of King Alexander III of Scotland. Queen Margaret died in 1283, but a daughter also named Margaret, the so-called 'Maid of Norway', survived her. On the death of King Alexander, the Scottish crown fell to this tender Norwegian princess, and Lord Bjarni spent the winter of 1286 in Scotland, attending to Princess Margaret's interests and ensuring her the crown. There can thus be no doubt that the account which the saga gives of its own origin is true, even though the English original has not come down to us. In style and language the story, as we have it, belongs to the end of the thirteenth century or the beginning of the fourteenth.[2]

The Norwegian saga or romance is about Charlemagne's sister Olif, who is said to have married a king named Hugon. Going to the chase one day the king left his wife in the care of Milon, the steward. He offered her his love, which she spurned. In revenge he made her drink a sleeping potion, and while she was under its influence he stripped her and put a black man in her bed. When the king came home, Milon led him to her bed. The king killed the black man on the spot. The queen offered to prove her innocence by various kinds of ordeal, which the king on Milon's advice refused. One of her knights then offered himself as her champion, but though he was victorious, Milon succeeded in persuading the king not to recognize this judgement of God on the ground that Olif must be a witch and the outcome of the battle due to sorcery. She was finally punished by being shut up with snakes and toads in a stone structure in the forest. The rest of the story, telling of the vindication of her innocence, does not interest us in this connexion. Olif ended her days in a nunnery.

The story of Olif is also found in an Icelandic song, *Landres*

---

[1] Cf. Leach, *Angevin Britain and Scandinavia*, pp. 68 f.
[2] See Unger's edition, p. xv.

Rímur, and in a Faroese ballad, *Óluvu Kvæði*, both probably derived from the romance. The ultimate source appears to be French; we possess a French and a Spanish version of the story in a different, and in some respects more original, form (see further pp. 123 ff.).

§ 15. 'The Earl of Toulouse'

Another English romance, *The Earl of Toulouse*,[1] is about an Emperor Diocletian of Germany and his beautiful wife. While the emperor was away, two of his knights, after trying in vain to obtain the empress's love, plotted together to revenge themselves. Under pretence of playing a trick to amuse her, they persuaded a youth of twenty to hide naked in her bedroom. After a while they roused the whole castle and went to her room, where they caught and killed the boy. The empress was to be burnt unless a champion could be found. Messengers were dispatched in all directions, and Sir Barnard, Earl of Toulouse, who greatly admired the empress, though he was the emperor's enemy, decided to fight for her. Disguised as a monk he first confessed her, thus assuring himself of her innocence. He then vanquished both her accusers, who were burnt instead of her. Sir Barnard afterwards hastened away, but was sent for by the emperor. The two were reconciled, and Sir Barnard was made steward of all the emperor's lands. After the emperor's death Sir Barnard married his widow and became emperor.

This poem was probably composed at the beginning of the fifteenth century.[2] Its immediate history is not known, but it professes to have been taken from some other source, which is called a 'story' (1070), a 'romaunse' (1203), and a 'lay of Bretayn' (1220). The 'gest' is said to have been 'cronyculyd yn Rome' (1219). We shall return later to the question of the place of this romance in the history of the motif in general (see § 43).

[1] Ed. Lüdtke, *The Erl of Tolous*. Also in J. Ritson's *Ancient Engleish Metrical Romanceës*, vol. iii; and in W. H. French and C. B. Hale's *Middle English Metrical Romances* (New York, 1930).

[2] This is the opinion of Lüdtke, p. 42. Sarrazin, *ESt*, vol. vii (1884), pp. 136-7, would place it about half a century earlier.

§ 16. *'Sir Tryamoure'*

Sir Tryamoure[1] is about a King Ardus of Aragon and his queen, Margaret. While the king was away on a crusade, Marrok his steward made love to the queen, but was repulsed. In revenge he calumniated her to the king on his return, telling him that he had seen a man lying with the queen and had slain him. The king banished her from the kingdom; she was sent away with a faithful old knight, Sir Roger, for escort. Marrok attacked them on the way, hoping to ravish the queen, but she escaped. Sir Roger was slain, but his trusty dog kept watch at his body. Yet one day hunger forced the dog back to the palace in search of food. The king saw a glimpse of it, recognized it, and grew suspicious. The next day the dog returned, and when it came the third day, it met Marrok and attacked and killed him. Meanwhile the queen had escaped to Hungary, where a Sir Barnard took care of her. She bore King Ardus a son, who was christened Tryamoure and grew up to be a brave knight. The rest of the story has little to do with our legend, except that Sir Tryamoure overcomes a mighty champion Burlond in single combat by first cutting off his legs at the knee and afterwards his head. Ardus and Margaret were reunited in the end.

This romance professes to have been translated from a story told 'in Romaynes' (Utterson's ed., l. 316), but no French original is extant. The English romance seems to date from about 1400.[2]

§ 17. *'Octavian'*

In *Octavian*, too, it is only the first part of the poem that concerns us. The Emperor Octavian of Rome married Floraunce, daughter of the king of France. His mother was jealous of her

---

[1] Edited from the MS. in the University Library, Cambridge, by J. O. Halliwell. Another copy is contained in the Percy MS., ed. J. W. Hales and F. J. Furnivall, 1867–8. There are also two early editions printed by Copland; one of them has been reprinted by E. V. Utterson, *Select Pieces of Early Popular Poetry*, vol. i (London, 1817).

[2] See Wells, *A Manual of the Writings in Middle English*, p. 121; and Hibbard, *Mediæval Romance in England*, p. 284.

daughter-in-law and spoke evil of her to her son, maintaining that she had a kitchen-boy for her lover. By the promise of a high reward she induced a scullion, 'lothly of face', to creep into Floraunce's bed while she was asleep, and she thereupon went and fetched her son to see it. He immediately smote off the scullion's head and had Floraunce cast into prison. The judges condemned her to be burnt. Arrangements had already been made and the fire had been lit, when Octavian took pity on her and ordered three barons to lead her and her two children out of the kingdom into a wild forest and leave them there. The rest of the story is about Floraunce and her two children's adventures until, five and twenty years later, Floraunce and Octavian were reunited. One of her sons had a fight with a giant, in which he stretched his opponent to the ground, cut off his head, and tied it to his saddle-bow.[1]

There are two Middle English versions, both dating from the middle of the fourteenth century, one of them from the south of England (summarized here), the other from the north.[2] Both versions go back to a French source (see further § 45).

§ 18. 'Florence of Rome'

The connexion of our legend with *Florence of Rome*[3] is less close than with the romances already mentioned. Florence, daughter of the Emperor Otes of Rome, was betrothed to Emere, but while he was engaged in war abroad, his brother Miles, to whose care Florence had been entrusted, importuned her with offers of love. He was unsuccessful and was put in prison, but was released at the news of Emere's return. Miles and Florence rode out to meet Emere, but on the way he carried her off into a wood and, after another unsuccessful attempt on her virtue, hung her up by her hair in a tree. She was rescued by Sir Tyrry and was in turn persecuted by his steward Macary, who

---

[1] Cf. the Norwegian version of our ballad (p. 13).
[2] Both edited by Sarrazin, *Octavian*.
[3] Ed. Viëtor and Knobbe. Also in Ritson's *Ancient Engleish Metrical Romanceës*, vol. iii.

tried to force her, but failed and took revenge by murdering
Tyrry's daughter and putting the bloody knife in the hand of
the sleeping Florence. Macary advised Tyrry to have her burnt,
but Tyrry took pity on her and sent her away into a forest. After
yet further adventures and attempts on her virtue, she reached
a nunnery, where she was well received. She cured one of the
nuns of a severe disease. Her fame soon spread. To her for heal-
ing came Emere, and also Miles, Macary, and the rest of her
persecutors. She made them confess as a preliminary to cure.
She was finally reunited to Emere.

This English romance is, by its own confession, taken from
a story told in French: 'Jn Romance as we rede' (1539), 'Sche
myȝt not speke, þe romance seyde' (1546), &c. In point of fact,
the French original is still extant.[1] Knobbe, the editor of the
English romance, suggests (pt. ii, pp. 12 and 52) 1400 as the
approximate date of composition. The story of the Empress of
Rome occurs also in the *Gesta Romanorum*. Besides English and
Anglo-Latin prose versions of the latter work, there exists a
metrical paraphrase of our particular story by Thomas Hoccleve.[2]

§ 19. '*Valentine and Orson*'

Only the beginning of *Valentine and Orson* concerns us here.
It is about an Emperor Alexander of Constantinople, who was
married to Belyssant, sister of King Pippin of France. The archbishop made love to her, but was repulsed. He took revenge by
slandering her to the emperor, saying that she had a lover, and
that she was planning to poison her husband in order to marry
her lover. The emperor went into her chamber and without
saying a word 'pulled her by the heer so rudely, that he threwe
her against the earth, and made her excellent face runne al on
bloude'. The emperor wanted to have her burnt, but spared her
for fear of her brother, Pippin. Instead she was banished from

---

[1] Ed. Wallensköld, *Florence de Rome*.
[2] Ed. F. J. Furnivall, *Hoccleve's Works*, vol. i (EETS, 1892), pp. 140 ff.
For further references see Wallensköld, op. cit., vol. i, pp. 112–13; and
Stefanović, 'Die Crescentia-Florence Sage', p. 495.

the empire, and departed in the company of a squire, Blendy-mayn, who had come with her from France. On the way they were attacked by the archbishop, but during the fight a merchant came up who knew the archbishop, and when the latter saw that he was recognized he fled. The merchant later revealed to the emperor what he knew. The archbishop asseverated his innocence and offered to prove it in single combat. After a fierce fight, the archbishop was vanquished by the merchant and put to death. The rest of the book is about the numerous adventures of Belyssant's two sons, who among other brilliant feats rescue their mother from the power of a giant.

In contrast with the other romances mentioned,[1] *Valentine and Orson* is in prose. It was translated into English shortly after 1500 by one Henry Watson, apprentice to Wynkyn de Worde. It is based on a French original composed between 1475 and 1489. This French prose story, which is found in a large number of translations, is a late version of an earlier metrical romance, *Valentine and Nameless*. The French original of this earlier version appears to be no longer extant, but it is possible to form an idea of the story from Dutch and German renderings. The two redactions of the story differ considerably: the later one omits a number of features, and substitutes others taken from elsewhere in the most arbitrary fashion (see further § 46).

---

[1] With the possible exception of *Olif*, which has not been preserved in its original form.

V

THE SCANDINAVIAN TRADITION

§ 20. *Introductory*

SCANDINAVIA has no historical record of a story similar to that told in the ballad. In versions A and H, Gunhild's husband is said to be Henry duke of Brunswick and Slesvig. This, as pointed out by Grundtvig (*DgF* i, p. 181), must be the famous Henry the Lion, who figures elsewhere in Danish balladry as duke of Brunswick (*DgF* 114). Slesvig was never, properly speaking, part of Henry's domains, but it was occupied for a while by his troops in 1156, when he interfered in the Danish civil war. Though Henry is famous in legend as well as history, a story like that in our ballad is nowhere else ascribed to him. There is perhaps a faint similarity between our ballad and the well-known story of Henry's long absence abroad and his return on the day when his wife was getting married to some one else,[1] a story repeated in a great many medieval romantic tales.[2] But the likeness is superficial. Henry's wife was not called Gunhild; he was married twice, first (1148) to Clementia, daughter of Conrad of Zähringen, and later (1168) to Matilda, daughter of Henry II of England.[3] Other details, too, fail to fit in. Henry the Lion did not live at Spire, i.e. present-day Speyer, the place mentioned in several of the Scandinavian versions[4] as Henry

---

[1] Summarized in Grimm's *Deutsche Sagen*, No. 520. See also Grundtvig's introduction to ballad No. 114.

[2] Cf. the British ballad of *Hind Horn*, Child No. 17.

[3] It may be this wife Matilda who, in some circuitous way, has been instrumental in getting the story attached to Henry the Lion. An adultery story is elsewhere (see p. 132) told of a Princess Matilda, daughter of King Henry (I or II) of England and married to a German emperor Henry. This Matilda is in another version said to be Canute's daughter. Our ballad may merely have carried the confusion one step farther.

[4] A, C, D, F, H, K, and P. B, E, G, I, and L leave out the name, while M and N substitute other names, *Ro* (M) and *Hæjler* (N), both probably imaginary and due to the exigencies of the rhyme. *Hæjler* bears a faint resemblance to the word *heelde* (='hall'?) used in A 18. It is perhaps this word that underlies the strange proper name *Valle* in version C (sts. 1, 9,

and Gunhild's residence. The name Speyer points to the Salian emperors of Germany, whose favourite city it was. We thus find the English tradition of Gunhild as the wife of a Salian emperor confirmed.

§ 21. '*Guðrúnarkviða III*'

A poem in the Elder Edda, *Guðrúnarkviða III*, relates an infidelity story about Guðrun, wife of Atli (= Attila), the famous king of the Huns. Herkja, Atli's bondmaid, who had previously been his concubine, accused Guðrun of adultery with Þjoðrek.[1] Guðrun denied the charge and asked to be allowed a trial by ordeal. She and Herkja had to dip their hands in a kettle full of boiling water, but while Guðrun's hand was unhurt, Herkja's was scalded. Herkja was led away and cast into a foul bog.

There is considerable divergence of opinion concerning the age of this poem.[2] The dates suggested vary from the end of the tenth to the beginning of the thirteenth century,[3] but the majority of scholars tend to regard the poem as one of the youngest in the Edda. It stands out from the rest by showing acquaintance with the Theodoric legend; it is the earliest evidence of the occurrence of that legend in Scandinavia. Later, about 1260, the full story of Theodoric's exile at Attila's court was told in *Þiðriks Saga*, based on north German legendary material. That *Guðrúnarkviða III* and *Þiðriks Saga* are independent of each other is evident, among other things, from the

and 21). See Bugge and Grundtvig's note, *DgF* iv, p. 731; and E. von der Recke, *Danmarks Fornviser*, vol. i, pp. 357–8.

[1] The MS. has *Þjoðmar* once, and it has been suggested that this might be the original name (*Þjoðmar* = German *Dietmar*, Theodoric's father), which was later changed by a scribe into the more familiar *Þjoðrek*. See Jónsson, *Den oldnorske og oldislandske Litteraturs Historie*, vol. i, pp. 295–6, and *Aarbøger for nordisk Oldkyndighed*, 3rd Ser., vol. xi (1921), p. 74; cf. also H. M. Chadwick, *The Heroic Age* (Cambridge, 1912), p. 154. The theory has been contested, for example, by Jiriczek, *Deutsche Heldensagen*, pp. 159–60.

[2] See Sijmons and Gering, *Die Lieder der Edda*, vol. iii. ii, pp. 317 ff.; and de Vries, *Altnordische Literaturgeschichte*, § 178.

[3] The former is suggested by Jónsson, the latter by Boer.

different forms of the names: Þjoðrek—Þiðrik, Herkja—Erka, &c. Both authors probably derived their information from north German songs or ballads. *Erka*, Attila's wife,[1] was at first unknown in the Scandinavian form of the Nibelungen legend, which knew only of Attila's quite unhistorical marriage to Guðrún. The author of *Guðrúnarkviða III*, unable to reconcile the two traditions, turned Herkja into a concubine.

The story of Guðrun's alleged adultery and ordeal is found nowhere else in Germanic legend. *Guðrúnarkviða III* no doubt represents the incorporation of a theme which did not originally belong to the Theodoric legend. Adultery stories were current in Germany about the Empresses Richardis and Cunegund (see § 35), and we saw in the last chapter how one of those stories appears to have spread to England, where it was attributed to Queen Emma. We must suppose that the author of *Guðrúnarkviða III* heard a similar story and transformed it to suit the Theodoric legend. It has been suggested that the author was an Icelander studying in Germany, but the story may also have been brought to western Norway by German merchants.[2]

Guðrúnarkviða III cannot be one of the ancestors of the Gunhild ballad, but it is very likely a lateral branch of the story (see p. 91).

§ 22. *Swanhild*

Another infidelity story is that of Swanhild, wife of Ermanaric, the Gothic king. It occurs both in poetry and prose.[3] A treacherous councillor, Bikki, urged Randver, Ermanaric's son by an earlier marriage, to make love to Swanhild, and he then accused them of adultery before the king. Randver was hanged,

---

[1] *Erka* is identical with the Κρέκα mentioned by Priscus (448) as Attila's principal wife. The German forms of the name are *Herche* and *Helche*.

[2] Cf. Sijmons and Gering, op. cit., p. 319.

[3] It is found in Bragi's *Ragnarsdrápa*, and in the Edda poems *Guðrúnarhvöt* and *Hamðismál*. In prose, we find the story told in Snorri's Edda and in the *Völsunga Saga*, chs. 41–43; it is also given by Saxo Grammaticus, bk. viii. The adultery theme is not directly mentioned in any of the poems; it is found in the prose introduction to *Guðrúnarhvöt*, as well as in the other prose versions mentioned. Bikki's treacherous counsel is also alluded to in *Sigurðarkviða hin Skamma* (st. 63 in Boer's edition).

while Swanhild was punished by being trodden under the feet of horses. Her brothers took revenge by attacking Ermanaric and cutting off his hands and feet.

It is not quite clear from the Norse versions of the story whether the accusation was a false one. It is certainly stated in Snorri and in the *Völsunga Saga* that the two young people liked Bikki's advice. There is thus some reason for the accusation, and the story does not quite belong to the type that we are here trying to trace. On the other hand, Saxo obviously believed that Swanhild was innocent. The main difference, then, between his story and the ballad one lies in the fact that in Saxo the lady's innocence is never vindicated. This, however, is an important difference, and any direct connexion with our ballad seems unlikely.

The earliest mention of Swanhild's cruel fate is found in Jordanes, the sixth-century historian.[1] As told by him, the story differs from the Scandinavian versions in many essential points. Sunilda[2] is not Ermanaric's wife. Her husband belonged to a subject tribe, the Rosomoni, and she was put to death[3] in punishment for her husband's treacherous revolt. Her brothers avenged her by plunging a sword in Ermanaric's side. Thus, the adultery motif is entirely unknown to Jordanes; moreover, we cannot tell when it was added to the story. If it was ever known in Germany and England in connexion with this story, it soon died out. Even the name Swanhild does not occur in German and English legend, though there may be some reason for regarding the Ealhhild mentioned in *Widsith* as identical with Swanhild.[4] It seems certain that the character of Bikki was known to the Anglo-Saxons,[5] but that does not imply a knowledge of

---

[1] See, for example, Mierow's translation, p. 87.

[2] The form of the name varies greatly in the MSS. On the possible etymology of the word, see Boer, *Die Sagen von Ermanarich und Dietrich von Bern*, pp. 8–9 and 16.

[3] In Jordanes she is not trodden to death, but is torn asunder by wild horses.

[4] Cf. Boer, op. cit., pp. 15–16; and Chambers, *Widsith*, pp. 21–28.

[5] The name occurs in *Widsith* and as part of various English place-names; see Chambers, op. cit., p. 20.

the adultery motif. German legend, too, has an evil counsellor, Sibiche (the Sifka of *Þiðriks Saga*), but no adultery incident.[1]

It is not at all certain that the adultery motif in this story was ever known outside Scandinavia.[2] Besides the addition of that part of the story, we find other changes made in the Scandinavian versions. Norwegian-Icelandic tradition connects the story with the Nibelungen legend; Swanhild is made a daughter of Sigurð and Guðrun, who after Atli's death is said to have married Jonak, by whom she had the sons who later avenged Swanhild's death. This added feature is unknown to Saxo, who in other respects, also, has preserved what is undoubtedly a more original form of the story,[3] for example the fact that Swanhild is unjustly accused. Ermanaric's son, according to Saxo, is called Broderus, not Randver. As shown by Herrmann (pp. 574–5), this may be explained as due to faulty recollection on the part of his authority, and it would thus indicate oral transmission. Saxo's version seems to be a compromise between the Norse form of the story and some other element, which may have belonged to either Danish or north German tradition (Herrmann, p. 577), and which was very likely in poetic form.

§ 23. 'Den kyske Dronning'

A late-fifteenth-century Danish metrical romance, *Den kyske Dronning*,[4] tells about a king of Poland who went on a pilgrimage and left his queen in the care of a knight named Scares. After a vain attempt upon her virtue, Scares induced a servant-boy to hide naked under her bed, and then went and surprised him there and killed him. On the king's return Scares told him that

[1] Ermanaric's seduction of Sibiche's wife, as told in *Þiðriks Saga* and the German *Heldenbuch*, serves only as a motivation for Sibiche's treachery. It is thus entirely different from the Swanhild story. It is doubtful, too, whether there is any connexion between Bikki and Sibiche; see Boer, p. 60; and Chambers, pp. 32–33.

[2] On the development of the Swanhild story see now Caroline Brady, *The Legends of Ermanaric*.

[3] See Herrmann, *Die dänische Geschichte des Saxo Grammaticus*, vol. ii, pp. 571–7. Guðrun appears in Saxo in the character of the sorceress Guthruna, who helps Swanhild's brothers to wreak their vengeance.

[4] Ed. Brandt, *Romantisk Digtning fra Middelalderen*, vol. ii, pp. 87–128.

the queen had been unfaithful. The king first banished her, but afterwards decided to have her burnt. Disguised as the Pope's legate, the king of Bohemia assured himself of her innocence by acting as her confessor, and then changed into a suit of armour and presented himself as her champion, still without revealing his identity. Scares was defeated in the combat and was burnt instead of the queen, who was taken into favour again. On the death of the king of Poland, the queen married her rescuer.

It will be noticed that this story in many respects resembles the English romance *The Earl of Toulouse* (see § 15). The two are undoubtedly related. The trick of the disguise and confession is the same in both; so is the feature of the boy hiding in the bedroom, and also the marriage between the queen and her rescuer after the death of her first husband. The main difference is that the queen has only one accuser in *Den kyske Dronning*, but this detail is found also in other stories belonging to the Earl of Toulouse group (see p. 135).

As for the relationship between *Den kyske Dronning* and our ballad, in certain details there is a striking similarity. In both stories the king goes away leaving Scares (Ravengaard) in charge of the queen and the country. When the king returns, he lands on the beach, and Scares (Ravengaard) rides down to meet him. The king asks forthwith, 'How stands it with my lands, and how is my beloved queen?' And Scares (Ravengaard) answers, 'All is well with your lands, my lord, but your queen has done amiss; I have seen her lie with another man.' The king rides straight to his palace, where he is greeted by the queen; but he chides her, saying, 'Ill hast thou done to me.'

The similarity between the romance and the ballad is emphasized by their having twice the same rhyme-pair. In Gunhild's reply to Ravengaard when he threatens to slander her, most of the Danish versions[1] have two lines somewhat like the following:

Ja lyv, ja lyv, til du faar Skam:
Sandhed for Løgn det gaar vel fram (B 8).

[1] B 8, G 6, H 8, I 5, K 16, L 6, and M 11. The rhyme-pair is a little different in A 9a (*skaam—graam*) and in the Faroese version E 10 (*skamm— mann*). Versions C, D, and F do not know the stanza.

Now *skam* and *fram* occur also in the queen's words to Scares when she repels his love-making, although the content of the lines is not the same:

> jech halp til ath drawe thik fram,
> hwi wilt thu giøræ mægh then skam? (ll. 173–4).

Similarly, when the king lands on the beach, we find the pair *land—strand* in both the ballad[1] and the romance, but the latter rhyme may be said to be so obvious that no particular value can be attached to it. *Skam—fram*, on the other hand, is a less common rhyme.

One cannot escape a general impression that there is a connexion between the romance and the ballad. Had Jep Jensen, the author of the romance, the ballad in mind whilst writing,[2] or was the ballad influenced by the romance? Or were both influenced by a common source? We know from the explicit statement of the romance itself that it was written in 1483. Now certain features of the ballad, such as the place-name Spire, point to a much greater antiquity (cf. pp. 43–44). It is probable that the story of Gunhild was known in Scandinavia before the thirteenth century and very likely in the form of a ballad (cf. pp. 108–9). On the other hand, the particular features in question, the king's absence and the steward's ride to the beach to welcome him on his return, cannot be paralleled in the German and English ancestors of the Scandinavian ballad and were therefore quite possibly borrowed from some romance (cf. pp. 110–11). Whether, however, that romance is identical with *Den kyske Dronning*, as we know it, remains an open question. The first written copy of the ballad, Danish A, dates from about 1550; the assumption of a loan from *Den kyske Dronning* would therefore mean that the

[1] B 9, G 7, I 6, and L 7. In a slightly different form (*land—sand*) we find the rhyme in D 11, E 11, F 9, H 9, K 17, and M 12. A and C alone of the Scandinavian versions (not counting, of course, the Norwegian version and the Danish fragments N and O) do not know the rhyme.

[2] Brandt, op. cit., vol. iii, p. 338, is of the opinion that the author wrote from memory. He bases this view on the absence of personal names, apart from Scares, and on the fact that the poem does not make an impression of being a translation.

ballad was reshaped between 1483 and 1550, at a time when ballad-making was becoming a dying art in Denmark. Though the possibility of a late revision cannot be excluded, it is equally possible that *Den kyske Dronning* had a forerunner no longer extant which served as a model at the revision of the ballad.

§ 24. 'Orm Ungersvend'

The fight between Ravengaard and Memering is fairly closely paralleled in another Danish ballad, *Orm Ungersvend og Bermer-Rise (DgF 11).*[1] As this part of the Gunhild story undoubtedly contains a strong folk-tale element, it is not surprising that we should come upon a similar fight elsewhere, but the similarity in this case is so close, at certain points, that direct borrowing seems probable. *Orm Ungersvend og Bermer-Rise* relates how the giant Bermer demanded the Danish king's daughter in marriage unless the king could find a champion to meet Bermer in single combat. The king went to the hall and asked of his men, 'Who among you would like to win a fair maiden?' All remained silent save young Orm, who sat at the far end of the table. He offered to fight if the king would grant him in reward the princess and half the kingdom. Orm then went to see his dead father in the mountain and obtained from him the sword Berting on condition that he avenged his father's death. When Bermer saw his youthful opponent, he contemptuously exclaimed that it befitted not a warrior to fight with a child.[2] But Orm was victorious: he cut off Bermer's legs at the knee because he could reach no higher. The rest of the ballad, telling how Orm avenged his father's death, is of no interest to us here.[3]

[1] Found in four sixteenth-century versions (A, B, C, D) and two nineteenth-century ones (E and F); E is only a fragment. There are five Swedish versions, which Grundtvig (*DgF* iv, p. 720) terms A, B, C, D, E; but A, D, and E are only fragments. Two Norwegian versions have been recorded, one by Landstad (No. 8) and one by Liestøl and Moe (3-vol. collection No. 47, 1-vol. collection No. 2).

[2] I follow version D. Most of the other versions have similar remarks; but in A it is the king who greets Orm with derision when he offers to fight.

[3] This part is missing in both the Swedish and the Norwegian versions.

This ballad is obviously composed of two distinct elements: (1) the story of how Orm acquired the sword Berting and avenged his father, and (2) the story of how he won the princess and half the kingdom by killing a giant. It has been pointed out by Bugge and others[1] that the ballad is probably descended from the legend of the sword Tyrfing, preserved to us in the *Hervarar Saga*. The second element, however, has been changed almost out of recognition. In its present form it is a folk-tale pure and simple. Countless examples could be cited of popular stories about the rescue of a princess from a giant or ogre, and the fact that it is the youngest and least promising who proves to be a hero is true to the folk-tale pattern; the offer of the princess and half the kingdom as a reward is, of course, a folk-tale common-place.[2]

Now what is the relation of this tale to the story of the fight in the Gunhild ballad? The latter, too, contains the feature of the unpromising youth who becomes a hero; but that in itself cannot prove borrowing. Even such a detail as the exchange of contemptuous remarks (cf. English A 40–41 and Danish C 23–24) is too common to prove anything.[3] But the similarity

---

[1] See *DgF* iv, pp. 705 ff. Cf. also Liestøl and Moe, *Norske Folkeviser fra Middelalderen*, pp. 15–17.

[2] For all three motifs see Thompson's *Motif-Index*.

[3] It seems to be part of the standard description of a fight with a giant, from the David-Goliath story upwards. One other instance occurs in English balladry, in *The Earl of Westmoreland*, Child No. 177, sts. 70–71. The latter passage may be a loan from the fourteenth-century romance *Libeaus Desconus*, which contains several combats with giants and other formidable opponents. One of these fights, with a giant called Maugis, begins in very similar fashion (ll. 1370–80). The English romance goes back to a French source, ultimately to Renaud de Beaujeu's *Le Bel Inconnu*, which dates from the end of the twelfth century. The relation of that romance to Chrétien de Troyes's *Erec*, which deals with much the same theme, is not quite clear, but they seem to have a common source; see E. Philipot, *Romania*, vol. xxvi (1897), pp. 290 ff. In *Erec*, too, a scene of the kind we are trying to trace occurs (ll. 4430 ff.) and that passage is reproduced very faithfully in the Norse translation, *Erex Saga*. Outside this set of related tales we find numerous giant-fights, some of them of our particular type, in the fifteenth-century romance *Sir Torrent of Portyngale*. Winifred Smith in her paper, 'Elements of Comedy in the English and Scottish Ballads', p. 85, n. 5, mentions more such 'flytings of warriors before battle'. Examples could easily be multiplied. Cf. also pp. 153 and 156 of this book.

extends farther: in most of the Danish versions[1] Orm conquers the giant by cutting off his legs (and in version F afterwards his head). The same trait is found in the early English prose versions of the Gunhild story as well as in the later Gunhild ballad, version A, but strangely enough in none of the Danish versions of that ballad. The cutting off of the legs is found elsewhere in English popular literature; we meet it in the romance of *Sir Tryamoure* (see § 16) and in the folk-tale of *Jack the Giant-Killer*. In the latter story Jacks meets a giant dragging a lady and a knight along by the hair; he attacks the giant and severs his legs below the knee, and when the giant tumbles to the ground, he cuts off his head and sends it to King Arthur.[2] How old this story is I do not know; it can be traced back to early-eighteenth-century chap-books, which probably utilized older folk-tales or folk-tale elements.[3]

It is curious that *Orm Ungersvend* should have this point in common with the English Gunhild ballad,[4] while the Danish versions of the latter ballad do not know it. Nor do the Swedish and Norwegian versions of *Orm* possess the feature. It is found, on the other hand, in the Icelandic poem *Ormars Rímur* (*c.* 1500), which tells the story of Orm in a way rather similar to the ballad.[5] Now *Hervarar Saga*, which, as explained above, probably represents an earlier form of the same story, has nothing

---

[1] All except the fragment E. The Swedish and Norwegian versions have not this feature, and Danish E, significantly, on several points tallies better with the Swedish versions.

[2] See Hartland, *English Fairy and Folk Tales*, pp. 11-13.

[3] See Bolte and Polívka's *Anmerkungen*, p. 43. In its present form *Jack the Giant-Killer* belongs to the Arthurian cycle. It shows a certain similarity to *Libeaus Desconus*. In the latter story the hero rescues a maiden from two giants; he kills them and presents the girl with their heads, which are afterwards sent to King Arthur (ll. 613 ff.). As *Libeaus Desconus* was extremely popular, it may have influenced the folk-book, but the cutting off of the legs is peculiar to the latter. On the other hand, Spenser, who was steeped in medieval romance, made his Prince Arthur use a very similar stratagem to overcome the giant Orgoglio (*Faerie Queene*, I. viii. 22-24).

[4] Bugge (*DgF* iv, pp. 704-5 and 709-10) has tried to prove that the English ballad corresponding to *Orm* is *King Estmere* (Child No. 60). If he is right in that theory, the above-mentioned connexion is so much more strange.

[5] See Grundtvig, *DgF* iii, pp. 775-7; and Þorólfsson, *Rímur fyrir 1600*, pp. 416-18.

corresponding to this episode; so the feature was presumably added at some later time. In England occurrences of the motif of the severed legs appear to be more frequent and to go back to a more distant past than in Scandinavia. If, therefore, there is a direct connexion, it seems more probable that the trait wandered from England to Iceland and Denmark.

In another point the Orm ballad agrees with the Scandinavian versions of the Gunhild ballad: the king's entry into the hall to ask who is willing to fight resembles the queen's appeal to the warriors in *Ravengaard og Memering*. In both cases all remain silent save one, the youngest. This, of course, is part of the very motif of the unpromising hero,[1] but the way in which it is told shows plainly that there must have been direct influence one way or the other. The rhyme-pair *ord—bord* occurs in the Danish versions A, B, D, and F and in the Swedish version A of *Orm*.[2] This is an extremely common rhyme in Danish balladry; yet the fact that it occurs in precisely the same place in all the versions and in the corresponding stanzas of *Ravengaard og Memering*, versions B, I, and K,[3] can hardly be accidental. The actual phrase used of Memering in B 18, G 15, and I 16 (cf. L 17), 'Memering (han) sprang over breden Bord', occurs, spoken of Orm, in D 13 of that ballad.[4] It is obvious that there must have been direct borrowing, but it is hard to determine to which of the ballads the passage belonged originally. The fact that in *Orm Ungersvend* the rhyme-pair *ord—bord* is chiefly confined to the Danish versions might indicate a loan from the Gunhild ballad,

[1] Consequently, we find it also in the early English tradition, but told in different terms: 'ceteris . . . refugientibus', &c.

[2] Danish C 7 has *Ord—tare* (= *torde*?), while E has a quite differently phrased stanza, which we find again in the Swedish version B. The rhyme does not occur in the Norwegian versions.

[3] G 15 has *jo—Bord*, which is undoubtedly due to corruption.

[4] This phrase occurs also in *Ormars Rímur* ('stökkr fram yfir stillis borð'), and, as shown by Bugge (*DgF* iv, p. 705), it can be traced back to *Hervarar Saga*. This is a very common expression, however, for the simple reason that the corresponding action was very common, owing to the special arrangement of the tables in the hall (see Grundtvig, *DgF* iv, p. 754, n. *c* to No. 19). The phrase is therefore of little value in itself, but its connexion with this particular rhyme in all the cases mentioned can hardly be due to chance.

which is not found in Sweden. On the other hand, the whole scene in the hall is found in all the versions of the Orm story, Icelandic, Norwegian, Swedish, and Danish; it is an original part of that story, while in the Gunhild tradition it is not known outside Scandinavia. It is, to my mind, more probable that the Gunhild ballad borrowed the hall scene from *Orm Ungersvend.* This view is borne out by certain considerations to be mentioned in the following section.

§ 25. *Folk-tale Elements*

If we compare the ancient English versions of the Gunhild story with the modern Scandinavian ones, we find the folk-tale element much more pronounced in the latter. In the former it is confined to the fight itself and consists in the idea of a dwarf unexpectedly conquering a giant; in the latter further folk-tale features have been added. Thus in all the modern Danish versions Memering wins Gunhild's hand by his fight; he is no longer the disinterested chivalrous defender of the fair sex. That this is a recent feature is confirmed by the fact that it does not occur in Danish A (dating from *c.* 1550), which ends with a re-conciliation scene between Henrik and Gunhild, similar to the one in the English and Scottish ballads. Now obviously this change is due to the influence of stories of wooing contests or of winning a princess by a fight with a giant, and very likely the influence has come, to some extent at least, from the ballad of *Orm Ungersvend og Bermer-Rise* mentioned in the last section.

In the light of this theory of progressive folk-tale influence the obscure features in the Norwegian version of the Gunhild ballad become perfectly intelligible. The beginning is generally believed to be missing: no reason is given for the fight; and the marriage, which one would expect to come at the beginning, is mentioned towards the end. The explanation undoubtedly is that the story has been so strongly exposed to the influence of folk-tale that the original main theme has been entirely forgotten; there is no longer any accusation of adultery. The story has become simply a story of rescuing a lady from the clutches of a giant, thereby winning her hand; and in true folk-tale fashion it is the youngest in her service, a mere boy, who succeeds where others fail. The marriage at the end is, of course, between Mimmer-Tand and Gunhild. Though the story has thus been completely changed, the proper names and certain snatches of phrase quoted by Strøm prove it to have been originally the same story as in the other versions.

The English ballad as found in the Percy Folio has only one added folk-lore feature: the dwarf has been made into a supernatural being. In Scott's version the figure of the dwarf has disappeared altogether, and in his place we find a perfectly normal human being, Sir Hugh le Blond: the story has been turned into an ordinary tale of chivalry.

§ 26. 'Sisibe'

The nearest approach in Scandinavian prose to a story like the ballad one is the tale of Sisibe, the mother of Sigurð, as told in Þiðriks Saga.[1] Summoned to arms to help his sister's husband, Sigmund entrusted his lands and his queen to the care of two of his nobles, Hartvin and Herman. Supported by Herman, Hartvin suggested to the queen that she should marry him, and that the two together should rule the kingdom. She refused indignantly and threatened him with the gallows. On the king's return, Hartvin and Herman went out to meet him and told him that during his absence the queen had had a handsome thrall for her lover and was with child by him. The king asked them how best to punish her, and Hartvin suggested leading her into a desolate forest, cutting out her tongue, and leaving her there to die. The king thought this good advice and commanded them to do so. When they got to the forest, however, Herman wanted to leave Sisibe unhurt and cut out the tongue of a dog instead to take back to the king. They quarrelled and fought over this, and Hartvin was killed. Sisibe gave birth to a son, Sigurð, and died.

Þiðriks Saga was composed by a Norwegian about 1260 from

[1] Bertelsen's edition, vol. ii, pp. 282–300.

north German legendary material, partly songs or ballads.[1] The story of Sisibe is not known from elsewhere. Presumably it goes back to the German source of the saga, and it is no doubt ultimately derived from a French tale (cf. p. 126).

[1] Cf. de Vries, *Altnordische Literaturgeschichte*, § 277; and the explicit statements by the author of the saga, vol. i, p. 2, ll. 13 ff., and vol. ii, p. 328, ll. 8 ff.

VI
HISTORY OF THE NAMES

§ 27. *Henrik and Gunhild*

THE etymology of the names of the two combatants in our ballad is linked to some extent with the history of the ballad itself. This is not the case, however, with Henrik (Henry) and Gunhild. Both of these are widely used names, whose histories are independent of that of the ballad. Neither is English in origin. Henry appears to be due mainly to Norman influence;[1] Gunhild is of Scandinavian origin and was the name of several members of the Danish royal family in England in the eleventh century.[2] On the Continent, Gunhild was a common name both in Germany and Scandinavia.[3] The Scandinavian name Henrik appears to be of foreign, probably German, provenance, since most of the bearers of that name recorded by Lind were foreigners.

§ 28. *Raadengaard*

Danish *Raadengaard*[4] is obviously the same name as English *Rodingar*. The latter is of rare occurrence; I have not encountered it outside the Gunhild story. The English forms of the name are: *Rodingar* (Ralph de Diceto's Rodingarus, John Brompton's Roddyngar), which is the normal equivalent of the Danish form, *Rodegan* (Life of St. Edward and, spelt *Rodogan*, Matthew Paris's *Chronica Majora*), *Rodingham* (Child B), and *Aldingar* (Child A). The form *Rodegan* has been explained above (p. 24),[5]

---

[1] Cf. Forssner, *Continental-Germanic Personal Names in England*, and Charlotte Yonge as quoted by E. Partridge, *Name this Child* (London, 1938).

[2] Cf. Björkman, *Nordische Personennamen in England*. See also pp. 95–96 of this book.

[3] Cf. Förstemann, *Altdeutsches Namenbuch*; Lind, *Norsk-Isländska Dopnamn*; and Knudsen, Kristensen, and Hornby, *Danmarks gamle Personnavne*.

[4] This is a variant and probably more original form of *Ravengaard*.

[5] The difference between *Rodegan* and *Rodingar* recalls the vacillation between *messager* and *messenger*, *nightegale* and *nightingale*, &c., found in late Middle English and early Modern English; cf. O. Jespersen, *Modern English Grammar*, vol. i (Heidelberg, 1909), pp. 35–37. It is doubtful whether

and *Rodingham* presents no difficulty: it is a variant of the kind
that is almost inevitable in oral tradition; it must be due to the
analogy of other names in -*ingham*, such as *Hardingham* and *Wal-
singham*. In *Aldingar* the loss of the initial sound was probably
caused by the preceding *Sir*, which occurs in none of the other
versions: the phrase Sir Rodingar may easily have been mis-
interpreted as *Sir Odingar* with a linking *r* at the end of *Sir*. The
l may have crept in under the influence of other names beginning
with *Ald-*: *Aldingham*, *Aldington*, &c.

The Scandinavian name is known from three different
ballads (see p. 59). The forms fall into several groups; dis-
regarding mere variations in spelling,[1] we can classify them as
follows: (1) Corresponding to *Rodingar* we have *Raadengaard*
(*DgF* 7 A and H; 12 C), *Radengaard* (*DgF* 7 G), *Radengaardt*
(*DgF* 7 I), *Radengårdh* (*DgF* 7, Swedish version),[2] *Rodenigår*
(*DgF* 12, Norwegian version),[3] *Raanegaardt* (*DgF* 12 B), *Rone-
gaardt* (ib.), *Ronnegaar* (*DgF* 13, Norwegian version), *Röngård*
(*DgF* 13 H). (2) The old Danish version (A) of our ballad has
Ravengaard (I have simplified the spelling), which form is also
found in *DgF* 7 D and 12 A. It is worth noting that all three of
the versions containing this particular form are taken from the
same manuscript, the Karen Brahe Folio. Yet the form of the
first element of the name can hardly be a mere caprice of Karen
Brahe's: we find it again in the modern Danish *Ravnlil* (*DgF*
13 B, G, K, L, M) and *Ravnhild* (ib. I), which have substituted
different endings, but have kept the first part. (3) *Rundkrud
Hagensgaard* (*DgF* 13 C) is peculiarly corrupt; it is not possible
to tell which of the older types it represents. (4) Faroese *Roysningur* and Icelandic *Rögnvald* differ so much from the rest of
the forms that it is doubtful if they are related to them at all (see
pp. 89 and 91).

there is any connexion: the phenomenon is considerably later than Matthew
Paris's time.
  [1] The spellings *aa* and *å* are different ways of representing the same
sound [ɔ:].
  [2] Arwidsson, *Svenska Fornsånger*, No. 4 B.
  [3] Liestøl and Moe, *Norske Folkeviser*, vol. ii, No. 52.

Outside balladry I know only a few instances of this name, at least in the particular form in which we meet it in the Gunhild story. It resembles AS. *Hrōþgār* (ON. *Hróðgeirr*, OHG. *Hrōdgēr*) and is very likely the same name with a middle syllable added. To *Hrōþgār*, *Hróðgeirr*, &c., corresponds MHG. *Rüedegēr*, the name of Attila's faithful margrave, Theodoric's friend, in the Nibelungen Story. We find this name in certain German sources as *Riedinger* (fifteenth century) and *Rudinger* (sixteenth century).[1] Further, in the thirteenth-century *Þiðriks Saga*, which is based on German legend, the same character is known as *Roðingeirr*. Though these forms come very close to *Rodingar* the two characters denoted are utterly unlike. There are indications, however, that the ballad name *Raadengaard* was associated with the Theodoric legend. In the Danish ballad *Kong Didrik og hans Kæmper* (*DgF* 7) Raadengaard figures as one of King Didrik's (Theodoric's) warriors. That this Raadengaard was considered, at least by some, to be identical with Gunhild's accuser, is shown by the fact that, in version A of the same ballad, Memering, Raadengaard's opponent in the Gunhild ballad, appears as another of King Didrik's retainers. Raadengaard occurs, moreover, in *Raadengaard og Ørnen* (*DgF* 12), a story which is probably also linked with the Theodoric legend.[2]

Though *Raadengaard* corresponds fairly closely to *Roðingeirr*, it is not the normal Danish equivalent. To ON. *geirr* and AS. *gār* would correspond Danish *gēr*. This is due to a change from *ei* to *ē*, which took place probably in the tenth century.[3] In the various German dialects the word became *gēr* at an even earlier date, perhaps as early as the seventh century; hence *Hrōdgēr*, *Rüedegēr*, &c.[4] We should therefore expect the ancient Danish form of the name to be something like *Rodinger* or *Rothinger*. As a matter of fact, this form did exist; I have found two instances.

[1] See Grimm, *Die deutsche Heldensage*, pp. 283 and 302.
[2] See Bugge, *Helgedigtene i den ældre Edda*, pp. 268 ff.
[3] Cf. Brøndum-Nielsen, *Gammeldansk Grammatik*, vol. i, §§ 172 and 145. 2.
[4] See, for example, Behaghel, 'Geschichte der deutschen Sprache', § 182, in Paul's *Grundriss*, pt. iii (1916).

The first occurs in the *Annales Slesuicenses*,[1] which have survived
in a manuscript in Anders Sørensen Vedel's hand (1542–1616),
but are of considerably earlier date. They form a consecutive
history of Denmark down to 1268, arranged first according to
kings and later in the form of annals. As these annals devote
particular attention to matters concerning Slesvig, there is
reason to believe that the author or authors of the original document must be sought in that district. In connexion with the
Emperor Henry I's invasion of Denmark in 934, during the
reign of Gorm the Old, we read:

> Tunc imperator Henricus ad restinguendam persecutionem in
> Dania . . . coloniam Saxonum uocauit et posuit ibi in monte castrum
> iuxta Haddeboth, ubi posuit marchionem Roythengerum.

And, again, of Gorm the Old's successor, Harold Bluetooth, we
read:

> . . . rebellare cupiens imperio marchionem Rodingherum cum
> legatis imperatoris trucidauit et coloniam Saxonum.

This Margrave Rodinger or Roythenger is not otherwise known
to us, and he may be quite unhistorical. Waitz is inclined to
identify him with the 'Ruedeger von Bechelaren' of the Attila-
Theodoric legend, and Haupt,[2] who believes that the author's
source of information was local Slesvig tradition, would see in
this document a proof of the existence of the Theodoric legend
in Slesvig.

The second instance is unconnected with the Theodoric
legend; it is the name of the Danish King Canute VI's cup-
bearer. In a document which Suhm[3] calls 'King Canute's will'
we are told that Canute bequeathed half his property to the
Church. His brother, Duke Valdemar, his mother, Lady Sophia,
and Sunni, the King's Marshal, made similar bequests, while
various other members of the royal household made smaller

---

[1] Ed. Ellen Jørgensen, *Annales Danici Medii Ævi*, pp. 132 ff. See also
Waitz, 'Zur Kritik dänischer Geschichtsquellen', pp. 33 ff.

[2] 'Zur niederdeutschen Dietrichsage', pp. 149–50.

[3] *Historie af Danmark*, vol. viii, p. 399. The document itself is printed on
p. 707.

donations. Amongst the latter items is the one that interests us in this connexion: '*Rothingerus* Pincerna marcam auri [dedit]'. Suhm ascribes the document to the year 1197; at any rate, it must belong somewhere within the period of Canute's reign, 1182–1202.

Rodenger or *Rothenger* could not have given *Raadengaard* by any regular development. Corresponding to the latter form we should expect an early Danish form ending in -*gārth*.[1] No such form has been recorded. In Nielsen's collection of Old Danish personal names we find only two names with that ending, *Salgarth* and *Thorgarth*, but at least twenty-five with the ending -*gēr*. Yet the possibility remains that there may once have existed a name *Rothengarth*, possibly under German influence.[2] Two somewhat similar forms have been recorded. The first, *Rotingar*, is found in a Latin document of the year 1177 in which the Danish King Valdemar I bequeathed some property to Ringsted Church. Among the witnesses to this deed was a certain 'miles' named Rotingar.[3] The second form, *Rotengaardt*, comes from a Latin title-deed of 1245. Here, unfortunately, the deed itself does not appear to have survived; it is known only from an entry in a list, compiled about 1600, of documents preserved at Skanderborg Castle.[4] The entry summarizes the deed in Danish, and one cannot escape a suspicion that the spelling of the name, as given in that summary, may have been modernized. Altogether

---

[1] The final syllable of a trisyllabic word like *Rothengarth* would normally tend to become weakened and would not be likely to produce -*gaard*; but the analogy of place-names might influence the development. Cf. such a name as Norwegian *Loðinsgarðr* > *Lodensgardi* (dative) 1344 > *Laadengaard* 1668; see O. Rygh, *Norske Gaardnavne*, vol. iv. 1 (Christiania, 1900), p. 206. It is worthy of note that the tune to version H of our ballad proves the stress to have been on the last syllable of the name *Röngård*, while that is not so in the versions that have altered the name to *Ravnlil*, &c.; see *DgF* xi, pp. 6–9.

[2] German *Hrōdgēr*, like most other German names in -*gēr*, has parallel forms in -*gar* and -*gard*. See Förstemann, op. cit., who explains the names in -*gar* as containing the OHG. word *garo* (= AS. *gearu*). The *a* would consequently be short and the syllable somewhat unlikely to produce -*gaard*. The etymology of the ending -*gard* is uncertain.

[3] See Suhm, op. cit., vol. vii, p. 502.

[4] See *De ældste danske Archivregistraturer*, ed. T. A. Becker, vol. i (Copenhagen, 1854), p. 266.

we cannot base any reliable conclusions on these two isolated instances. The forms do not tally completely with the name Raadengaard, and, moreover, neither of the persons in question seems likely to have bequeathed his name to the ballad character.

A far more likely prototype is the English form *Rodingar*.[1] The latter name must be presumed to have had a long *a* like other early English names in *-gār*. This vowel later, both in England (south of the Humber) and in Scandinavia, developed into a rounded vowel, the one found in modern English *gore*. In Scandinavia this sound is denoted by *aa* or *å*. There is thus almost perfect agreement between *Rodingar* and the Norwegian forms mentioned above, *Rodenigår* and *Ronnegaar*. The Danish forms end in *d* or *dt*, but we cannot be certain that these letters were ever sounded. It is a regular feature of modern Danish pronunciation to leave out *d* in the noun *gaard* and words of similar structure. This goes back to an early loss of *þ* in the combination *rþ* (written *rth*, *rdh*, or *rd*), which took place in the fourteenth and fifteenth centuries.[2] This development led to a certain amount of confusion; we sometimes find words which were never pronounced with a final *d* written with one. Very likely, *Raadengaard* belongs to the latter group.[3] The spelling with a *d* is no doubt due to the influence of the common noun *gaard*.

It is not possible, from philological evidence alone, to date the passage of our name from England to Scandinavia with more than very rough accuracy. Opinions differ as to when the rounding of *ā* took place in England. Spellings with *o* are encountered from about 1150, and, according to Wyld,[4] the change would seem to have been completed in the first quarter of the thirteenth century. Luick,[5] on the other hand, would place the completion

---

[1] This suggestion was first made by Bugge in *Helgedigtene i den ældre Edda*, pp. 270-1.

[2] See Brøndum-Nielsen, *Gammeldansk Grammatik*, vol. ii, § 402.

[3] The solitary Swedish instance of the name, *Radengårdh*, is due to Danish influence. The stanza in which it occurs, Arwidsson 4 B 14, is simply a translation of *DgF* 7 H 22. Cf. Grundtvig, *DgF* i, pp. 64-65.

[4] H. C. Wyld, *A Short History of English* (London, 1927), § 156.

[5] K. Luick, *Historische Grammatik der englischen Sprache* (Leipzig, 1921), § 369.

of the change considerably later, in the northernmost area involved (southern Yorkshire) not till about 1400. Now it is unlikely that English *Rodingār* ever became *Rodingore*; such a
development is contradicted by the modern forms *Aldingar* and
Rodingham.[1] These must be due to a shortening of the vowel of
the final syllable, by which it escaped the rounding which over-
took long *a*. It thus appears that the change from *ā* to *å* in our
name took place on Scandinavian soil. Consequently, the name
must have been exported to Scandinavia before *ā* had been
shortened, and as this shortening must of necessity have happened before the completion of the rounding process in England,
i.e. before 1400, that year may be considered as the final limit
for the passage of our name from England to Scandinavia. This
terminus ante quem is confirmed by the Scandinavian evidence.
Here, too, opinions differ as to the precise date of the rounding
of *ā*, and probably the process was not simultaneous in the
whole of the Scandinavian area. In Denmark the rounding
seems to have taken place in the latter half of the thirteenth
century; in Norway probably not much later and certainly before 1400.[2] The latter date, then, is upheld as the final limit for
the migration of our name; but most probably the event took
place some time, perhaps a long time, before that year. We shall
return to this question later.

In view of the rarity of the name, it is probable that the
borrowing is connected with the passage of our story from
England to Scandinavia. As will be shown in the next chapter,
the strange name *Mimecan* appears to have followed the same
route. In Scandinavia the name *Rodingar* probably became
associated with the *Rodenger* or *Roðingeirr* of the Theodoric

---

[1] Cf. also place-names containing the related AS. word *gāra*: modern
Langar (Nottinghamshire) and *Bredgar* (Kent); see A. Mawer, *The Chief
Elements used in English Place-names* (Cambridge, 1924). The title of Gilbert
and Sullivan's opera *Ruddigore* somewhat resembles the name that we are
trying to trace, but this similarity is probably purely accidental.

[2] See Brøndum-Nielsen, op. cit., vol. i, § 138; Noreen, 'Geschichte der
nordischen Sprachen', §§ 88 and 139; and M. Hægstad, 'Vestnorske Maalføre
fyre 1350', pt. ii. 2, vol. i (*Videnskapsselskapets Skrifter*, ii. Hist.-Filos. Klasse,
1915, No. 3, Christiania, 1916), pp. 88–89.

legend. That would account for the appearance of *Raadengaard*
as one of King Theodoric's warriors (see p. 59).

The variant form *Ravengaard*, found in one of the Danish
manuscripts, may indicate German influence. This form, it will
be recalled, is unknown in Norway. It resembles the German
name *Ravengar*, to which it probably owes its first element,
while the second element is due to *Raadengaard*.

How far back the name *Rodingar* dates in England it is impossible to say. The ending *-gār* goes back to an earlier *-gair*.
The change from *ai* to *ā*, which took place probably in the sixth
century, meant a break with the continental form of that ending
(which later became *-gēr* in many dialects: see p. 59); but even
after that date a translator may have had a general impression
that the normal English equivalent to *ai* or *ē* would be *ā* and
may have substituted that sound when introducing the name
Rodingar. On the other hand, although *Mimecan*, as we shall see,
is of continental origin and appears to have come over with the
story itself, it is not necessary to assume the same to have been
the case with *Rodingar*. That name may have been added in
England (cf. p. 32).

§ 29. *Place of Memering in Balladry*

Memering[1] occurs in all the Scandinavian versions of the
Gunhild ballad except the Icelandic one. In the Faroese versions, however, the figure is quite out of place and has obviously
been imported from Denmark (cf. p. 14). In all the Danish
versions, except A, G, and L, Memering is described as little
(cf. p. 13 n.). His smallness is particularly stressed in the Norwegian version, where the queen taunts him by saying that he
had better stay at home and tend his sheep. The Faroese
versions appear to have preserved some original lines, now
lost in the other versions, about Memering's diminutive size.

[1] The spelling of this name varies considerably in the different versions.
For convenience' sake I generally use the above form except in quotations
containing a different spelling.

Faroese D, which is partly in Danish, has among its Danish stanzas:

> 27. Gunhild gaar neder til den Strand,
> mødte hende liden Mimmering Tand.

> 28. Mødte hende liden Mimmering Tand,
> han var den eneste christen Mand.[1]

Version E, which is entirely in Faroese, has the second of these stanzas in what is undoubtedly an older form:

> 25. Hàr møtti henni Mimmering Tann,
> hann vàr tann minsti kristin mann.

The phrase *den eneste* ('the only') does not make sense, while *tann minsti* ('the smallest') fits in perfectly. Further proof of this theory comes from Strøm's summary of the lost Norwegian version. He quotes a few phrases from the ballad, among which is 'Mimmer-Tand, den mindste kristne Mand'.[2]

It is strange that these lines, which appear to have been the standard description of our hero, his leitmotif so to speak, should have got lost in all the Danish versions of our ballad. There are a few faint traces of them in C:

> 31. Ak, hvem udi mit ganske Land
> har hugget Rundkrud, den store Mand?

> 32. Ja, Memring, den mindste Mand,
> har hugget Rundkrud, den store Mand.

As will be shown presently, there are also traces of them elsewhere in Danish balladry.

Memering occurs in three other Danish ballads. In version A (sixteenth century) of *DgF* 7, *Kong Didrik og hans Kæmper*, he figures side by side with Raadengaard among King Didrik's

---

[1] Translations of the Scandinavian versions of the Gunhild ballad are given in the Appendix. On the peculiar name *Tand* see later (pp. 74 ff.).

[2] Strøm gives it as 'den mindste kristne Mand paa Runda'; but this, as pointed out by Grundtvig (*DgF* ii, p. 645), is evidently because he mistakes the refrain *paa Runda* for part of the sentence.

(Theodoric's) warriors. The stanza in which he is mentioned runs as follows:

> 53. Ther skinner y denn thiennde skioldt,
> der skinner y itt spiudt:
> thenn fører hannd liidenn Memerinng Thannt,
> for inngenn vill hanndt fly.[1]

DgF 14, *Memering*, is about him alone. The ballad exists only in a few versions, the oldest of which is found in a sixteenth-century manuscript.[2] It relates how Memering, the smallest man ever born in King Karl's land, wore a coat of mail before he could walk; and as soon as he was able to carry a sword he set forth in quest of adventure. After slaying a knight who spurned the offer of his services because of his tiny size, he met Vidrik Verlandsen (the Viðga, son of Velent, of *Þiðriks Saga*) and challenged him to a fight. They fought for two days; but as neither could conquer the other, they swore brotherhood in arms. The opening stanza of this ballad runs as follows:

> Mimering vor den mindste mandt,
> som fødd vor paa Karl kongens landt.[3]

Finally, we meet Memering in two versions of *DgF* 16, *Grev Genselin*. This ballad exists in three Danish versions (A, B, and C), all sixteenth century, and in one Norwegian and three Faroese versions (printed in *DgF* iv, pp. 732–42), all nineteenth century.[4] The versions that concern us here are Danish C and the Norwegian version, which I shall call N. The action of the ballad is very slight and is mainly concerned with a fight between Genselin

---

[1]   There shines on the tenth shield,
There shines on it a spear:
That carries little Memering Thannt;
For no one will he flee.

[2] The name Memering occurs only in this one version. It is unknown in the two Norwegian variants (see p. 73). Two fragments of ballads recorded in Jutland in the 1870's may be versions of this ballad, but they do not contain the name Memering; see *DgF* x, p. 6.

[3]   Mimering was the smallest man
Who was born in King Karl's land.

[4] The version given by Vedel (pt. i, No. 6) is made up of Danish B and C; see Grundtvig, *DgF* i, pp. 222 and 229–30. This highly 'edited' variant exists also in a Swedish translation: Arwidsson No. 6. Both Vedel and Arwidsson have a stanza mentioning Memering, based on C 30.

and a certain Ivar Blaa, who is conquered and offers Genselin his sweetheart. Genselin declines, but says that he will have Ivar's sister (C: sister's daughter) instead. The rest of the ballad is a description of the festivities in connexion with Genselin's wedding. The burlesque character of this part gives an impression of late origin;[1] it is missing in the Faroese versions, which end with Genselin's betrothal. It is in this latter part that Memering comes in, and this very fact must, of course, make us suspicious.

Among the wedding guests mentioned in C are several of Theodoric's warriors. In the final stanza Memering occurs:

> 30. Den mindste kempe, i dantzen vaar,
> vaar femtan alne neden kne:
> uden hin lille Mimmering Tand,
> hand vaar den eniste christen mand.[2]

The absurdity of the phrase *den eniste* ('the only') is even more apparent here than in the stanza from the Gunhild ballad mentioned above. The talk is about size only; moreover, as Genselin earlier in the same ballad (st. 11) invokes the aid of 'Jesus, son of Mary', Memering cannot have been the only Christian present. Altogether, the stanza makes a very corrupt impression, and it is easy to prove that it did not belong to the ballad originally. Its rhyme-scheme differs from that of the rest of the ballad, which has *abcb*. Stanza 30 is quite irregular: the first two lines have no rhyme at all, while lines 3 and 4 rhyme together. Now the first two lines appear as lines 3 and 4 of the preceding stanza:

> 29. De begynte en skrecker-rey
> fra Ribe oc indtil Slie:
> Den mindste kempe, i dantzen vaar,
> vaar femtan alne neden kne.[3]

---

[1] Cf. Grundtvig, *DgF* i, pp. 222–3; and von der Recke, *Danmarks Fornviser*, vol. i, pp. 129–30.

[2]   The smallest warrior in the dance
        Was fifteen ells below the knee,
        Saving little Mimmering Tand:
        He was the only Christian man.

[3]   They began a skrecker-rey [a kind of dance]
        From Ribe right to Slie.
        The smallest warrior in the dance
        Was fifteen ells below the knee.

Obviously, C 30 is a later addition made up simply by taking the last two lines of st. 29 and tacking on to them two lines borrowed from another ballad with a different metrical structure, probably *Ravengaard og Memering*. The removal of the figure of Memering from *Grev Genselin* does not affect the story in the slightest.

What suggested the addition was first of all the phrase *den mindste kempe*, which recalls the standard description of Memering as *den mindste mand*.[1] There is reason to think that the former phrase itself was borrowed from another ballad. The last two lines of st. 29 are practically identical with the ending of the Faroese version A of *Kong Didrik og hans Kæmper* (*DgF* 7):

> 61. .   .   .   .   .   .
>   tann minsta kempa í dansinum
>   var fýra alin til kníggja. (*DgF* iv, p. 617.)

Although it is not possible to determine for certain which of the ballads borrowed from the other, or whether they both borrowed from a common source, I am inclined to think that *Kong Didrik* (though not necessarily the Faroese version: the stanza may have occurred, but got lost, in other versions) was the giver and *Grev Genselin* the receiver. The lines serve to emphasize great stature and thus fit in well with a description of King Theodoric's warriors. In other respects, also, *Kong Didrik* seems to have influenced *Grev Genselin* (see pp. 70 and 72), no doubt because of the presence of some of Theodoric's warriors at Genselin's wedding feast.

In version N Memering plays a more active part than in C. Special Norwegian popular heroes are here substituted for Theodoric's warriors. Vidrik and Memering are still among the wedding guests, however, and when Vidrik slays Grenjehetta, one of the bridesmaids, because of her rowdy behaviour, Memering protests:

[1] A contributory cause may have been the occurrence of a bridesmaid named *Gyndehelte* (= Gunhild): see p. 70.

30. De va' då den minste Mimring,
    han sine hendanne sló:
    'Kven tóre slíkt våge,
    å drepa tóre mi mór?'[1]

But Vidrik finds it hardly worth while to use his sword: he kills Memering with a single blow of his fist.

The phrase *den minste Mimring* ('the smallest Mimring') is very peculiar. We find it again in st. 32, the final stanza, where *mimring* is used apparently as a common noun:

32. Der kom í so ædelig en dans
    uppå golvet slette:
    den minste mimring, í dansen va',
    va' femten alner ti knétti.[2]

This stanza may afford a clue. It will be noticed that it is almost the same as C 29 quoted above. The main difference is that the word *mimring* has crept in instead of *kempe* 'warrior'. This is probably due to a faint, but faulty, recollection of C 29–30 (or the corresponding stanzas of a now lost version). C 29, as explained above, suggests the figure of Memering, who is thereupon introduced in the following stanza. Stanza 32 of the Norwegian version is simply C 29 with Memering introduced in the stanza itself. The use of the word as a common noun is not without precedent; *mimring* is sometimes used in Scandinavia to denote a 'dwarf', a meaning probably derived from the proper name (see § 31). Here this meaning hardly makes sense; but then the version as a whole makes an even more confused impression than the Danish versions and is obviously a late composite of elements taken from elsewhere. The incident of Vidrik and Memering was, in my opinion, added after st. 32 had received its

---

[1] It was the smallest Mimring,
He beat his hands together:
'Who dares to do a deed like that,
Who dares to kill my mother?'

[2] There began a noble dance
Upon the floor so smooth:
The smallest mimring in the dance
Was fifteen ells up to the knee.

present form. Hence the phrase *den minste Mimring* in st. 30, which makes some sort of sense when *mimring* is taken as a common noun, but none whatever if the word is a pure proper name.

It is possible to some extent to follow the growth of the Genselin ballad and to watch the way in which extra scenes have been added. The extant Faroese versions undoubtedly present a more original form of the story.[1] The wedding scene, found only in the Norwegian and Danish versions, must have been taken principally from *Tord af Havsgaard* (*DgF* 1), but also from the Faroese ballad *Ismal*.[2] The latter ballad seems to have supplied the names of the bridesmaids, Brynild and Kremold (i.e. Grimhild) in A and B, and Gyndehelte (i.e. Gunhild) or, very corruptly, Grenjehetta in C and N. It is doubtful whether this Gunhild has anything whatever to do with the Gunhild of *Ravengaard og Memering*, but the mere fact that the names Gunhild and Memering are coupled in that ballad may have served to attract Memering to *Grev Genselin*. Significantly enough, the figure occurs only in the two versions which have a bridesmaid called Gunhild.

In the Danish versions, as in *Tord af Havsgaard*, it is the bride who gets rowdy, and in A and B she has a fight with the giant Langben Risker. In the Norwegian version (N) this part is played by Grenjehetta, and her fight, as we have seen, is with Vidrik, not Langben. This is no doubt a later development. There is a reminiscence of Langben Risker in N 28, which is modelled on a stanza of *Kong Didrik og hans Kæmper*, A 16.[3] The latter ballad opens with a fight between Vidrik and Langben, and st. A 16 refers to Langben. In *Grev Genselin*, version N, the corresponding stanza (28) is assigned to Vidrik, and it has been slightly modified under the influence of A 29 and B 32 of the Genselin ballad.

Yet another circumstance is of importance in order to under-

---

[1] Cf. Grundtvig, *DgF* i, pp. 222–3; and von der Recke, *Danmarks Fornviser*, vol. i, pp. 129–30.

[2] Hammershaimb, *Sjurðar Kvæði*, p. 78.

[3] The stanza is found in a corrupt form in several of the other versions of *Kong Didrik*.

stand how the Vidrik incident came to be included in *Grev Genselin*; the legendary name for Vidrik's sword is *Memering* (*Mimring*, &c.). At any rate, that is the commonest form of the name in Scandinavian ballads;[1] elsewhere in Germanic legend, for example in the Middle High German poem *Biterolf*, the Norse *Þiðriks Saga*, and the Anglo-Saxon poem *Waldere* (i. 3 and ii. 4–5), the name has a somewhat different form without an *r*: *Miming* (*Mimung*,[2] *Mimming*, &c.). *Miming* is said to be Weland's work, but the name appears to be derived from the smith *Mime* mentioned in *Biterolf* and *Þiðriks Saga*.[3] In the latter work, *Mime* (*Mimir*) is stated to be Weland's teacher. It is doubtful whether the name was originally applied to Vidrik's sword, although, to be sure, it was a sword-name in its origin. In Saxo,[4] *Mimingus* is the name of a wood-spirit who dwells in a cave, and whom Hother robs of a magic sword in order to kill Balder. The motif of the sword undoubtedly represents a late change in the story of Balder's death; a magic sword has been substituted for the original branch of mistletoe. The plant-name *mistletoe* seems to have been kept as a name for the sword,[5] and this then caused the original name of the sword to be transferred to its owner.[6] That *Miming* was originally the name of the sword

[1] Found, e.g., in *DgF* 7 A, B, C, E, and the corresponding Swedish ballad, Arwidsson 3 A; *DgF* 10 A, B, C, D, F, G, and Arw. 5 A. Arw. 5 B has *Vimmering*, which is undoubtedly a mistake, perhaps due to *Vidrik*. Another Swedish variant has *Mörding* (see Arwidsson, vol. i, pp. 27 and 406), and Arw. 3 B 17 has the peculiarly corrupt line: 'Min brynia heeter mit godhe sverdh' ('My byrnie is the name of my good sword').

[2] The form *Mimung* is also found in the Faroese version A (late eighteenth century) of *DgF* 7: see *DgF* iv, p. 615, st. 16. The other Faroese version of that ballad (early nineteenth century) has *Mimaring*: see ib., pp. 617 ff., sts. 21, 67, and 92. In Svabo's collection one Faroese ballad (*Disja Dølgur*) has *Miming* and another (*Engankaari*) has *Mimmaring*; see Matras's edition pp. 91 and 294.

[3] Cf. H. Falk, *Altnordische Waffenkunde* (Christiania, 1914), pp. 55–56. On sword-names in *-ing* derived from personal names, see also Olrik, *The Heroic Legends of Denmark*, p. 146.

[4] Bk. iii. Holder's edition, pp. 70–71.

[5] Cf. *Hrómundar Saga Greipssonar*, where Hromund attacks a ghost in a barrow and steals a sword called Mistletoe. A sword of the same name is mentioned in *Hervarar Saga*, ch. ii.

[6] Cf. Herrmann, *Die dänische Geschichte des Saxo Grammaticus*, vol. ii, pp. 221–2.

itself is confirmed by the thirteenth-century Danish *Annales Ryenses*,[1] where we are told that Hother 'inuenit in quodam nemore Suecie gladium, qui Mimming dictus est, cum quo Balder occidit' (p. 64*a*). The sword-name *Miming* thus appears to have reached Denmark independently of the legend of Vidrik; but later, in folk-ballads, we find the two traditions merged.

When *Miming* became *Mimring*, &c., it coincided in form with the name of Gunhild's champion; indeed, it is possible that the change took place under the influence of the latter name. *Memering*, the dwarf's name, is of a different origin (see § 30), but it is obvious that the two names were sometimes confused by ballad-singers. Thus, in *Ulf van Jærn* (*DgF* 10), version A, Vidrik's sword is called *Memerick-tand*, though elsewhere the curious addition *tand* belongs to the dwarf's name alone.

To return to *Grev Genselin*: what suggested the Vidrik-Grenjehetta-Mimring incident in version N was (*a*) Grenje-hetta's (Gunhild's) association with Mimring, (*b*) Vidrik's association with Langben Risker, and (*c*) Vidrik's association with *Mimring* as the name of his sword. It is worth noting that the stanza in *DgF* 7 A following the one which, as shown above, was adapted for use as st. 28 of *Grev Genselin*, contains a line mentioning *Mimring*, Vidrik's sword. In *Grev Genselin*, the following stanza (29) tells how Vidrik killed Grenjehetta, and in st. 30 Mimring comes in as her avenger. In a sense he performs the same function here as in the Gunhild ballad, though not with equal success.

One other parallel to the Vidrik-Mimring incident might be urged: in the ballad *Memering*, mentioned above (p. 66), Memering and Vidrik fight an indecisive battle, after which they swear brotherhood in arms. It is probable, however, that Memering did not originally belong to this ballad. Being the hero, the figure cannot of course be left out; but it looks as if the ballad was at first about two entirely different people, to whom the names Memering and Vidrik were later attributed. These names occur only in the one Danish version, found in a sixteenth-century

[1] Ed. Ellen Jørgensen, *Annales Danici Medii Ævi*.

manuscript. Two Norwegian ballads[1] which are generally considered to be variants of *Memering* relate a fight between Lagi (Lagje) and a strange knight Bjönnevald (Herbjönn); but neither Memering nor Vidrik is mentioned.[2]

This leaves us with only two other ballads in which Memering occurs. *Kong Didrik og hans Kæmper* and *Ravengaard og Memering*. In the former he plays an entirely subordinate part, whose removal would not seriously affect the story. Very significantly, too, he occurs only in one version (A) of that ballad. We thus come back to the Gunhild ballad as the probable home of the Memering figure in Scandinavian balladry. Since his opponent, Raadengaard, figures at the same time as one of King Theodoric's warriors (cf. p. 59), it is but natural that Memering should come to be included in the list of warriors mentioned in *Kong Didrik og hans Kæmper*. I can give no specific explanation of how Memering and Vidrik came to be substituted for the original names in the ballad *Memering*; but as Lagi, too, is said to be little, that would form a point of contact. In addition to the spread from ballad to ballad, we have other evidence that the picturesque figure of Memering was a popular one (see § 31), and the ballad *Memering* in its Danish form may be imagined to have been composed in order to satisfy a natural curiosity as to its hero's other exploits besides his championship of Gunhild.

§ 30. *Derivation of Memering*

The sword-name *Memering* has already been dealt with (pp. 70–72). We are here concerned to find the origin of the personal name *Memering*. This name occurs with a number of different spellings, but most of them represent pronunciations differing only slightly, if at all, e.g. *Mimmering* (versions D, K, L of our ballad) and *Mimring* (G). *Nimmering* (version H) must be a corruption, though I cannot explain how it arose. *Immerik*

---

[1] Landstad, *Norske Folkeviser*, No. 90; Bugge, *DgF* iii, p. 782.

[2] E. von der Recke, *Danmarks Fornviser*, vol. i, No. 22, adduces evidence in favour of a theory that the Danish ballad is of Norwegian origin. This would confirm our view that Memering and Vidrik are unoriginal.

(version M) is also clearly a mistake; the ending -*ik* may be due to such names as Henrik and Frederick; cf. also *Memerick-tand*, the name of Vidrik's sword in *DgF* 10 (see p. 72). The most peculiar thing about the name is the little word *Tand*, which is sometimes tacked on. This form of the name occurs in: *DgF* 7 (*Kong Didrik*) A 53 *Memerinng Thannt*; *DgF* 13 (Gunhild ballad) D *Mimmering Tand*, E *Mimmaring Tann*, H *Nimmering Tant*; *DgF* 16 (*Grev Genselin*) C 30 *Mimmering Tand*.[1] Finally, in a class apart, there is the form found in the Norwegian Gunhild ballad: *Mimmer-Tand*.

Tand, pronounced [tan'],[2] is the Danish word for 'tooth'. The Faroese and Swedish form of the name, *Tann*, does not, however, mean 'tooth' in those languages; for that idea Faroese has *tonn*[3] and Swedish *tand*. This does not necessarily imply that the name never meant 'tooth'. Both the Swedish and Faroese stanzas in question are translations from the Danish, and the form *Tann* may have been adopted for the sake of the rhyme. On the other hand, this etymology leaves us as puzzled as ever.

Another explanation has been suggested by Arwidsson (vol. ii, p. 477), who thinks that *Tann*, Danish *Tand*, is 'undoubtedly a corruption of Icelandic *þegn*, early Swedish *þegen*, German *Degen* "warrior, hero" '. A transition from *þegn* to *tann* would, however, be quite unparalleled, contrary as it is to the ordinary laws of sound-development. It is true that Danish and Swedish have a word *thegn* (*tägn*), which sometimes occurs as *than* (*tan*), but these forms are due to English influence in the nineteenth century. Altogether the word appears to have been almost forgotten until it was brought into use again at the romantic revival.[4]

---

[1] The addition is also found in Vedel's heading and introduction to *DgF* 14 (*Memering*) as *Tandt*; and in his and Arwidsson's versions of *Grev Genselin* (see p. 66, n. 4) as *Tand* and *Tann* respectively.

[2] The phonetic symbol ' indicates the glottal stop, *stød*.

[3] See M. A. Jacobsen and C. Matras, *Færøsk-Dansk Ordbog* (Thorshavn and Copenhagen, 1927–8).

[4] See Dahlerup's *Ordbog over det danske Sprog*; Kalkar's *Ordbog til det ældre danske Sprog*; and Söderwall's *Ordbok öfver svenska Medeltids-Språke t*.

Bugge (*DgF* iv, p. 622) suggests an etymology which fits in perfectly with what we have already discovered about the derivation of Raadengaard. The Norwegian form *Mimmer-Tand*, says Bugge, is probably 'a corrupt form of English Mimicon, Mimecan, where -con, -can are diminutive endings; cf. Scots memerkyn'. To understand how *Mimecan* could have become *Mimmer-Tand* one must realize that there may never have been a *d* in the pronunciation of the latter name. Assimilation of *nd* to *n(n)* took place at an early date in Danish and several other Scandinavian languages.[1] After the completion of the process, i.e. after *c.* 1450, we frequently find *nd* written for original *n(n)*. The form *Mimmer-Tand* may be such an inverted spelling, covering an original *Mimmertan*. In this form the word is remarkably close in structure to *Mimecan*. The chief difference is between *c* (*k*) and *t*, and this may be explained as due to palatalization; a palatalized *k* will often sound, particularly to a foreign ear, like a variant of *t*, and vice versa.[2]

Mimetan on its adoption in Norwegian would naturally become reinterpreted in terms of Scandinavian nomenclature. There was already a name *Mime* or *Mimir* (see p. 71), and nothing is more natural than for *Mimetan* to be understood as *Mimertan* or *Mimer-Tand*. As, moreover, the smith *Mimir* gave his name to a sword *Miming* or *Mimring*, a name which in Saxo, and presumably also in his source, is transferred to the owner of the sword, there is nothing very surprising in the personal name *Mimer-Tand* becoming *Mimring-Tand*.

Three of the forms of the second part of the name as listed above (p. 74) offer some slight difficulty in the way of this theory: the sixteenth-century *Thannt* and *Tandt*, and the nineteenth-century *Tant*. The last form, which follows modern spelling rules, appears to cover a pronunciation [tan't],[3] and

[1] Cf. Brøndum-Nielsen, *Gammeldansk Grammatik*, vol. ii, § 341; and Noreen, 'Geschichte der nordischen Sprachen', §§ 132 and 184.

[2] It is also possible to explain the change from *Mimecan* to *Mim(m)e(r)tan* as due to palaeographical confusion between *c* and *t*, two letters not always clearly distinguished in medieval script.

[3] Yet in *DgF* 13 H 20 *Tant* rhymes with *kan*!

it is possibly the same pronunciation that is indicated by the other two spellings. Even those forms, however, may go back to a previous *Tan*: similar excrescent *t*'s after *n* are encountered elsewhere, both in older and modern Danish.[1]

That the two names *Mimecan* and *Mimmer-Tand* should turn out to be connected was only to be expected: the characters they represent resemble each other closely and are not paralleled elsewhere.[2] If the two forms *Mimecan* and *Mimetan* are regarded by themselves, a development from the latter to the former is quite as probable as one in the opposite direction. Considering, however, that the name *Raadengaard* appears to have passed from England to Scandinavia, it is more likely that *Mimecan* went the same way. Furthermore, Danish *Memering Tand* can hardly have developed into *Mimetan*, so if we assume that the name went from Scandinavia to England, it seems to follow that the word arose in Norway and spread from there both to England and to Denmark. Such an assumption is not supported by any other evidence. It would still leave the question of the ultimate origin of the name *Mimetan* unsolved, while, if we adopt the theory here proposed, the name *Mimecan* gives very little difficulty in that respect (see § 32).

§ 31. *Memering and Mimecan as Common Nouns*

One more possibility with regard to the origin of *Memering* remains to be discussed. The word exists (or existed) in parts of Scandinavia as a generic term for a puny, dwarfish person. Is this use of the word derived from the proper name or vice versa? The earliest record of the common noun is in a Danish dictionary published in 1626,[3] where the word is listed under the form

---

[1] Cf. Brøndum-Nielsen, op. cit., § 356.

[2] Except in the story of Gundeberg (§ 36). The similarity between Mimecan and Memering extends even to such a detail as that Mimecan (Memering) had been in Gunhild's service before her marriage and had come with her to her new home. This feature is found in the ancient English prose versions (§ 8) and in several Scandinavian versions (A 22*b*, K 35, M 22; D 29, E 26), where Memering says that he served Gunhild's father for fifteen (K and M: eleven; D and E: eight) years; cf. p. 12.

[3] Colding, *Dictionarium Herlovianum* (Copenhagen, 1626). See Kalkar, *Ordbog til det ældre danske Sprog*, s.v. 'mimring'.

mimring and is defined as 'a person dainty in appetite or small of stature, Lat. nanus'. According to Dahlerup's *Ordbog over det danske Sprog*, the word is also recorded in a manuscript dictionary compiled by M. Moth about 1700. Dahlerup himself has a quotation from Oehlenschläger's *Palnatoke* (1809). Finally, we come upon the word in a mid-nineteenth-century version of *Orm Ungersvend og Bermer-Rise* (*DgF* 11 E). This ballad, as shown above (§ 24), has some kind of connexion with the Gunhild ballad. In all the versions there is an exchange of derisive remarks before the fight between Orm and the giant, and in version E the giant calls Orm a 'mimmering', against which Orm indignantly protests: 'I am not a mimmering.' The corresponding stanzas in most of the other versions have *møsseling* or *mysseling* or some other word or phrase meaning a child or tiny person; but according to Bugge (*DgF* iii, p. 778) *mimring* is also used in a Norwegian version of *Orm Ungersvend*, and the word is still in independent use in several districts of Norway as a designation for a puny, weakly person.[1] The occurrence of the word in the Norwegian version of *Grev Genselin* has already been commented on (pp. 69–70).

All four ballads in which the character of Memering occurs are extant in sixteenth-century manuscripts. We can thus trace the proper name almost a century farther back than the common noun. Although this in itself is no proof of seniority it is at least some indication. As, moreover, the assumption that the common noun is the earlier leaves the question of the ultimate origin of the word unsolved, it is a far more likely explanation that the common noun is derived from the ballad character Memering, whose name we can trace back to the corresponding English name.

This development from proper name to common noun seems to have an exact parallel on the other side of the North Sea: *Mimecan*, too, occurs in later times as an ordinary word for a dwarf. The *Oxford Dictionary* records an early-sixteenth-century Scots word *mimmerkin* or *mymmerken*, which it hesitatingly

[1] Cf. Ross, *Norsk Ordbog*, and Torp, *Nynorsk etymologisk Ordbok*.

takes to mean 'a dotard'. It is equally uncertain about the
etymology, but suggests that the word may come from the
Middle Dutch verb *mimmeren* 'to dote'. The improbability of
this etymology has been shown by Bense,[1] who points out that
the Dutch suffix *-kijn* or *-ken* can only be added to substantives,
and there is no substantive *mimmer* in either Middle or Modern
Dutch. The meaning which the *N.E.D.* suggests is equally
questionable; it seems based mainly on the supposed etymology
of the word, so with the refutation of the etymology we may also
abandon the meaning. Jamieson[2] is undoubtedly right when he
explains the word as 'a contumelious term, apparently expres-
sive of smallness of size'. He ends his remarks on the etymology of *mimmerkin* with the following words: 'As it seems
doubtful whether an O.E. word, of an indelicate sense, does not
enter into the composition, I shall leave it without further investigation.' Whether we have missed anything by this piece of
misplaced tact it is hard to say, but I must confess my inability
to see what O.E. (what we should now call Middle English) word
Jamieson is thinking of. The form and the meaning of *mimmerkin*
prove beyond a doubt that the word is connected with *Mimecan*.

The common noun is not found in southern standard English,
but that it has had currency south of the Border is shown by
modern English dialects, where the word is still in use. Wright's
Dialect Dictionary mentions a substantive *mimmock*, 'a person
with a dainty and fastidious appetite or manner', and a corresponding verb meaning 'to play with one's food, to have a poor
appetite'. There is also a participial form *mimmocking*, (1) 'dainty
in appetite; puny, sickly, weakly'; (2) 'affected in manner'; (3)
'grimacing'. It is the participle in particular that interests us
here. Sense 1 is apparently the most common; it is the only one
that is illustrated by examples. The word in this sense seems
everywhere to be applied only to small weakly children (or sometimes animals), but never to inanimate things: 'a little mim-
mockin thing' (Herefordshire); 'Her's a poor little mimmickin

---

[1] *A Dictionary of the Low Dutch Element in the English Vocabulary.*
[2] *Etymological Dictionary of the Scotch Language* (Edinburgh, 1808).

thing, hardly worth rearing' (Somerset). Nobody can fail to notice the striking similarity, both in form and in meaning, between the word as it occurs in these examples and the proper name *Mimecan*. The so-called participle is probably older than the substantive *mimmock*. In my theory it was derived direct from *Mimecan* (or *Mimekin*), but as it looked like a participle it came to be used like one, with the result that a verb and a noun *mimmock* were formed by subtraction of the supposed ending.

Note 1. Besides *mimmock*, modern dialects have other forms of the word, such as *mammock* and *mummock*.[1] This change of vowel is not unparalleled: a similar word, which the *N.E.D.* records under the form *maumet* and derives from *Mahomet*, is found also as *mammet* and *mommet*. No further explanation is needed here than a reference to such imitative words as *flip, flap, flop* and *slabber, slubber, slobber*, &c. That imitative elements enter into *mimmock* I have no doubt; my contention is, however, that these are only secondary influences which did not come into play till after the word had been created in another way. The same applies to *maumet*. Both words are particularly suited to sound-symbolism. *Mimmock* with its *i*-sound is suggestive of something tiny (cf. O. Jespersen on 'The Symbolic Value of the Letter I' in *Linguistica* (Copenhagen, 1933)). *Maumet*, especially in the form *mommet*, reminds one of *mummery*, a word which is probably of purely imitative origin. The forms *mummock* and *mammock* will naturally, because of their vowels, be closer to *mommet* than to *mimmock* in meaning (see Wright's *Dialect Dictionary*). Finally, let me point out that the substitution of the ending *-ock* for the original *-ick(in)* is, of course, due to the analogy of other diminutives in *-ock*.

Note 2. A single instance of an adjective or participle *mimmering* is recorded in the *Oxford Dictionary*. It occurs in George Darley's *Sylvia* (London, 1827), Act II, scene iv: 'A half-brain'd loon! A mimmering driveller!' Where Darley got this word from I do not know. The *N.E.D.* thinks it may be pseudo-archaic; does that mean that it is simply a product of Darley's imagination, or had he a prototype? Irish influence, I suppose, is out of the question, so perhaps the *N.E.D.* is right when it suggests that the word may be due to the

---

[1] The verb *mammock* is known, e.g., from Shakespeare's *Coriolanus*, I. iii. 71, 'Hee did so set his teeth, and teare it. Oh, I warrant how he mammockt it' (i.e. tore it to shreds).

influence of Middle Dutch *mimmeren* and may mean 'doting, dreaming'. But had the verb *mimmer* ever any oral currency in English? The word is common to several Germanic dialects: Low German has *mimern*, and Danish has *mimre*. The latter form, which suggests age and weak-mindedness, has undoubtedly influenced *Mimering-Tand* and helped to keep it alive, although it has nothing to do with its origin.

§ 32. *Etymology of Mimecan*

Though there can be no doubt that the proper name *Mimecan* and the dialectal forms *mimickin* and *mimmerkin* are one and the same word, that does not necessarily imply that the latter forms go back to the proper name. We have to consider the possibility that there may have existed an early noun *mimickin* or some similar form, of which the modern dialectal word is a descendant, and which was used as a proper name for the dwarf in the Gunhild story. In fact, that is what the passage in Matthew Paris's chronicle would seem to imply: '. . . qui nanus erat et propter corporis parvitatem Mimecan dicebatur.'

Various etymologies of *Mimecan* have been suggested. Grundtvig (*DgF* i, p. 193, n. ***) very cautiously asks whether it might be connected with *manikin* or *minikin*. Child (vol. ii, p. 37, n. ‡) attributes to Bugge an opinion which I have not been able to trace; he says: 'Danish and Norwegian Mimecan, Mimmering, Memering, English mimicking, mimocking, and probably minnikin, Scottish memerkyn, mynmerkin, all denote a man or object of small size, and point to Icelandic minni = minor, minnkan, a minishing, &c.; as Bugge remarks.'[1] On the contrary, Bugge (*DgF* iv, p. 722) says that *Mimecan*, &c., is hardly identical with English *minikin*, but is probably of Romance origin, and he points to Portuguese *meiminho* 'little finger', Italian *mimma* 'little girl', and French *môme* 'little boy', as possibly related forms.

Bugge's etymology, while perhaps not improbable, seems too

---

[1] Altogether this note makes a very confused impression. *Mimecan* is placed among the Scandinavian forms! I also doubt whether any of the words mentioned, apart perhaps from *minnikin*, can denote an inanimate object.

remote; it must at best remain an unproved hypothesis. Besides, though Bugge is fully aware that *-can* is a diminutive ending,[1] he fails to see that this dispenses us from looking for a word with a diminutive meaning in itself. The addition of the suffix will automatically give any word that implication of smallness which seems to underlie the remark in Matthew Paris's chronicle.

In Ralph de Diceto's chronicle, it will be recalled, the dwarf's name has a slightly different form: *Mimekinus* (cf. also the later dialectal forms mentioned above). This seems to show that *-can* is identical with the well-known suffix *-kin*. This diminutive ending is due to Dutch influence; in Flanders and the Netherlands forms in *-kin* appear as early as the tenth century.[2] In England the forms are encountered in the twelfth century,[3] and in the thirteenth they are evidently in familiar use. They appear to have been used at first only as personal names; many examples of such names can be adduced from the thirteenth and fourteenth centuries, for example from Langland and Chaucer. As Christian names they seem to have gone out of fashion shortly after 1400, and in modern English they survive only in surnames

[1] Cf. his note on the etymology of *Mimmer-Tand* quoted on p. 75.

[2] Cf. for this and the following statements in this paragraph the *N.E.D.*, s.v. '-kin'.

[3] Various attempts have been made, not very successfully, to prove that the ending was known in England in Anglo-Saxon times: see E. Björkman, 'Hæðcyn und Hakon', *ESt*, vol. liv (1920), pp. 24–34.

The *N.E.D.* has noted no examples earlier than 1250. One of the earliest instances of a *kin*-name in England that I have come across is in Matthew Paris's *Historia Anglorum*, vol. i, p. 381. Talking of the Earl of Leicester's Flemish mercenaries in 1173, Matthew Paris says: 'quando ad aliquam planitiem gratia pausandi diverterant, choreas ducentes patria lingua saltitando cantabant,

'Hoppe, hoppe, Wilekin, hoppe, Wilekin.
Engelond is min ant tin.'

It is significant that this early occurrence is in a dance-song of Flemish origin.

Another *kin*-name is found in Theodoric's account of the Cursed Dancers of Kölbigk (see § 3), where one of the girls is called *Vibecyna* (Orderic Vitalis MS.) or *Uuibeccina* (Fairfax MS. 17). Both these MSS. date from the twelfth century, but the account itself purports to go a century farther back. It is indeed possible that the name occurred in some records at Wilton Abbey, which Theodoric is reported to have visited in the latter half of the eleventh century, but we have no evidence that the name had any currency in England at that time.

like *Wilkins(on)*, *Dickins(on)*, *Watkins*, &c. Instances of the ending being added to common nouns do not appear till the fourteenth century and remain rare till a century or two later.

One of the earliest occurrences of *Mimecan* (*-kin*, &c.) is that in Matthew Paris's *Chronica Majora*, the original compilation of which dates back to a time not later than the beginning of the thirteenth century (cf. pp. 21–22). Ralph de Diceto's reference is roughly contemporaneous, dating from about 1200 or just before. Now at that time, as we have seen, names in *-kin* were used only as names of persons; common nouns in *-kin* are of later date. This, then, gives us the proof that we wanted: *Mimecan* was a personal name originally, and it was only later that it became a generic term for a small person. No doubt, the later use of the word was at first meant as a direct reference to Gunhild's champion. This, in its turn, shows that Mimecan's story must have been widely known both in England and in Scotland, presumably in the form of a ballad. It is strange to reflect that Mimecan, the most popular of the characters in our ballad, should have lost his name in the surviving British versions.

It is evident from the foregoing discussion that the name *Mimecan* cannot be much older on English soil than its first occurrence in the Gunhild story. It may be a native formation or, what is more likely, it may have been imported with the story itself from the Continent (cf. p. 106).

We still have not solved the problem of the first part of Mimecan's name. I cannot offer any quite satisfactory etymology, but can only suggest, very hesitatingly, that it may be the word *mime* 'minstrel, jester, buffoon'. The difficulty is that this word is not recorded in either Middle or Modern Dutch, and in English the earliest quotation in the *N.E.D.* is from 1616 (Ben Jonson). Though not a genuine vernacular word till comparatively late, it was fairly widely known in the Middle Ages[1] and

---

[1] The word is used once in an Anglo-Saxon text. The *Old English Martyrology* (ed. G. Herzfeld, EETS, 1900), under the date 25 August, has: 'on þone ylcan dæg bið þæs martyres tid sancti Genesi; se wæs ærest sumes kaseres *mima*, þæt is leasere, ond sang beforan him scandlicu leoð ond plegode scandlice plegan.' In spite of the anglicized ending *-a* for *-us* the word is

may well have formed the basis of *Mimekin*, which is possibly of semi-learned origin (cf. pp. 104–5).

This derivation of the word leaves the problem of its place of origin undecided; it may equally well be of Flemish or of English origin. After its adoption or formation in English, the first syllable of *Mīmekin* would regularly undergo shortening to *Mĭmekin*[1] (= mod. *mimickin, mimmerkin*).

obviously an unusual word needing special explanation. It is not quite clear whether it has the classical Latin sense of 'actor' or the specific medieval sense 'buffoon', &c., which we must presuppose for our etymology. The translation *leasere* points to the latter sense.

[1] See H. C. Wyld, *A Short History of English* (London, 1927), § 176.

VII

HISTORY OF THE BALLAD

§ 33. *Anglo-Scandinavian Relations*

H. G. LEACH in his book *Angevin Britain and Scandinavia* (p. 358) says that 'in not a single instance has the history of the loan or translation of a ballad from English to Danish been definitely traced'. I do not know what Leach means by 'definitely traced',[1] but in the case of the ballad with which we are concerned there can be no doubt that the names Raadengaard and Memering are a loan from the English ballad.[2] Moreover, as shown in § 28, it is possible to fix the time of borrowing within fairly narrow limits. It was in no circumstances later than 1400 (see p. 63), and it cannot have been earlier than the tenth century, when *kin*-names first began to appear in Flanders. It is unlikely, however, that this type of name appeared in any great number in England till the latter half of the twelfth century (cf. p. 81), and in any case we must allow a certain length of time between the adoption of the name from Flanders and its re-exportation to Scandinavia. We can therefore, with a fair degree of certainty, fix 1200 and 1400 as the probable limits within which the passage of our ballad from Britain to Scandinavia took place.[3] If it went from Britain to Denmark, it must have happened before 1300; if it reached Norway first, it must have been before 1400.

Of the two countries, Norway and Denmark, Norway is the

---

[1] It would appear from certain remarks on p. 370 that the definiteness that Leach is thinking of is mainly in the matter of dating the passage from Britain to Scandinavia.

[2] I take it for granted that the two names were borrowed at once. The possibility that they were adopted at different times is highly improbable.

[3] This bottom limit tallies with the other evidence for the history of Scandinavian balladry. Verrier, *Le Vers français*, vol. iii, pp. 63–64, thinks that ballads go back to the twelfth century, or 1200 at the latest, in Denmark, to roughly the same period in Norway, and to the thirteenth century in Sweden.

more likely to have been the importer of the ballad. Though there were close relations, diplomatic and commercial, between England and Denmark in the time of the Valdemars (1157–1241),[1] the bonds were not nearly so close as those between England and Norway. 'In the royal writs and passports from this period [1060–1300] preserved in the Public Record Office at London, documents referring to Norwegians occur approximately ten times as often as those which refer to Danes' (pp.36–37). Leach doubts whether Anglo-Danish trade 'was of much significance in the development of higher or artistic culture. Trade in Denmark, unlike that of Norway, was not the approved avocation of nobility and clergy' (pp. 32–33). Moreover, in the course of the thirteenth century Danish trade with England was largely taken over by the Hansa merchants. Furthermore, England was never a necessary market for Danish trade. Denmark had the Continent at her door, while for Norway England was the nearest door. Besides, Denmark after the Norman Conquest had no colonial possessions in the British Isles. Norway, on the other hand, had colonies extending from the Shetlands and Orkneys through Caithness and Sutherland down the west coast of Scotland to the Isle of Man.

Intercourse between England and Norway was particularly intimate during the long reign (1217–63) of Hakon Hakonarson, nicknamed the Old. Outside the Scandinavian group England during this period was the country with which Norway maintained the closest relations in commerce and diplomacy. Traffic with France was almost non-existent. King's Lynn was the favourite rendezvous of Norwegian ships, while in Norway the trade with England was practically monopolized by Bergen.

With Scotland during the same period relations were rather strained. The Norwegian possessions were a thorn in the side of the Scottish kings, and in 1263 it came to open hostilities. After the cession, in 1266, of Man and the Hebrides, relations im-

[1] See Leach, op. cit., pp. 26–34. The following account of Anglo-Scandinavian relations is based almost entirely on Leach's book, from which all quotations not otherwise indicated have been taken.

proved. In 1281 King Erik Priesthater married a Scottish princess, Margaret, who died two years later; but in 1293 he married another Scotswoman, Isabella Bruce, sister of the famous Bruce of history. This alliance with the Bruce family, in connexion with the failure of the plan to marry the English King Edward I's son to the 'Maid of Norway', Erik and Margaret's daughter (see p. 37), led to an estrangement in diplomatic relations between Norway and England. Norway turned to France instead.

Political estrangement also affected trade relations. 'True, there was some trade with England for a quarter of a century after 1290, not as formerly in the hands of courtiers and clerics, but due to the initiative of the townsfolk' (p. 60). There was a good deal of ill feeling, however, which 'came to a head in 1312, when some English fishermen off the Norwegian coast killed a tax-collector and two[1] other men of importance. This was followed by wholesale arrests and reprisals upon Englishmen in Norway. Henceforth the English were all but excluded from Bergen, although as late as 1375 they made ineffectual attempts to regain a footing there. After 1350 English and Norwegian merchants almost ceased to cross the North Sea' (p. 61). There was a deeper cause for this cessation of trade than petty riots and fights. The Hanseatic League had obtained concessions in Norway towards the end of the thirteenth century, and in the first half of the fourteenth century it established itself firmly in Bergen and monopolized Norwegian trade with England. From then onwards Norwegian fish was brought to England in Hanseatic bottoms.

In Norway, in the thirteenth century, unlike the rest of Europe with the exception of Italy, commercial activity was not considered beneath the dignity of the nobility and clergy. 'Government officials, bishops, and abbots sailed in person as merchants, while the archbishop and even the king sent their own private ships on trading voyages to English ports' (p. 67).

---

[1] This should be *ten*: see Leach's authority, A. Bugge, 'Handelen mellem England og Norge', and Rymer's *Foedera*, vol. ii. p. 294.

Leach thinks it but natural that these men of rank should have taken an interest in the arts and literature of Britain, and doubtless, he says, they had much to do with the importation of Anglo-Norman culture. As a concrete example he mentions the case of Bjarni Erlingsson of Bjarkey (see § 14), who, after a diplomatic mission to Scotland, brought back with him to Norway in 1287 the romance of *Olif* and had it translated into Norwegian.

In ecclesiastical matters relations between Norway and England had been intimate since earliest times. The Norwegian Church was founded by Englishmen, and English influence remained predominant till after 1290. Norwegian cathedrals reproduced English models. 'Norwegian sculpture, also, from the first half of the thirteenth century, shows either the hands of Englishmen or those of careful Norwegian students of British art' (p. 95). The high clerics of Bergen frequently served as emissaries to the court of London; between 1215 and 1309 at least sixteen such missions are mentioned in the English rolls (p. 99). English clerics, in their turn, often acted as diplomatic envoys to Norway.

Best known of all these clerical envoys to Norway is Matthew Paris of St. Albans.[1] The financial affairs of the Benedictine monastery of Nidarholm in Norway had got into such a state that the monks had to call for assistance, and Matthew Paris was first asked to help in freeing the monastery from the claims of usurers in London. But although the temporal difficulties of the monastery were smoothed out, the spiritual position remained in a bad way. The archbishop threatened the monks with expulsion as ignorant and void of discipline. Again a request for help was directed, this time through the Pope, to Matthew Paris, who was asked to come to Norway. He arrived at Bergen in the summer of 1248, and after successfully accomplishing the object of his mission, he returned to England. We do not know how long he stayed in Norway, but he can scarcely

---

[1] His own account of the mission is found in the *Chronica Majora*, vol. v, 42–45. See also Madden's edition of the *Historia Minor*, vol. iii, pp. xv ff.; and Leach, op. cit., pp. 103–5.

have returned before 1249; he was certainly back in England in 1251. From the way in which the letter to the Pope refers to Matthew Paris as a most particular friend of King Hakon (*familiarissimus regi nostro et amicissimus*), it would appear that he had been on a previous visit to Norway, but we have no certain evidence of that.[1]

Such, then, is the background against which the importation of our ballad must be seen. Philological evidence tells us that the ballad must have been imported between 1200 and 1400 if in Norway, and between 1200 and 1300 if in Denmark. Historical evidence shows that the event most likely took place in Norway in the thirteenth century.[2] In that period commercial, cultural, and diplomatic relations between England and Norway were as close as never before or after, and much more intimate than between England and Denmark.

This is as near as we can ever hope to get to tracing the passage of our ballad to Scandinavia. It is tempting to see in Matthew Paris the man who brought the ballad to Norway, but we have no decisive proof. There is much to be said, however, in favour of this theory. Matthew Paris went to Norway at least once. Besides being a clerical reformer, he was a writer and an artist. At Faaborg in Norway there is a painting of St. Peter which Dr. Lindblom of Stockholm considers to be the work of either Paris himself or one of his school, and which is probably connected with Paris's visit to Norway in 1248–9.[3] As shown by Liestøl,[4] it appears probable that the transfer to Norway of the other-world legends of Tundale and Thurkill was also due to Matthew Paris. Very likely, then, his mediation extended to other legends. Moreover, Matthew Paris knew the Gunhild story well and made a drawing of the combat scene. On the other hand, the form Rodegan (Rodogan), which appears not only in

---

[1] Cf. Madden, op. cit., p. xvii, n. 1.

[2] As philological evidence in favour of Norway one may regard the fact that the Norwegian forms of the names of the two opponents, *Mimmer-Tand* and *Rodenigâr*, are considerably closer to the English forms than are the Danish.

[3] See Montagu James's edition of the Life of St. Edward, pp. 29 and 31–32.

[4] *Draumkvæde*, pp. 125–6.

the Life of St. Edward, where it can be explained as due to the rhyme, but also in the St. Albans chronicle (cf. pp. 23–24), speaks against this theory. Raadengaard and the other Scandinavian forms show clearly that it was the form Rodingar that was adopted in Norway.

§ 34. *Different Strata in Scandinavia*

A most important problem remains to be dealt with: the Scandinavian tradition cannot be explained as sprung entirely from the English Gunhild story. Our evidence for the borrowing is confined chiefly to the two names Raadengaard and Memering. Now in the Faroese and Icelandic ballads the first of these names occurs in a form so strange that it may be quite a different name or two different names, Roysning(ur) and Rögnvald. Memering does not appear in the Icelandic ballad at all, and in the Faroese tradition the figure is obviously a loan from the Danish versions. This is no doubt connected with the fact that these ballads have no judicial combat, but an ordeal. A further difference is that the king's name is Theodoric, not Henrik. Gunhild is thus the only character in these versions whose name can be identified with certainty. Is it possible that this name is a loan, so that in reality we are here concerned with an entirely different ballad which has come under the influence of the Gunhild ballad?

We have other evidence against the theory that the Scandinavian form of the story is a direct descendant of the English tradition. The place-name Spire, which occurs in both the Dano-Norwegian and the Faroese-Icelandic tradition (see § 20), cannot be explained as a loan from the English ballad. It occurs neither in the ancient English prose versions nor in the later ballad versions. As the name is connected with the Salian emperors of Germany, it must ultimately go back to the German Gunhild tradition, and it may never have been known in England. In the absence of any evidence of an English provenance, we must assume that the name came to Scandinavia direct from Germany.

It thus looks as if we have to reckon with three different variants which have coalesced to form the Scandinavian versions of the Gunhild story as we know them: (1) some tradition associated with the name Theodoric and perhaps with Rögnvald or Roysning(ur); (2) the German Gunhild story, containing the name Spire; (3) the English version of that story, containing the names Rodingar (Raadengaard) and Mimecan (Memering).

Apart from the names, the similarity not only of action, but even of phraseology, between the Faroese and the Danish ballad is so close that the former, in its present form, may certainly be said to tell the same story as the Danish ballad, except for the substitution of an ordeal for the single combat. This close similarity must, however, to some extent be due to direct borrowing, as evidenced by the Danish stanzas in D, which have been adopted without being translated. In E some of these stanzas occur in a word-for-word translation. The Icelandic version differs more; and yet, to pronounce this a different ballad would imply the assumption of a vast amount of borrowing from a Danish or possibly a Norwegian version. When one considers that the Faroese and Icelandic ballads in certain respects form a separate tradition, that, further, the Faroese versions are much closer to the Danish tradition, and that all three traditions, Icelandic, Faroese, and Danish, have a certain stock of incident and phrase in common, the best theory to explain these facts appears to be one of successive waves of influence from the south or south-west (England). One may imagine that there was a substratum which was later partially covered by a second tradition, somewhat similar to the first, but different in important details. There was probably even a third invasion from the south. On this showing, the Icelandic ballad would represent the first stratum more faithfully than the Danish and Faroese ballads.[1]

[1] E. von der Recke, *Danmarks Fornviser*, vol. i, Introduction to No. 23, advances a theory that the Faroese-Icelandic versions go back to the tradition of the Danish islands, as opposed to the Jutland tradition represented by the extant Danish versions. If this is true, the mixing is a case not of several successive waves of influence from the south, but of adjoining local traditions,

The exact nature of this first stratum is difficult to determine. It must be identical with variant 1 mentioned above (p. 90), which is characterized by (*a*) the name Theodoric, (*b*) the name of the accuser, Rögnvald or Roysning(ur), and (*c*) an ordeal instead of a combat. As will be shown later (p. 99), there is some reason for believing that variant 2, the German Gunhild story, also contained an ordeal; the fact that there appears to be no trace whatever of a fight in the Faroese-Icelandic tradition seems to indicate that this peculiarity was shared by variants 1 and 2.

Concerning the original name of Theodoric's wife in variant 1 it seems futile to speculate.[1] The name Gunhild, as found in the extant Icelandic and Faroese versions, is undoubtedly due to variants 2 and 3. Theodoric is, of course, the famous legendary hero, but no story like the one in our ballad is attributed to him elsewhere. We have seen examples before, and shall see more presently, of the arbitrary way in which infidelity stories are attributed now to one and now to another historical or legendary personage. It is small wonder, then, that a story of this type should also have been told of King Theodoric. In *Guðrúnarkviða III* (see § 21) Theodoric figures in an adultery story, but there is no reason to suppose any direct connexion between that poem and our ballad; they may have arisen independently. As to when and where variant 1 arose, nothing definite can be said except that it was presumably earlier than variants 2 and 3, and variant 3 must be placed in the thirteenth century. Variant 1 may never have been known in Denmark.

With regard to the origin of the names Roysning(ur) and Rögnvald I can offer no satisfactory explanation.[2] It is strange that the name of the traitor should differ in the Faroes and in

each probably of southern origin, influencing each other. My theory, however, seems to cover the facts better, especially the progressive differentiation when proceeding from Denmark to the Faroes and Iceland.

[1] In *Þiðriks Saga* his first wife is called Gudilinda, a name which has a certain similarity to Gunhild. The fact that Roðingeir's wife in *Þiðriks Saga* is also called Gudilinda may, or may not, be significant. Most likely not, since Roðingeir does not seem to have been among the characters in variant 1.

[2] Grundtvig (*DgF* i, p. 193, n. **) suggests some not very probable etymologies.

Iceland. *Roysningur* is the Faroese word for 'walrus' and is not a normal personal name. It is at least closer than Rögnvald to Rodingar and may be a corruption of the latter. Rögnvald is a fairly common name in Scandinavia.[1]

While variant 2, the German Gunhild story, reached as far as Iceland, as testified by the occurrence of the name Spire, variant 3, the English form, never got farther than the Faroes. Even there it is obviously a late admixture: in D the stanzas about Memering have not even been translated, but have been left in the original Danish. In E a rough translation is given (sts. 25 and 26), and the following stanza (27) has been altered so as to give Memering a certain purpose in the story, namely, to assist Gunhild in carrying out the ordeal. It thus seems established that variant 2 preceded No. 3.

As we find the name Gunhild even in the Icelandic version, which does not appear to have been under English influence, that name, too, apparently came to Scandinavia direct from Germany as part of variant 2. Most likely, then, the name Henrik is also of German provenance.

A difficult feature to place is Gunhild's distribution of gifts. It is found in the Faroese and Icelandic versions and in Danish A. In the Icelandic ballad it occurs at the beginning: Gunhild gives a present to everybody in her service, and to Rögnvald she gives a red shield. The next stanza contains Rögnvald's speech asking her to become his mistress. In the Faroese versions the feature is put at the end, after Gunhild's innocence has been proved: on Christmas Day she distributed gifts, and to Roysning she gave a red ring. In the Danish version the feature occurs in the speech in which Memering pities Gunhild and talks of her former glory. Strangely enough, in this version it is not Gunhild who is said to distribute the gifts, but apparently her father, whom Memering says he served for fifteen years.[2] There is something incongruous when we are told that 'To Ravengaard

---

[1] See Lind, *Norsk-Isländska Dopnamn.*

[2] At least, he is the most likely person to whom Memering's 'hand' ('he') can refer; Henrik seems out of the question, since he has not been mentioned for several stanzas past.

he gave most of all; yet he has forsaken you first of all' (st. 22). Did Ravengaard, too, serve Gunhild's father?

I am inclined to think that the incident of the gifts rightly belongs to the beginning of the story; it seems entirely out of place at the end. The giving of a gold ring (in the Faroese versions) is said to symbolize hanging;[1] but why, then, did Gunhild give presents to the others as well? And why are we told that the occasion was Christmas Day? Placed at the beginning, the episode might serve as a motivation for Rögnvald's action as related in the following stanza. In the same sort of way an innocent remark by the Lombard Queen Gundeberg about a certain nobleman's figure was misunderstood by him and led to an indecent proposal[2] (see § 36). The Danish version, too, gives us to understand that the giving of presents was prior to Ravengaard's accusation, and it stresses his ungratefulness.

The question is now, to which stratum did this feature belong originally? At any rate, not to the English Gunhild story. There is nothing about gifts in the British versions that have come down to us, and the only Scandinavian version that seems free from English influence, the Icelandic one, is alone in having the incident in the original form and place. This theory also explains why the feature later changed its place in the other versions: the English story in its early form contained a different opening, Gunhild's wedding, or rather her dispatch from England. The Faroese versions chose to move the distribution of gifts to the end of the story and to give it a symbolical meaning. The Danish version has kept more of the original character of the incident; but its original significance in the plot has been lost, and a discrepancy has crept in: we know nothing of Ravengaard having

---

[1] See Bugge, *DgF* iv, p. 729; and J. Fritzner in *Historisk Tidsskrift*, published by the Norwegian Historical Society, vol. i (1871), pp. 401–3.

[2] The Scottish ballad opens with a scene which bears a faint resemblance to this Lombard story. Rodingham assures the queen that he loves her well, and the queen in reply says, quite innocently, 'So do I thee,' whereupon Rodingham makes his proposal. This similarity may be purely accidental. If it is not, it should be viewed in conjunction with the other evidence, such as it is, suggesting a partially independent Scottish tradition: see pp. 11 n., 109–10, and 158.

served at Gunhild's father's court. Whether the incident belonged originally to the Theodoric element or to the German Gunhild story, I do not know.

To sum up: The English version of the Gunhild story reached Norway in the thirteenth century. The German form of that story containing the names Henrik, Gunhild, and Spire, was already known in Scandinavia, and in the Faroes and Iceland that form had blended with a story about King Theodoric. Both the German story and the Theodoric legend ended with an ordeal. The most important new feature in the English version was the fight between little Mimecan and big Rodingar. This incident became even more popular in Scandinavia than in Britain, and the figure of Memering (= Mimecan) was later introduced into several other ballads. The fight was never incorporated in the Icelandic and Faroese versions, which held to the original ending. At a much later date the figure of Memering was introduced into the Faroese versions, while the Icelandic version never underwent any English influence. This is true also of another innovation brought to Scandinavia from England: the story of Henry and Gunhild's wedding. That incident ousted the old beginning, the distribution of gifts, everywhere but in Iceland.

§ 35. *Historical Basis of the Story*

While the story of Gunhild's accusation and trial must have come to England from the Continent, the account of the bride's progress was almost certainly added in England, where the event is said to have happened (cf. §§ 8 and 11). This part of the story, found in the early English prose versions and (in a somewhat altered form) in Scandinavia, but not in the extant British ballad versions, is probably the only part that has any historical basis. The English chroniclers seem in many ways to have been badly informed.[1] Gunhild did not marry Henry in the second year of Hardicanute's reign, 1041, as maintained, for example, by John Brompton. The marriage had probably been arranged just

---

[1] Cf. Freeman, *The Norman Conquest*, vol. i, Appendix NNN.

before Canute's death,[1] and according to contemporary German chroniclers the wedding took place in June 1036.[2] To all appearances, Queen Gunhild lived happily with her husband till 1038, when she died of the plague in Italy (Steindorff, pp. 41–42). Gunhild was never empress of Germany; Conrad II reigned till 1039, and Henry was not crowned emperor till 1046.

While, so far as I can discover, no story of Gunhild like the one in the ballad is known to German chroniclers, a very similar one is recorded of one of her predecessors, the Emperor Henry II's wife Cunegund. It is extremely probable that the story told about Gunhild, Canute's daughter, is really due to a confusion of the two queens. After her coronation in Germany, Gunhild assumed the name Cunegund.[3] Now the two Cunegunds were almost contemporary; on her husband's death Henry II's queen retired to a nunnery, where she died in 1033, three years before Gunhild's coronation.[4] How easy, therefore, for a story in oral circulation to become attached to the second Cunegund instead of the first!

A further circumstance contributing to the confusion was the existence of several Gunhilds besides the heroine of our ballad. Gunhild was a common name in the Danish royal family in England in the eleventh century, and several of its bearers took refuge on the Continent in the troubled years before and after the Conquest. Our heroine's cousin, Canute's sister's daughter,

---

[1] See Steindorff, *Jahrbücher des deutschen Reichs unter Heinrich III*, vol. i, pp. 33–34.

[2] See Steindorff, op. cit., pp. 35–36. Suhm, *Historie af Danmark*, vol. iii, p. 744, very ingeniously tries to reconcile the conflicting statements by supposing that Canute before his death sent Gunhild to Denmark as a first stage of the journey to Germany. This would explain the splendour displayed, which is unlikely to have happened in 1036, during the reign of Gunhild's half-brother Harold Harefoot, who was hostile to any children of Queen Emma. Suhm then supposes that Hardicanute in 1036, in the second year of his reign in Denmark, sent his sister on to Germany.

[3] See Steindorff, op. cit., p. 36. The entry in the *Annales Hildesheimenses* runs: 'regina, Cunihild nomine, quae ibidem in natali apostolorum regalem coronam accepit, et mutato nomine in benedictione Cunigund dicta est.' There is a good deal of vacillation in contemporary records between her baptismal and her adopted name.

[4] Bresslau, *Jahrbücher des deutschen Reichs unter Konrad II*, vol. ii, p. 79.

was called Gunhild. In 1044, after the death of her second
husband, Earl Harold, she was banished from the country together with her two sons.[1] She went first to Bruges, where she
stayed for some years, and then on to Denmark. Another exile of
the name of Gunhild was Earl Godwine's daughter, Harold's
sister. After the flight of her family from England she lived as a
recluse in Bruges, where she died in 1087. She had taken a vow
of virginity and spent the years of her exile in pious activities;
she was 'hilaris et modesta, erga extraneos benivola & justa,
pauperibus larga, suo corpori admodum parca', to quote her
epitaph. She was interred in the Church of St. Donat at Bruges,
where her sepulchral inscription was discovered by some work-
men in 1786. Another, probably spurious, inscription from the
same church bears witness to the prevailing confusion by stating
that the Gunhild buried there was Henry the Black's (i.e.
Henry III's) wife, who 'post acceptam gravissimam a marito
injuriam' came to live as a nun in Bruges, where she died in
1042.[2] A third bearer of the name was the last-named Gunhild's
niece, Harold's daughter, but nothing definite is known of her
later life,[3] though it was probably spent on the Continent.

The most important of these Gunhilds for our purpose is
Godwine's daughter. From her epitaph she seems to have been
regarded as something of a saint; nothing would be easier, therefore, than for a legend to grow up round her memory. Moreover,
she was known to be of noble birth.[4] Now if there was already a
tendency to mix up the two Cunegunds and to attribute to the
younger Cunegund (= Queen Gunhild) the legend belonging to
the first Cunegund (= Henry II's wife), that inclination would

[1] Freeman, op. cit., vol. ii, p. 71.

[2] Cf. Freeman, op. cit., vol. iv, pp. 159 and 756-7; Ellis, *Introduction to
Domesday Book*, vol. ii, pp. 136-8; and Grundtvig, *DgF* i, p. 183, n. ****.
Further literature on the subject is listed in U. Chevalier, *Répertoire des
sources historiques du Moyen Âge*, vol. i (Paris, 1905), s.v. 'Gunnilde'. The
Church of St. Donat was destroyed in 1804, but the inscription is preserved
in the Church of St. Sauveur at Bruges.

[3] Cf. Ellis, op. cit., vol. ii, p. 127.

[4] According to some sources, her mother, Gytha, was a sister of King
Canute. This is undoubtedly a mistake; cf. Freeman, vol. i, Appendix EEE.

be considerably strengthened if there was actually (or had been) a nun of the name of Gunhild living in Bruges. In several versions of the story of Queen Gunhild, it will be recalled, she is said to have taken the veil after the vindication of her chastity.

The story of the accusation and trial of Cunegund, Henry II's wife, is found in no contemporary records; it does not emerge in literature till the twelfth century.[1] We then find it in two different redactions. One occurs in the Pöhlde Annals (*Annales Palidenses*) of the late twelfth century[2] and was later translated and embodied in the *Saxon World Chronicle* generally ascribed to Eike of Repgow[3] (first half of the thirteenth century). In this form of the story a duke is mentioned as playing a certain part in the accusation; another characteristic is that before undergoing the ordeal Cunegund prays for help: 'O Lord, who savedst Susanna, help thou also me in my dire need'; after the ordeal the king falls at her feet and asks her forgiveness. The second redaction is first found in Adalbert's *Vita Heinrici Imperatoris* of the middle of the twelfth century.[4] This version is very brief and contains none of the above details, but it was later considerably expanded by the author of the *Vitæ Sancti Heinrici Additamentum*.[5] In the latter version there is no mention of a duke, but we are told that the devil in the shape of a young knight (*miles*) had been seen several times leaving Cunegund's bedchamber; Cunegund's prayer contains no reference to Susanna; the feature of the king falling at her feet after the ordeal is included. In both redactions Cunegund states publicly that she had never known any man, not even her husband; the *Additamentum* adds that this remark caused the bashful emperor to strike her with his hand to stop her talking. The story as told in the *Additamentum* was in its turn translated and versified by Ebernand of Erfurt[6] in his *Henry and Cunegund* (first half of the thirteenth

---

[1] Cf. Bresslau, *Jahrbücher des deutschen Reichs unter Heinrich II*, vol. iii, pp. 360–1 and 368–70.

[2] Pertz's edition, p. 66.   [3] Weiland's edition, p. 167.

[4] Pertz's edition, p. 805.   [5] Pertz's edition, pp. 819–20.

[6] Bechstein's edition, chs. xix–xxiii.

century). Finally, the story is told in the Pope's letter of canonization of the year 1200,[1] but that version is too bare of detail to allow of any classification.

The two earliest occurrences of the Cunegund story that we we possess are thus Adalbert's and the one in the Pöhlde Annals. Both appear to rest on a now lost Saxon *Chronicle of the Emperors* composed probably by a nun of Gandersheim in the reign of Lothar III (1125–37).[2] This chronicle, so far as it is now possible to reconstruct it, must have been quite unhistorical in its method. It was simply a collection of legends about the emperors of Germany, told for their edifying value. The stories seem to have been drawn exclusively from oral tradition.

If that theory is correct, the story of Cunegund's trial goes back at least to the first half of the twelfth century; but the fact that no contemporary annals or chronicles know it makes it extremely doubtful whether it has any historical foundation. This view is confirmed by the discovery that the same or a very similar story was told about another German empress, who lived over a hundred years earlier. Abbot Regino (d. 915) reports in his chronicle[3] that in 887 the Emperor Charles the Fat publicly accused his wife Richardis of adultery with Bishop Liudward of Vercelli. The emperor announced at the same time that although he and his wife had been married for over ten years, their relationship had always been of an ascetic nature. His wife, in her turn, announced with pride that she had never had carnal relations with any man, not even her husband, and she offered to prove the truth of this statement by a single combat or an ordeal of ploughshares. We are not told whether any such test was ever held, but Regino says that Richardis divorced her husband and retired to a nunnery, which she had herself caused to be built.

In the case of Richardis, too, it is problematical how much truth, if any, there is in the story, which is known from no other

[1] Ed. Migne, *Patrologia*, vol. cxl, col. 221.
[2] See Bernheim, 'Die sagenhafte sächsische Kaiserchronik aus dem 12. Jahrhundert', pp. 51 ff., esp. pp. 59 and 93.
[3] Migne's edition, *Patrologia*, vol. cxxxii, col. 125.

contemporary source.[1] It is possibly purely fictitious, built up around the fact of the dismissal of Bishop Liudward, Charles's chief adviser, and the empress's decision to take the veil. Certain it is that the subject was seized upon and embroidered by later chroniclers, who report for a fact that an ordeal took place, though they are not agreed on the exact form of the ordeal and none of them mentions walking over red-hot ploughshares.[2] Whether or not the story is true, it is extremely likely that it influenced the later story of Cunegund. The saintly character of both the women lends itself to confusion; Cunegund, too, ended her days in a nunnery. The public announcement of conjugal chastity is the same in both stories, and in the twelfth-century *Kaiserchronik* we are told that Charles after hearing the accusation against Richardis went up to her room and beat her.[3]

As the name Gunhild seems to have come to Scandinavia direct from Germany (see p. 92), the confusion of the two Cunegunds—and the consequent association of an adultery motif with Gunhild—must be of German origin and not, as supposed by Grundtvig (*DgF* i, p. 183), due to a mistake by the English chroniclers. It is perhaps significant, therefore, that there are certain particular points of resemblance between the Scandinavian Gunhild ballad and the German chroniclers' stories of Richardis and Cunegund. In the first place, Gunhild, wife of Theodoric, undergoes an ordeal, and there is no indication that any other ending to the story was ever known in Scandinavia till the English version was brought to Norway (cf. p. 91). Secondly, in all the Scandinavian versions Henrik (Theodoric) beats his wife on hearing the accusation. This may be a parallel to the blows which Richardis and Cunegund had to endure.[4] Thirdly, all the Scandinavian versions except

---

[1] See Dümmler, *Geschichte des ostfränkischen Reichs*, vol. ii, pp. 284–6. Though the *Annales Fuldenses*, A.D. 899, report a similar crime committed by the Empress Uta, they are silent on the subject of Richardis.

[2] See Dümmler, op. cit., p. 286; and Grundtvig, *DgF* i, p. 190.

[3] Schröder's edition, pp. 360–2.

[4] The validity of this comparison appears to be seriously shaken by the romance of *Valentine and Orson* (see § 19), which in this detail forms a much closer parallel to the Scandinavian ballad than do the German Cunegund

one[1] say that the supposed lover was a clergyman, and in some versions (A, C, and F) he is said to be an archbishop. This reminds one of the charge brought against Richardis.[2]

Certain incidents in the German legends of Richardis and Cunegund have parallels in English tradition. The taking of the veil in the Richardis story reminds one of the final sentence in William of Malmesbury's story of Gunhild. Other points are paralleled not in the English Gunhild legend, but in the story of Emma. We find there the bishop as a lover and the ordeal of ploughshares. In some respects the Emma story resembles more closely that of Cunegund's trial, especially as recounted in the Pöhlde redaction. Emma, like Cunegund, prayed for help to 'God, who saved Susanna', and when King Edward saw her innocence proved, he fell at her feet and asked her forgiveness.

It is hard to untangle this web of incident. It appears that there is scarcely a single point in the German Richardis-Cunegund-Gunhild tradition which cannot be paralleled in England. We have good reason to believe that the story told about Emma in England is no other than the story of Richardis and Cunegund with the names and one or two details changed. In what way it travelled from the Continent to England we do not know. The English Gunhild story as such, however, owes much less to the German tradition than does the Scandinavian story. One very important part of the English tradition, the fight between Rodingar and Mimecan, must have had a different source, and we are fortunate enough to possess the record of an event, true

and Richardis stories. The account of how the king (emperor) took his wife by the hair and threw her on the ground is remarkably alike in the ballad and in *Valentine and Orson*. This incident, however, is one of those added only in the late version of the romance. In the early, metrical version we are told that Phila (= Belyssant) tore her accuser's hair and bit off his nose. Where the late version borrowed the detail from I do not know, but it is not unlikely that on this point *Valentine and Orson* and the ballad ultimately go back to the same source.

[1] H, which does not particularize the accusation.

[2] In the versions of Cunegund's story which mention a lover, he is either a duke or a knight; but if, as seems likely, all the extant accounts of that story go back to a *Chronicle of the Emperors* written by a nun for the purpose of edification, an original archbishop as a lover would naturally have been expunged.

or untrue, which has all the appearance of being one of the ancestors of the English ballad: the story of Queen Gundeberg.

§ 36. *Gundeberg Story*

Gundeberg was queen of Lombardy in the seventh century. The earliest record of her story is found in Fredegar's *History of the Franks*,[1] which is almost contemporary with the event. In bk. iv, chs. 50–51, we are told how King Adalwald (616–26) was deposed and Charwald, who was married to Adalwald's sister Gundeberg, was elected king (626–36). Now Gundeberg one day happened to praise a certain Adalulf's figure, whereupon he made her an indecent offer. She spurned it indignantly and spat in his face. Fearing for his life, Adalulf went to the king and said that Gundeberg and a Duke Taso were plotting to poison the king in order that they might marry. Charwald believed the accusation and put Gundeberg in prison. By the intervention of the Frankish King Chlothar, Gundeberg's kinsman, a single combat was arranged between Adalulf, her accuser, and a man named Pitto. The latter was victorious, and Gundeberg, who had by then spent three years in prison, was released and restored to her former dignity.

This story is retold, with little difference of detail, but considerable difference of phrase, by the ninth-century historian Aimoinus the Monk.[2] The story is also told briefly by Paul the

[1] For convenience' sake I sometimes talk of Fredegar's chronicle as if it were entirely the work of Fredegar. The question of authorship is of minor importance in this connexion, since the chronicle is undoubtedly a seventh-century work. Schnürer, in *Die Verfasser der sogenannten Fredegar-Chronik*, thinks that our passage was written by the author whom he calls B, and who, he thinks, lived in the south of France and wrote about 642 or 643. He was probably a royal notary and drew his knowledge of Lombard affairs from one Aubedo, who had been on frequent diplomatic missions to the Lombard court.

[2] *Historia Francorum*, bk. iv, ch. 10. He differs from Fredegar in the form of several of the names: *Charwald* is termed *Ariwald*, and *Caumellum* (the castle where Gundeberg was imprisoned) is *Amello*. *Pitto*'s name is unaltered. It is not clear to me how Entwistle (*Sir Aldingar*, &c., p. 105) can understand the account to mean that Gundeberg's deliverer was French (if by 'deliverer' he means champion). Aribert, Gundeberg's cousin, made the arrangements for her defence, but neither Fredegar nor Aimoinus says anything about Pitto's nationality.

Deacon[1] (d. 801), whose account, however, differs in several essential points. The queen is here accused of adultery, and she is defended by her own servant, whose name is Carellus. Moreover, Paul makes Gundeberg the wife of Rodwald, not Ariwald (= Charwald). Rodwald, as a matter of fact, was Gundeberg's own son by Rothar, King Ariwald's successor, whom she married after her first husband's death.[2]

These two redactions of the Gundeberg story, Aimoinus the Monk's and Paul the Deacon's, have been copied by later chroniclers. The former is included, in a rough French translation (c. 1300?), in the *Chroniques de St. Denis*.[3] The champion's name is here said to be *Putons*, but that must be due to a misreading of the manuscript, *itt* being read as *ut*; the -*s*, of course, is the nominative ending. Paul the Deacon's version, a good deal changed in phraseology, but sentence for sentence the same story, is found in the *Chronicon Universale* formerly ascribed to Ekkehard, Abbot of Aura, but according to more recent research compiled by Frutolf (d. 1103), Prior of the Monastery of Michelsberg near Bamberg.[4]

Besides direct literary copying and imitation, the story seems to have also had oral currency. Gaston Paris thinks that before Gundeberg's time there was very likely some earlier poem, Lombard or Frankish, on the theme of the queen unjustly accused and vindicated by a judicial combat, and this poem was later adapted to the story of Gundeberg. At any rate, it is obvious

---

[1] *De Gestis Langobardorum*, bk. iv, ch. 49.

[2] See L. M. Hartmann in the *Cambridge Medieval History*, vol. ii. The list of kings, arranged schematically, looks like this:

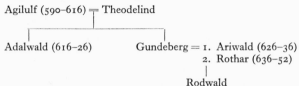

[3] Bouquet's edition, pp. 280–1.

[4] Pertz's edition, p. 146. Also in Migne, *Patrologia*, vol. cliv, col. 799. On the question of authorship see Bresslau, 'Die Chroniken des Frutolf von Bamberg und des Ekkehard von Aura'.

that after Gundeberg's time the story was kept alive by word of mouth; otherwise we cannot account for the discrepancies between Fredegar's and Paul the Deacon's versions, such as the change from Pitto to Carellus. The change of the accusation to one of adultery is typical of medieval romance (see p. 113).

This oral tradition that we have postulated was more probably Frankish than Lombard, although it may have existed in both countries. It will be recalled that it was a protest from the Frankish king that led to the release of Gundeberg from her imprisonment, and Gundeberg herself was descended from the Frankish royal house. The Franks, consequently, were more interested in perpetuating the story, since it reflected glory on them. It should be borne in mind, too, that the relevant part of Fredegar's chronicle was probably written by somebody who lived in the south of France, and that before writing his history of the Lombards Paul the Deacon spent several years (782–6) at Charlemagne's court, where he may have heard the story. Charlemagne himself, we know, was fond of old ballads.[1]

The question of whether there is any historical truth in the Gundeberg story has been debated by Rajna,[2] Nyrop,[3] and Paris.[4] Rajna says, and Paris agrees, that it is hard to believe that the story has no foundation of fact at all, seeing that it was written down so soon after the event is supposed to have happened. Nyrop, on the other hand, cannot agree with this view; he supports Grundtvig, who believes that the story is only a variant of the widespread legend of the accused queen, of which I shall have more to say in the next chapter. It is natural that Grundtvig, who knew only Aimoinus' and Paul the Deacon's accounts, should have arrived at this view; but one must admit with Rajna that Fredegar's almost contemporary evidence cannot be dismissed altogether: he can hardly have invented the whole story. On the other hand, there may be very little historical

---

[1] See Einhard's *Vita Caroli Magni* (ed. Migne, *Patrologia*, vol. xcvii), ch. 29.

[2] *Le Origini dell' Epopea Francese*, pp. 179–98.

[3] *Storia dell' Epopea Francese*, p. 122, n. 1.

[4] 'Le Roman du Comte de Toulouse', pp. 19 n., 26, and 28 ff.

truth in the account. Presumably, Gundeberg was really in prison for three years and was only released by the intervention of King Chlothar,[1] but the rest of the story could easily have been built up around these two facts. There are obvious folk-lore elements in the story. Pitto and Carellus seem both to be nick-names indicating a person of small stature.[2] We find the same feature in the English and Scandinavian Gunhild ballad; it is undoubtedly borrowed from the folk-tale motif of a fight be-tween a dwarf and a giant.[3] The story itself, that of the accused queen, is a common one both in folk-tale and in more ambitious romantic literature. The theme is far too universal to go back to this one story. Moreover, and this is the most important point of all, it is found centuries before Gundeberg's time in the Bible story of *Susanna and the Elders* (cf. p. 114). We cannot prove the existence of a direct literary connexion between the stories of Susanna and Gundeberg; neither can we link up the Gundeberg story with the German Richardis-Cunegund tradition. But the connexion may be there, though hidden to us; folk-tales now lost may have formed the missing link or links.

On the other hand, it does seem possible to establish a direct connexion between the Gundeberg story and the English Gun-hild tradition. It is not stated expressly that Gundeberg's champion was a dwarf, but that seems implied in the names Pitto and Carellus. We have here an obvious parallel to the figure of Mimecan; the latter name, too, is a diminutive (§ 32). Carel-lus was Gundeberg's servant, and Mimecan performed some domestic function in Gunhild's household (cf. p. 19, n. 1). One

---

[1] In chs. 70–71 of Fredegar's chronicle (in the part supposed to have been written by B) we are told that during the reign of her second husband, Chrothar (= Rothar), a religious conflict arose between Gundeberg and the king, as a result of which she was in prison for five years and was only released by the intervention of the Frankish King Chlodevech. On this occasion Aubedo, B's authority, himself acted as emissary. The two im-prisonments have sometimes been considered to be one and the same event, but Schnürer entertains no doubt that Gundeberg was in prison twice. The real reason why she was imprisoned the first time may also have been a religious conflict. Cf. Hartmann, op. cit., pp. 202–3.

[2] See Bugge, *DgF* iv, p. 730; and Child, vol. ii, p. 39.

[3] See Thompson's *Motif-Index* under L 311.

cannot escape an impression that Mimecan is simply a Germanic translation of Carellus. Gaston Paris thinks that the hypothetical poem relating the story of Gundeberg was in some Germanic dialect; but the names Pitto and Carellus show that it was at any rate meant partly for Romance listeners, or listeners with some knowledge of a Romance tongue. Otherwise the nicknames would be lost on them, even if, as is very likely, the poem contained some remark that the man was called Carellus 'because he was so little'. As the story spread northwards to populations which had no contact with Romance-speaking people, this passage would naturally be altered: either the explanatory line would be dropped or a Germanic name substituted. This is the way in which we may imagine that the name Mimecan came into being. I would go so far as to suggest that the relevant words in Matthew Paris's chronicle (*propter corporis parvitatem Mimecan dicebatur*) are simply a translation of the corresponding passage in the early English Gunhild ballad. In my opinion, it is this very line which in the Scandinavian ballad has become the standard description of Memering: 'han var den mindste kristne Mand' ('he was the smallest Christian man'). The rhyme *Tand—Mand* probably goes back to the English version, and one of the reasons for keeping the peculiar word *Tand* in Scandinavia was that it formed part of the rhyme. In the Scandinavian ballad the connecting word 'because' was dropped; Memering was no longer felt to be a diminutive.[1]

§ 37. *Provisional Conclusion*

That there is a connexion between the Lombard story of Gundeberg and the English story of Gunhild seems sufficiently established; it appears probable, moreover, that it was through France that the Gundeberg story reached England. But did the merging of the two legends take place on the Continent, before

[1] Having ventured on to the thin ice of hypothesis, we may perhaps go a step farther and attempt a retranslation into Middle English ballad metre, as for example:

He was ycleped Mimecan,
For þat he was þe leste man.

they reached England? Or did they come to England separately, and, in that case, which of them came first?

We saw above (pp. 96–97) that the formation of the Gunhild legend most probably took place in Bruges. Now there is a good deal of evidence pointing to that city as the place where the name *Mimecan* (-*kin*) was also formed. English names in -*kin* were adopted from Flemish, and the type does not seem to have taken root in England till shortly before *Mimecan* appears. Although the diminutive meaning of -*kin* seems to have been well understood in England, it is not very likely that the formation of the word should have taken place on English soil. The name, as well as the story, was more probably imported from the Continent. From about the time of the accession of Edward the Confessor, diplomatic and commercial relations between England and Flanders were close.[1] William the Conqueror was accompanied by a host of volunteers from various parts of western Europe, the most important of whom were Flemings. Flemish colonists settled in different parts of the country; there was a considerable influx of Flemish merchants and craftsmen, and Flemish mercenaries became a common sight. It has already been mentioned that Matthew Paris quotes a dance-song supposed to have been sung by the Earl of Leicester's Flemish troops in 1173. This song contains the name *Wilekin*; very likely *Mimecan* was brought to England in the same way.

All that this argument proves, however, is that the change from *Carellus* to *Mimecan* probably happened on the Continent. The Gundeberg story in its changed form may have spread to England and may only there have been combined with the Gunhild story. This would make it easier to understand how Scandinavia received the Gunhild story unalloyed, so to speak, without the incident of the judicial combat (cf. § 34). We do not know how the story reached Scandinavia, but there was a good deal of traffic in the Middle Ages between Bruges and the

[1] Cf. Bense, *Anglo-Dutch Relations*. See also Forssner, *Continental-Germanic Personal Names in England*, pp. xxxviii ff.; and Häpke, *Brügges Entwicklung zum mittelalterlichen Weltmarkt*, ch. 5.

Danish port of Ribe in Jutland, and, at least in later times, there was a Danish Street in Bruges.[1] The legend could therefore easily have been carried to Ribe by Danish sailors. This tallies well with the fact that the ballad has only been found in Jutland, not in the Danish islands. Considering, however, that this is the only argument we can bring forward against the assumption that the Gunhild and Gundeberg legends were combined in Flanders and not in England, the theory cannot be regarded as refuted. The evidence either way is inconclusive. Personally I incline to the view that the fusion did take place in Flanders, where the Gunhild legend was formed and the Gundeberg story was altered. There may have been, at the same time, two different Flemish versions of the story of Gunhild, one of which travelled to England and the other to Denmark.

In the absence of further proof we shall have to leave the matter at that. But wherever the fusion took place, it appears that the story of the queen accused of adultery with a bishop and vindicated by an ordeal of ploughshares also reached England independently and was in that form attributed to Queen Emma, Gunhild's mother. The combined Gundeberg-Gunhild story was perhaps joined to the tale of Gunhild's magnificent wedding (or progress). This is the form in which the story is told by the early English chroniclers, and the wedding scene is found again, with all the appearance of being a loan, in the Scandinavian ballad. On the other hand, not all the British versions seem to have had that feature added: there is no trace of it in the two extant versions of the British ballad.

We have thus arrived at the genealogy shown on the next page. As explained above, some of the details are a little doubtful; the most certain of all is the secondary influence from England to Norway. With regard to chronology, the early stories have been sufficiently dealt with in §§ 35–36. The original Flemish version of the Gunhild story must be placed somewhere between Gunhild's death (1038) and William of Malmesbury's chronicle (c. 1130), probably not till after the death of

[1] Cf. Häpke, op. cit., p. 123.

Gunhild's namesake, Godwine's daughter (1087), and presumably a few years before 1130. It is impossible to say when exactly the Gunhild story reached Scandinavia, but it must have been before the English version was brought to Norway in the thirteenth century.

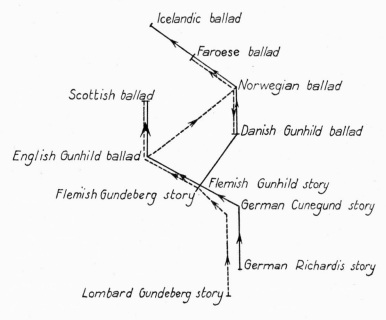

The above pedigree represents first and foremost the evolution of the story as such. How far the tradition was in ballad form is a different question. The Gundeberg story was undoubtedly preserved largely by oral transmission and very likely in poetic form; but whether that poem was anything like the type of song that we understand by a ballad (cf. § 2) is extremely doubtful. We have no certain evidence of the existence of ballads in our sense of the word till a considerably later date than the first version of the Gundeberg story (cf. § 3). We have reason to believe, however, that the early English Gunhild song or songs had the specific ballad structure, since by that time the ballad genre had emerged. The immediate Flemish prototype may also have been in ballad form; it is possible, too, that the Gunhild story spread to Scandinavia in the form of a ballad.

While most of these points can never be settled satisfactorily unless we discover the actual songs or ballads concerned, we do at least know that the story at a later date existed in ballad form in Scandinavia. The oldest of the manuscripts, the Karen Brahe Folio, goes back to *c.* 1550; but the ballad itself must be somewhat older than the manuscript. There are many verbal resemblances between the various extant Scandinavian versions, and all of them are in the well-known two-lined four-beat stanza.[1]

With the exception of the names, the modern British versions show no verbal resemblance to the Scandinavian ballad; but what is more remarkable, they show no mutual resemblance. I cannot find a single line or phrase which the two British versions may be said to have in common. Both are in the form of seven-beat couplets arranged, as usual, in stanzas of four lines. The English version, the older of the two, goes back to the Percy MS. of *c.* 1650 and is probably, in its present linguistic form, not much anterior to that date.[2]

There are several other indications that the British ballads in their present form are of comparatively recent date. The ancient English prose versions resemble the Scandinavian Gunhild ballads much more than they do the extant English and Scottish ballads. There are two points in particular which are common to

---

[1] Danish A is written down in four-lined stanzas, but that is due to a mistake of the scribe's. In a large number of stanzas, e.g. 6, 9, 12, 15, 24, 27, 28, and 35, a new incident is narrated in the second half; sts. 8, 10, 11, 14, 17, 25, 32, and 36 are divided between two speeches, each taking up half the stanza; and parallel couplets like 7*a* and 12*b*, 27*a* and 28*b*, and 30*b* and 33*a*, occur in different halves of the stanzas.

[2] Certain rhymes in A (*nest—east*, st. 20; *east—best*, st. 27; *child—old*, st. 28; *hee—nigh*, st. 38; and *shold—wall*, st. 52) may indicate a greater antiquity, but no safe conclusions can be built on these sporadic instances. Ballad rhymes are not very reliable evidence. Although the rhymes in sts. 28 and 38 seem to point to a time before the diphthongization of long *i*, we cannot be sure, since ballad-makers are often content with very imperfect rhymes. It may be significant, however, that these two stanzas refer to Gunhild's tiny champion. Stanzas 30 and 34 contain a phrase, 'When bale is att hyest, boote is att next', which must obviously have had internal rhyme originally, presumably *hext—next*. But the proverbial nature of the phrase makes it worthless as evidence.

the Scandinavian ballads and the Matthew Paris version, but are not shared by the modern British ballads: (1) the wedding at the beginning of the tale, and (2) certain features in the description of Gunhild's champion. The modern British versions no longer remember the original name of her champion; in the English ballad he has no name at all, while in the Scottish ballad he is given a name belonging to a Scots noble family (cf. p. 18). The Scottish ballad describes him as an ordinary human being of normal size; the English ballad remembers that he is a dwarf, but has made him into a supernatural being. The information that Mimecan had served Gunhild's father and had come with her to her husband's country, which is preserved in Scandinavia, has got lost in the modern British versions.

Conversely, the modern British versions contain several details which are found neither in Matthew Paris nor in the Scandinavian versions. These are: (1) a leper is put in the queen's bed to prove the alleged truth of the accusation; (2) the queen has a dream presaging her coming misfortune as well as her rescue; (3) the queen is to be burnt if she fails to prove her innocence; and (4) messengers are dispatched in all directions to find a champion, who comes riding from afar at the last moment. Since all four of these points can be paralleled elsewhere in medieval literature, they are undoubtedly due to borrowing (cf. pp. 157-8.).[1] Finally, we may mention a detail found in Scandinavia, but not in any of the British versions ancient or modern. In all the Scandinavian versions except the Icelandic we are told that the king goes away to the wars and leaves Raadengaard in charge of his lands and his queen. This can

[1] As dreams are fairly frequent in ballads (cf. Gerould, *The Ballad of Tradition*, pp. 159-61), it might seem unnecessary to go outside the sphere of balladry to look for the origin of the queen's dream. This particular dream, however, is 'more like the elaborately symbolical dreams of medieval chronicle and romance' (Gerould, p. 160). The queen dreams that a griffin is trying to carry away first her crown and kirtle of gold and afterwards herself; but she is rescued by a hawk, which kills the griffin. Now in the Carolingian and Arthurian legends griffins and hawks are familiar apparitions in dreams, and a griffin always signifies an enemy, while the hawk is the dreamer's friend and helper. See Mentz, *Die Träume in den altfranzösischen Karls- und Artus-Epen*, §§ 58, 60, 88, and 90.

hardly have been part of any of the variants mentioned in § 34, and hence is probably also a loan from romance; we find parallels elsewhere (cf. pp. 161–2).

In order to substantiate these statements about borrowing from romance we shall have to go into the question of the motif in general.

VIII

THE MOTIF IN GENERAL

§ 38. Introductory

WHAT we have been doing so far might be described as tracing the lineal descent of the Gunhild story. The motif as such is much more widespread both in imaginative and in historical and pseudo-historical literature. We may define it as the theme of the accused and exculpated wife (often a queen). It is possible and, indeed, probable that the various stories of this type do not all go back to the same source: the theme represents something so central in human nature that it may conceivably have been invented over and over again. We can divide our material, i.e. the instances that we have discovered of the theme in literature, into certain groups of stories which seem to be genealogically related. The various groups can often be shown to have influenced each other, but whether their relationship is a closer one than that is highly dubious. The question is made all the more complicated by the existence of numerous folk-tales on the same theme. A detailed treatment of the history and development of the motif is outside the scope of the present work.[1] Our purpose is to find the immediate sources of the British and Scandinavian ballads, but a survey of the ramifications of the theme is necessary in order to show where the Gunhild story fits in.

[1] The motif of the accused queen in folk-tale and romance has been admirably dealt with by Margaret Schlauch in her book on *Chaucer's Constance and Accused Queens*. Grundtvig and Child's introductions are useful, though now out of date. Hempel's treatment of the subject in *Nibelungenstudien*, pp. 179–99 and 230–64, suffers from a certain super-ficiality, no doubt due to its being only incidental to the treatment of a different subject (cf. p. 135, n. 6). Special groups of stories are dealt with in the books and papers by Wallensköld, Stefanović, Huet, Lüdtke, Krappe, Dickson, and others, mentioned below and in the Bibliography. In my bibliographical notes to this chapter I have not attempted completeness; my aim has been to mention the most important or most recent books, which will generally contain references to the rest of the literature.

§ 39. *Folk-tale and Romance*

Our theme is one that has never failed to grip the imagination and stir people's sympathy: it is but one form of the more general motif of the innocently suffering, patient heroine, as told in numerous stories such as *Cinderella*, *Snow-White*, and *Griselda*. Our particular type of story is distinguished (*a*) by having a married woman for its heroine, and (*b*) by the accusation motif. In medieval romance this subject is given the added zest of a love element, which often entails a different type of accuser and a different ending. In genuine folk-tales the accusation is not one of adultery, but generally of witchcraft, or of having eaten her children or given birth to animals. The persecutors are witches, co-wives, mothers-in-law,[1] or step-mothers. The vindication of the queen's innocence is brought about in various ways, but often the queen's exposed child or children grow up to be her saviours.

These folk-tales, ranging through the whole of Europe and at least part of Asia and Africa,[2] have furnished material for numerous romantic stories in medieval literature. That the romances are based on folk-tales, and not vice versa, is in itself a natural assumption, and this is further borne out by certain changes in the plot which often occur when the stories are adopted by conscious romantic literature. The stories become more sophisticated. The primitive accusations give way to the more modern ones of treason and adultery, and the witch or mother-in-law as persecutor is supplanted by a villain whose motive is either ambition or thwarted love. The whole setting changes from that strangely remote and mysterious atmosphere of primitive folk-tale society to the jealousies and intrigues of a

---

[1] In the mother-in-law as persecutor Margaret Schlauch would see a reminiscence of a matriarchal state of society.

[2] See Schlauch, *Chaucer's Constance*, ch. ii. Examples from Grimm are Nos. 9 (*The Twelve Brothers*), 25 (*The Seven Ravens*), 49 (*The Six Swans*), and 96 (*The Three Little Birds*). Since the appearance of Margaret Schlauch's book, R. D. Jameson in a paper 'On the Making of a Maerchen' (in *Three Lectures on Chinese Folklore*, pp. 105–33) has dealt with the occurrence of this type of folk-tale in China and its relation to an historical event.

medieval court. This transition from folk-tale to romance can sometimes be viewed in the process. Many romances, like *Octavian* (see § 45) and Chaucer's *Constance* (*Tale of the Man of Lawe*), have preserved primitive features side by side with more modern ones. 'Moreover, certain definite story-cycles, which have been preserved both in older and more recent stages of development, show the actual process of dropping the märchen machinery in favor of more modern devices.'[1]

Though the transition from primitive folk-tale to romance as described above is perhaps best and most frequently illustrated in medieval literature, the development is not, as one might gather from Margaret Schlauch's book, confined to the Middle Ages. The sophisticated type of story can be traced much farther back. The earliest example that I know is the apocryphal Bible story of *Susanna and the Elders*, added as a thirteenth chapter to the Book of Daniel. The story dates from shortly before 100 B.C., and it assumed its present form some time during the former half of the last century of the pre-Christian era.[2] It was no doubt circulated orally before it was reduced to writing. It is an embodiment of two folk-tale motifs, 'the falsely accused lady' and 'the wise boy'. The latter motif, that of the little boy giving judgement when his elders are at their wits' end, is a common one in oriental tales. It is impossible to tell whether the combination of the two motifs is a Jewish innovation; nor do we know at what date it took place.[3]

The fact that the story of *Susanna* is centuries earlier than other treatments of the theme seems to me never to have been sufficiently stressed by writers on the subject of accused queens.[4] It is also significant that the story was widely popular in the Middle Ages; allusions to Susanna belong almost to the

---

[1] Schlauch, op. cit., p. 113. Among the stories referred to are *The Swan Children* (see pp. 143 ff.) and *Valentine and Orson* (§ 46).

[2] See Dr. Oesterley in T. W. Manson's *Companion to the Bible* (Edinburgh, 1939), p. 86.

[3] See Baumgartner, 'Susanna'. Cf. also Eissfeldt, *Einleitung in das Alte Testament*, p. 646.

[4] Schlauch, op. cit., p. 104, makes only a brief reference to the story, Hempel and other writers none at all.

commonplaces of stories of falsely accused women.[1] The story
is told in full in a fourteenth-century poem probably by a
Scotsman named Huchown, and the subject received dramatic
treatment in France in the fifteenth century.[2] The story is also
included in the German collection of *exempla* entitled *Der Seelen
Trost* (fourteenth century), which was later translated into
Dutch, Danish, and Swedish.[3] After 1500 the story became a
favourite both in dramatic and in pictorial art.[4] In Shakespeare's
day a broadside on *The Constancy of Susanna* was current;[5] two
lines of it are sung by Sir Toby Belch (*Tw. N.* ii. iii. 87 and 93).
Though direct borrowing is hard to prove, it is scarcely a mere
coincidence that two accusers occur both in *Susanna* and in
The Earl of Toulouse (cf. p. 128, n. 1).

Our ballad, too, though it goes back to a relatively distant
past, represents a late stage in the development from the primitive to the sophisticated type of accusation. Its solution appears
to be an innovation. Though trial by battle no doubt reaches

---

[1] The earliest example that I know is in Florent's life of St. Rusticula
(Krusch's edition, p. 344), which dates from the former half of the seventh
century. Rusticula was falsely accused, though not of adultery, but the spectators 'illum poscebant defensorem e caelis, qui sanctae Susannae ab impiis
condemnatae sanctum Danielem praemisit liberatorem'. The references to
Susanna in the twelfth-century stories of Cunegund and Emma have already
been mentioned (pp. 33, 97, 100). Early in the following century Gautier
de Coincy makes a similar allusion in his poem *De l'Empereri Qui Garda sa
Chastéé par moult Temptacions* (ll. 1037 ff.), which belongs to the Crescentia
type (see § 41). This allusion is kept in the late-fourteenth-century dramatic
treatment of the same story, *L'Empereris de Romme* (ll. 1463 ff.). From about
the same period date the allusions in Chaucer's *Constance* (*Tale of the Man
of Lawe*, l. 541) and in the English romance *Cheuelere Assigne* (ll. 89–91).
The similarity between all these passages is so striking that it can hardly be
purely accidental.
[2] See L. Petit de Julleville, *Les Mystères*, vol. ii, pp. 371 ff. Cf. also *Le
Mistère du Viel Testament*, vol. v (ed. Baron Rothschild), ch. 41.
[3] See Thorén, *Studier över Själens Tröst*.
[4] See Baron Rothschild's bibliography of dramas on Susanna in Greek,
Latin, French, Italian, Spanish, English, Dutch, German, Danish, and
Czech (op. cit., pp. lxvi ff.). Cf. also Pilger, 'Die Dramatisierungen der
Susanna im 16. Jahrhundert'. A sixteenth-century Ladin drama has been
edited by Ulrich, *Susanna. Ein oberengadinisches Drama des XVI. Jahrhunderts*. Susanna is the subject of paintings by Tintoretto, Veronese,
Altdorfer, Rubens, Van Dyck, Rembrandt, and others.
[5] See *The Roxburghe Ballads*, vol. i, pp. 252 ff.

farther back than the Middle Ages,[1] the judicial combat was apparently revived in the early feudal period, and it came to enjoy a certain popularity under the auspices of chivalry, which vested it with a romantic hue originally alien to it. It formed a regular institution in the Assize of Jerusalem.[2] In our ballad, however, this chivalric conception is practically absent, particularly in Scandinavia, where Memering in the later versions is no longer a disinterested champion, but fights Raadengaard in order to win Gunhild's hand (cf. § 25). This conception is carried to its extreme in the Norwegian version, where the accusation has dropped out altogether. But even in the early English versions the fight savours more of folk-tale than of romance, and this is further stressed in the later English ballad, where a supernatural element is added. The Scottish version alone represents the chivalric ideal.

Margaret Schlauch makes no mention of the fact that we do find folk-tales containing an accusation of adultery and a steward or butler or some similar person as accuser. This type is listed as No. 883 A (*The Innocent Slandered Maiden*) in Aarne and Thompson's *Types of the Folk-Tale*; it has been recorded in Finland, Estonia, Russia, and Spain. The Spanish version,[3] the only one with which I am personally familiar runs as follows.

A girl's parents went away on a pilgrimage to Santiago, leaving their daughter in the care of the butler (*mayordomo*), a negro. He made love to her, but was rebuffed. He then sent a letter to her parents accusing her of trying to seduce him. The parents believed the accusation and ordered their son to turn his sister out of the house, kill her, and tear out her eyes. He took pity on her, and left her unhurt. While asleep under a tree, she was found by the king, who fell in love with her and married

<hr/>

[1] See R. Thurnwald in Ebert's *Reallexikon der Vorgeschichte*, s.vv. 'Gottesurteil' and 'Zweikampf'; and R. Hübner in Hoop's *Reallexikon der germanischen Altertumskunde* under the same words. Cf. also Jordan, 'Zur Entwicklung des gottesgerichtlichen Zweikampfs in Frankreich', and Hibbard, *Mediæval Romance in England*, p. 132 n., where further literature is mentioned.

[2] See Gibbon's *Decline and Fall*, ch. 58.

[3] Espinosa, *Cuentos Populares Españoles*, No. 106.

her. The king's mother did not like her son's marriage to a
foundling. One day when the king had gone away, the queen
went out accompanied by a black servant. He attempted to
seduce her, but she escaped. He returned to the court and said
that she had run away. On his return the king set out with the
black servant to find his wife. She, meanwhile, had dressed up
in men's clothing and had opened a hostel for travellers. The
king put up at this hostel, as did also the girl's parents. A general
recognition scene followed.

If Margaret Schlauch is right in her theory, this tale must
have been considerably influenced by romance. The only primitive survival is the fact that the queen's mother-in-law is
antagonistic to her, but that feature plays no part whatever in
the present form of the story.

§ 40. *Chaucer's 'Constance'*

The repeated persecutions in the folk-tale just mentioned are
a feature often encountered in stories of this kind. We meet
it, for instance, in Chaucer's *Tale of the Man of Lawe*, where
Constance is accused first of murder and later of having given
birth to a monster. The first of these accusations comes from a
knight who makes love to her, but is repelled. In revenge he
kills her benefactress, Hermengild, one night, and puts the
bloody knife in Constance's hand while she is asleep. This may
be a modernized version of the accusation of child-murder so
common in folk-tales. Very similar accusations are met with in
a large number of romances.[1] The second accusation, of having
given birth to a monster, comes, in true folk-tale fashion, from
her mother-in-law.[2] She obtains her purpose by falsifying letters
passing between the king, who is away at the wars, and the man
left in charge of Constance. This Exchanged Letter motif occurs
over and over again in folk-tale and romance. In the Constance

---

[1] e.g. in *Crescentia*. See p. 119.
[2] Unlike the other versions in this group, Chaucer's tale opens with an
account of yet another persecution by a wicked mother-in-law, Constance's
first husband's mother.

story, as in the Spanish folk-tale, the queen's innocence is
proved neither by an ordeal nor by a judicial combat; Constance
is put in a boat with her little child and cast adrift. The story
ends with a scene of recognition and explanation. Both these
features, the recognition scene and the boat scene, are common
to a large number of stories of accused queens.[1]

Chaucer's *Tale of the Man of Lawe* belongs to a large group
of stories of practically the same structure;[2] but apart from this
general mention we shall leave them aside in the present survey,
which deals mainly with queens accused of adultery. Another
group of stories, which also contains repeated persecutions and
a recognition scene at the end, comes within our purview: the
Crescentia type.

§ 41. *The Crescentia Type*

Stories belonging to this group have enjoyed an enormous
popularity in a large number of countries, and versions have to
be counted in hundreds.[3] The story occurs in prose, verse, and

---

[1] The former is found, e.g., in *Crescentia*, and the latter in the *Miracle
du Roy Thierry* (see p. 163, n. 3). On exposure in a boat see also Thompson's
Motif-Index under S 141.

[2] The earliest certain occurrence of the story in England is in the *Vitæ
Duorum Offarum* (c. 1200) by an unknown writer of St. Albans. In the
fourteenth century we find the story in an Anglo-Norman chronicle by one
Nicholas Trivet and in the romance of *Emare*, as well as in Chaucer's *Tale
of the Man of Lawe* and Gower's *Confessio Amantis*, ii, ll. 587 ff. Cf. Schlauch,
Chaucer's Constance, pp. 62 ff.; the same author's '*The Man of Law's Tale*';
and Wells's *Manual*, pp. 113, 129–31, and 701–2. Siefken, in *Das geduldige
Weib in der englischen Literatur*, deals not only with the Constance story,
but also with some of the related types mentioned in the following pages.
It is possible that the story was known in Anglo-Saxon England: see
Klaeber's *Beowulf* (3rd ed.), pp. 196–7, and the literature mentioned there
and in his Bibliography, iv. 98–106. This view has been contested by
Krappe, 'The Offa-Constance Legend'. Cf. also this book, p. 120, n. 4.
For versions in other languages see Suchier's Introduction to the works of
Philippe de Beaumanoir; Bolte and Polívka's *Anmerkungen zu den Kinder-
und Hausmärchen der Brüder Grimm*, vol. i, pp. 298–301; and Schlauch,
Chaucer's Constance, p. 69.

[3] See especially Wallensköld, 'Le Conte de la Femme Chaste convoitée
par son Beau-Frère'; the same author's Introduction to *Florence de Rome*;
and his 'L'Origine et l'évolution du Conte de la Femme Chaste', &c. See also
Stefanović, 'Die Crescentia-Florence-Sage'; Hilka, 'Zum Crescentiastoff';

dramatic form. It is found, for example, in the *Gesta Romanorum* and in Vincent of Beauvais's *Speculum Historiale*. An English metrical version has been mentioned in an earlier chapter under the title of *Florence of Rome* (§ 18). A characteristic feature of this group of stories is that the lady is persecuted first by her brother-in-law[1] and a second time by someone in the service of the man who rescued her from her first persecutor. The second persecution takes the form of an accusation of murder, very like the one of which Constance was the victim.[2] This is how we first meet our story in the earliest recorded version, *Crescentia*, which occurs in the Old High German *Kaiserchronik* of *c.* 1150.[3] In later versions, such as *Florence of Rome*, the number of trials the heroine has to endure has increased, and in some stories we get as many as five successive persecutions. The story ends with a scene in which the heroine heals her persecutors, stricken with punitive maladies, after they have confessed their sins.

While all the other versions in the group are about fictitious personages, Hildegard, the heroine of a well-known subgroup,[4] is said to be Charlemagne's wife. Her story differs in some respects from the rest of the stories in this group: there is only one persecutor, Talandus, who is Charlemagne's half-brother. According to one theory, represented by Wallensköld,[5] the story of Hildegard goes back to a Bavarian schoolmaster, Johannes Birck, who in 1484 or 1485 introduced it into the Annals of the Abbey of Kempten, simply as a variation of his own invention, in which he attributes the role of heroine to the patroness of the abbey, Queen Hildegard. This theory has

Teubert, *Crescentia-Studien*; and Hibbard, *Mediæval Romance in England*, pp. 12 ff.

[1] In some versions, e.g. *Florence of Rome*, the heroine is not accused or slandered, but directly wronged by her brother-in-law.

[2] For other instances of this kind of accusation, probably borrowed from the Constance or the Crescentia type, see p. 150, n. 4.

[3] Schröder's edition, pp. 298–314. For a detailed account of the versions and MSS., see Stefanović, op. cit., pp. 468–70.

[4] Her story is told in Grimm, *Deutsche Sagen*, vol. ii, No. 437.

[5] See his 'Conte', &c., ch. viii (pp. 65 ff.), or his Introduction to *Florence de Rome*, pp. 125 ff.

been strongly contested by Stefanović (pp. 500–11), who holds that the Hildegard story is based on a popular tradition independent of, and earlier than, Birck's version. It is a fact that the story of Hildegard has remained alive in popular tradition to the present day.[1]

Views differ considerably with regard to the origin of the Crescentia type. The story exists in several oriental versions, for example in the Persian story-book known as the *Tuti-Nameh* from the first half of the fourteenth century, in a Turkish version from the fifteenth century, in a Tartar version, in the *Arabian Nights*, and in several other collections of oriental tales. The question to be decided, therefore, is whether the oriental or the occidental branch can claim seniority. Grundtvig (*DgF* i, p. 203) and later Stefanović have put forward the view that the story is of Germanic origin. Grundtvig urges the complexity of structure of the extant oriental versions, and Stefanović their late date. The opposite view has been taken by Mussafia,[2] who believes in two successive importations of an Eastern tale, first in a simple and later in a more complicated form, and by Wallensköld, who maintains that all the European versions go back to an oriental tale, which was introduced into Europe about the end of the eleventh century.[3]

We cannot here go into this question in detail, but considering that the Crescentia type is of much later date than the earliest traces of the Gunhild story,[4] and that the structure of the

---

[1] See Graber, 'Hildegard von Stein'.

[2] 'Über eine italienische metrische Darstellung der Crescentiasage', pp. 680–1. See also the same author's 'Eine altspanische Prosadarstellung der Crescentiasage'.

[3] Teubert, op. cit., thinks that the author of the earliest version drew chiefly on the Clementine *Recognitions*, but was also influenced by the tale of *Apollonius of Tyre*. This theory leaves the question of ultimate origin unsolved. With regard to the later history of the type, Karl, 'Florence de Rome et la vie de deux saints de Hongrie', has put forward a theory that the story was modified to fit certain facts in the life of St. Elizabeth of Hungary (d. 1231). Hence the frequent references to Hungary in several branches of the tradition.

[4] Stefanović (pp. 546 ff.) tries to trace the Crescentia story back to the Anglo-Saxon poem *The Wife's Lament*. Cf. also his paper 'Das angelsächsische Gedicht "Die Klage der Frau"'. Others (see p. 118, n. 2)

Crescentia story is considerably more complex, it seems certain that, whatever its origin, *Crescentia* cannot belong to *Gunhild's* ancestors. She is more likely to be a second cousin once removed. It is possible, however, though far from certain, that the Crescentia story influenced the ballad at a later stage. In the former we find the episode of the treacherous seneschal or steward (second accusation) and the features of the king's absence at the war while his queen is being persecuted (first accusation). Both these incidents, however, are found elsewhere, sometimes in romances which also on other points offer close parallels to the ballad and which are therefore more likely to have been its direct source.

§ 42. *The Sibilla Type*

Another group of stories, which it is customary to term the Sibilla group after the heroine of one of the versions, resembles the Gunhild story by having only one persecutor, generally the king's steward or seneschal. As in numerous other tales of persecution, for example the first part of the Crescentia story, the king is away, either at the chase or at the war, while the steward makes love to the queen. In other respects, also, this story recalls the Crescentia type: the queen is sent out into a wood for punishment, and lives in exile for many years before her honour is finally vindicated. In contrast with the Crescentia type, the heroine bears a son in her exile, who plays a certain part in bringing about the reunion of his parents (cf. p. 113). Many of the versions have also some form of single combat, which, however, does not lead to the immediate rehabilitation of the queen. The accusation is generally of adultery with some dwarf or slave or servant, and practical proof of the alleged crime is often furnished by smuggling somebody into the queen's bed. The type seems to have arisen in France.

Sibilla, so the story goes, was Charlemagne's wife. A treacherous

would connect this poem with the Constance story. The evidence either way is inconclusive.

knight Macaire[1] tried to seduce her, but unable to obtain her love he took revenge by persuading a dwarf to creep into her bed while she was asleep. Sibilla was to be burnt, but on the intercession of the highest men in the realm she was banished instead, and was sent off in company with a squire named Aubri. On the way they were attacked by Macaire, who killed Aubri, while Sibilla escaped. Aubri had a greyhound, which kept watch at his corpse. Returning to the palace for food one day, it attacked Macaire and wounded him. Charlemagne and his court grew suspicious, and the emperor ordered the greyhound to be followed, should it come again for food. In this way the crime was detected. Macaire denied everything and offered to prove his innocence by a single combat. Nobody dared to meet him in the lists, but somebody then suggested that the greyhound, the real accuser, ought to fight with Macaire. The duel took place, and Macaire was conquered, and afterwards duly punished. After many adversities Sibilla was reunited with Charlemagne.

As told here, the story is a reconstruction of the supposed original. It was the subject of an early French *chanson de geste*, but that poem is now preserved only in an italianized version,[2] in which the queen's name is Blanchefleur. Guessard, who has tried to restore the poem to its original French form, believes it to date from the end of the twelfth century. A different version of the same story occurred in a later poem in alexandrines, *La Reine Sibille*, of which only a few fragments survive.[3] There exists also a fifteenth-century French prose version of the story,[4] a Dutch and a Spanish prose translation, and a fourteenth-century German poem about an unnamed queen of France, who is no other than our heroine.[5] In England we find

---

[1] Note that this name occurs also in *Florence of Rome* (see § 18). Cf. below, p. 147.   [2] *Macaire*, ed. F. Guessard.

[3] Published by Scheler, 'Fragments uniques d'un roman du XIIIe siècle sur la Reine Sebile'. Cf. also Baker, 'Nouveaux fragments de la chanson de la Reine Sibile'. A Latin summary of this version of the poem is given by the thirteenth-century chronicler Alberic of Trois-Fontaines.

[4] Cf. Léon Gautier, *Les Épopées françaises*, vol. ii (Paris, 1892), p. 554.

[5] See Guessard's Preface, esp. pp. lxiii ff. The Spanish version is printed

the story in the romance of *Sir Tryamoure* (§ 16), in which the incident of the dwarf is suppressed. There appears to have also existed a Latin prose rendering. In the Matricularium of Peterborough Abbey Library,[1] which in the opinion of Montagu James dates from the fourteenth century, there is mentioned a book on the following subject: 'Qualiter Sibilla Regina posita sit in exilium extra Franciam, et quomodo Makayre occidit Albricum de Mondisdene'. This book is no longer extant.[2]

The episode of the dog has had the remarkable fortune of being remembered long after the rest of the story had fallen into oblivion. The fight was for a long time believed to be an historical event supposed to have taken place during the reign of Charles V.[3] It was no doubt originally taken from Plutarch's story of Pyrrhus' dog.[4]

Variations on the theme of Sibilla are numerous. One of them, the story of *Olif*, has been summarized above (§ 14) from the thirteenth-century Norse version. Though Olif offers to undergo an ordeal, and though in fact one of her knights fights a joust with her accuser, the decision of that combat is overruled, and it is only after many years that the queen's innocence is finally proved through the efforts of her son Landres.

According to its own explicit statement, the Norse version is a translation of an English romance. It is included in the second redaction of the *Karlamagnús Saga*, the rest of which is based

by A. Bonilla y San Martín, *Libros de Caballerías*, pt. i. The German poem can be found in von der Hagen, *Gesammtabenteuer*, vol. i, pp. 165 ff.; and in Hertz, *Schondochs Gedichte*.

[1] Published by James, *Lists of Manuscripts formerly in Peterborough Abbey Library*.

[2] The catalogue seems to indicate specifically whenever a manuscript is in one of the vernacular tongues, and also when it is in verse. As none of these indications (*Gallice*, *Anglice*, *versifice*, &c.) is found after the above entry, the book was presumably in Latin prose.

[3] Cf. Guessard's Preface, esp. pp. lxxxiii f.; see also L. Clédat, *Chrestomathie du Moyen Âge* (11th ed.), pp. 62–65; and *La Grande Encyclopédie*, s.v. 'Aubry de Montdidier'. Several encyclopedias still describe the incident as if it were an authentic historical fact.

[4] Besides Guessard, loc. cit., cf. also Hibbard, *Mediæval Romance in England*, pp. 286–7; and Hempel, *Nibelungenstudien*, p. 242.

on an Anglo-Norman or a French model.¹ The English Olif
story, too, goes back to a French original; it is related to the
chanson de geste, Doon de la Roche. To the same group belongs
a Spanish prose story, *Historia de Enrrique fi de Oliua.* In the
north the story is also found in a Faroese ballad, *Óluvu Kvæði,*²
and in an Icelandic poem, *Landres Rímur.*³ The three Scandinavian versions form a separate tradition;⁴ the two songs or
ballads probably go back to the *Karlamagnús Saga.* I reproduce
Huet's genealogical table:

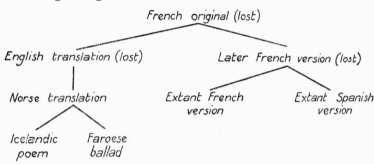

---

¹ See Paris, 'La Karlamagnus-Saga'; and de Vries, *Altnordische Literaturgeschichte,* § 289.

² Printed by Hammershaimb in *Færøsk Anthologi,* vol. i, No. 25. Cf. also
the same author in *Antiquarisk Tidsskrift,* 1846–8, pp. 279–304; and Thuren,
Folkesangen paa Færøerne, pp. 81 and 92–94.

³ Printed by Jónsson in *Rímnasafn,* vol. ii. Cf. Þorólfsson, *Rímur fyrir
1600,* pp. 390–3.

⁴ For example, in the north, Olif is Pippin's daughter, Charlemagne's
sister, while in the French and Spanish versions she is Pippin's sister. This
is doubtless a deliberate alteration on the part of the Norwegian translator
in order to fit the story into the saga of Charlemagne. The translator seems
also to have added certain details. Thus, Landres's foster-mother gives him
a sword called *Mimung* and a horse named *Kleming* (ch. 15). This recalls
the passage in *Þiðriks Saga* where Velent presents his son Viðga with the
sword *Mimung,* which he himself has made, and with a horse called *Skem-
ming.* The sword is known from other sources as Viðga's sword: see pp. 71–72.
The feature of the snake-pit appears also to be of Scandinavian origin; it
does not occur in the French and Spanish versions. On the relative age of
the two branches of the group, see Huet's Preface to his and Meyer's edition
of *Doon de la Roche,* pp. lxxi ff.; Hempel, *Nibelungenstudien,* pp. 247 ff.;
Schlauch, *Chaucer's Constance,* pp. 95 ff.; and Smyser, 'The Middle English
and Old Norse Story of Olive'. Smyser's paper suffers from certain in-
accuracies, some of which have been pointed out by Larsen, 'Olive and
Landres'. See also Smyser's reply, 'Olive Again'.

The surviving French version appears to have been composed about 1200, which probably means that the lost original belonged to the middle or early part of the twelfth century.[1]

Perhaps the best-known variation on the Sibilla theme is the story of *Geneviève of Brabant*,[2] whose husband is said to have been a Count of the Palatinate named Siegfried. Going to the wars he entrusted his wife to the care of his seneschal, Golo, who betrayed his trust and acted the usual part of seducer and accuser. He told Siegfried on his return that his wife had sinned with a servant. She was led into a forest to be killed, but the men took pity on her and cut off the tongue of a dog to take back to Siegfried. Geneviève lived for six years in the forest. Her little child (who, incidentally, plays scarcely any part in the story) was suckled by a hind, and one day when Siegfried was out hunting he caught sight of this hind and pursued it till he came to his wife's hiding-place. Geneviève was restored to her former dignity, but died soon after.

This story has been told over and over again in popular literature; but although it contains many old and familiar features, it is probably of comparatively recent date. The oldest existing versions go back to the fifteenth century. The legend appears to be almost certainly the story of Sibilla adapted to local tradition in the district of Maifeld in western Germany, where St. Geneviève, patroness of Paris, was held in high honour. The story is probably, at least in part, of learned origin.[3]

A faint echo of the Geneviève legend is found in the story of *St. Ida of Toggenburg*.[4] Here, too, there is an accusation of

---

[1] Cf. Huet, op. cit., pp. xxxvii f. and xciii, n. 2.

[2] See, e.g., Grimm's *Deutsche Sagen*, vol. ii, No. 532; and Weckerlin, *Chansons Populaires*, vol. i, pp. 206–11.

[3] The latest treatment of the subject is in Kentenich, *Die Genovefalegende*. Cf. also Schlauch, op. cit., pp. 106–7; and Brockhaus's *Konversations-Lexikon*. Hempel, op. cit., pp. 186–9, places the origin of the Geneviève legend in the twelfth century. Cf. also p. 126, n. 5.

[4] See Grimm, *Deutsche Sagen*, No. 507. Cf. also Schlauch, op. cit., pp. 107–8, and Brockhaus, op. cit. I have not seen L. M. Kern, 'Die Ida von

adultery, and vindication after years spent in exile, but many of the characteristic episodes of the Sibilla-Geneviève type are missing.

A further tale related to our legend is told of Wolfdietrich's mother in version A of the *Wolfdietrich Saga*.[1] There are many discrepancies, however, which seem to prove that the story was not originally part of the saga, but was later adapted for inclusion.[2] The *Wolfdietrich Saga*, like the Sibilla story, is probably of Frankish origin.[3]

Finally, we must mention the story of *Sisibe*, Sigurð's mother, in *Þiðriks Saga* (see § 26). This saga, too, has adopted numerous French stories and story elements, among which is undoubtedly the tale of Sisibe.[4] As in the Wolfdietrich story, the ending differs from that of the Sibilla legend. The two accusers in the Sisibe story seem to have been borrowed from another group of stories, shortly to be mentioned, the Earl of Toulouse type.[5]

The Sibilla story has one interesting point in common with the later English Gunhild ballad: the man smuggled into the bed.[6] On the other hand, it differs from the story of Gunhild in the way in which the queen's innocence is proved. In this respect *The Earl of Toulouse* forms a much closer parallel to the Gunhild story.

Toggenburg Legende', *Thurgauische Beiträge zur vaterländischen Geschichte*, vol. lxiv/lxv (Freiburg dissertation, Frauenfeld, 1928).

[1] The only existing MS. dates from the sixteenth century, but the poem was probably composed in the first half of the thirteenth century. See Schneider, *Wolfdietrich*, pp. viii and xx.

[2] See Scheludko, 'Versuch neuer Interpretation des Wolfdietrich-Stoffes'. Cf. also Schlauch, op. cit., pp. 100–2.

[3] Besides the works already cited, cf. Heinzel, 'Über die ostgothische Heldensage', pp. 78–79.

[4] See Krappe, 'Une Version norroise de la Reine Sibille'.

[5] Hempel, op. cit., pp. 179–98, on the basis of certain similarities between the stories of Geneviève and Sisibe, classes these two as a separate group parallel to the Crescentia and Sibilla types.

[6] This feature appears to be of oriental origin. On European soil it is found, outside *Sibilla* and *Sir Aldingar*, in *The Earl of Toulouse* (see p. 135) and in *Octavian* (p. 149). A faint reminiscence occurs in *Hirlande* (see p. 153). Cf. Huet, op. cit., pp. lxxxi–lxxxii; Krappe, op. cit., p. 587; and G. L. Kittredge, *Harvard Studies and Notes*, vol. viii (1903), p. 188, n. 1.

§ 43. *The Earl of Toulouse Type*

I have named this type after the English romance summarized in an earlier chapter (§ 15). Among other representatives of the type I have also had occasion to mention the Danish romance *Den kyske Dronning* (§ 23). Lüdtke, who has investigated the origin of this group of stories,[1] thinks that they are all founded on an event which happened during the reign of Louis the Pious, whose second wife Judith was accused of adultery with Bernard, Count of Barcelona and perhaps also of Toulouse,[2] and chamberlain at the imperial court. They both cleared themselves by oath, but Bernard, before taking the oath, challenged anyone who dared to accuse him to a single combat; no such person presented himself. It is also possible that Judith offered to undergo an ordeal.

The legend would thus, according to Lüdtke, go back to the ninth century. The earliest certain occurrence of the story known to us is found in Desclot's Catalan chronicle, *Cronica del Rey En Pere*,[3] which dates from shortly before 1300. The heroine is a Bohemian princess married to the emperor of Germany. Two of the emperor's councillors, the queen's enemies, accused her of infidelity, and the emperor believed them and gave orders that she was to be burnt unless she could find a champion within a year and a day. No German knight dared to fight against her accusers, who stood high in the emperor's favour; but there lived at court a minstrel (*juglarets*) who, when he saw the empress's distress, went out in search of a champion. He travelled from court to court till he came to Barcelona. The count of that town decided to defend the empress's honour. He set out in company with another knight

[1] See his edition of *The Erl of Tolous*, esp. pp. 98 ff. Although this is still the best study, it must now be supplemented by others. See Paris, 'Le Roman du Comte de Toulouse'; Rubió, 'Les versions catalanes de la llegenda del bon comte de Barcelona i l'emperadriu d'Alemanya'; Hibbard, *Mediæval Romance in England*, pp. 35 ff.; and Hempel, *Nibelungenstudien*, pp. 190–2 and 238 ff.

[2] Cf. F. Lot, *Le Moyen Âge*, 2nd Ser., vol. viii (1904), pp. 150 and 152.

[3] Ed. Buchon, *Chroniques étrangères*, pp. 565 ff. The passage is summarized by Lüdtke, pp. 170–2, and (very briefly) by Rubió, pp. 259–60.

and arrived at Cologne three days before the year and the day were up. He did not reveal his identity, but merely passed himself off as a Spanish knight willing to fight for the empress. He obtained permission to visit her in prison in order to hear from her own mouth that she was innocent. To her he told who he was, and she gave him a precious ring as a token that he was to be her champion. The next day the duel took place, and the count was victorious; but soon after the combat he secretly left Cologne and returned to Spain. The empress now revealed to her husband who her champion was, and the emperor, wishing to reward him, told his wife to go to Barcelona and fetch her rescuer back to Germany. When the count arrived, the emperor gave him Provence as fief.

The resemblance to *The Earl of Toulouse* is obvious. We have here the features characteristic of the group as a whole, particularly of the older branch of the tradition: two accusers;[1] the empress is to be burnt unless a champion can be found; at the last moment a knight comes riding from afar; he does not reveal his identity to the others (in some versions not even to the empress herself), obtains a conversation with the empress in prison, receives a ring from her (in *The Earl of Toulouse* and some of the later versions this incident is placed earlier in the tale), conquers her accusers, and leaves before the emperor has had time to reward him; he is recalled and duly recompensed.

The story of the empress of Germany and her rescue from death at the stake by a count of Barcelona has been told by numerous later Catalan chroniclers and imaginative writers.[2] Some of these versions are based on Desclot; others seem to

---

[1] Lüdtke would see their historical counterparts in the Empress Judith's two enemies, Counts Hugo and Matfrid. Outside this group of stories, two accusers occur in *Susanna* (see pp. 114–15) and in the story of *Sisibe*, which probably borrowed the feature from the Earl of Toulouse type (see p. 126). Faint traces are also met with in *Valentine and Orson* (see p. 150) and in *Hirlande* (see p. 155). Lüdtke (pp. 114–15) and Hempel (p. 239) maintain that two accusers are only suitable in stories where the motive is ambition or envy, and that it is a disadvantage for the English romance to have kept the two accusers after the motive had been changed to unrequited love.

[2] As late as in 1923, according to Rubió, it formed the theme of a classical tragedy in alexandrines, *Matilde d'Anglaterra*, by Ferran Soldevila.

draw upon some independent source, which may well have been a poem of a popular nature. Rubió, who has made a detailed study of the tradition, has found no certain instance of the tale in the fourteenth century, but in the following century there are several. An anonymous historical compilation, *Flos Mundi*, dating from shortly after 1400, gives a version in which the name of the emperor is Henry (Enric), 'emperor of the Romans and king of the Germans', and that of the empress is Matilda (Matildis); the defender's name is said to be Ramon Berenguer, and the combat takes place at Aix-la-Chapelle. Later chroniclers identify the defender with one of the reigning counts of Barcelona, Ramon Berenguer III or IV, more often with the former. The names Henry and Matilda recur in the *Crónica General* of Beuter (1551), who says that the empress was an English princess, and they are found in most subsequent versions. Nearly all the Catalan chronicles state that Provence was given to the count of Barcelona in reward for his chivalrous defence of the empress.

The theory of an oral tradition in Catalonia, rendered probable by the popularity of the theme and by certain differences between the written versions,[1] finds corroboration in the existence of a Castilian ballad about a Count Ramon of Barcelona who delivered an unnamed empress of Germany from death at the stake.[2] This ballad is first found in a collection printed in 1520; in its present form it can scarcely be older than the first half of the fifteenth century. In this ballad as in the later Catalan versions, starting with Carbonell's *Chroniques de Espanya* (c. 1495), the count's interview with the empress to assure himself of her innocence takes the form of a scene in which he disguises himself as a monk and acts as her confessor. This scene, it will be recalled, occurs also in *The Earl of Toulouse* and in *Den kyske Dronning*.

Outside this group of stories about a count of Barcelona and

---

[1] See Rubió, op. cit., pp. 258 and 278–9.
[2] Menéndez y Pelayo, *Romances Viejos Castellanos*, vol. i, No. 162. Also in Durán, *Romancero General*, vol. ii, pp. 210–12.

an empress of Germany there exist versions in Spain obviously belonging to our type but about purely fictitious personages. A fifteenth-century Catalan prose romance, *Curial y Guelfa*, is about an unnamed duchess of Austria and her alleged lover, Jacob of Cleves; while on a pilgrimage to Santiago he was recalled by the duchess to defend her honour. A Castilian ballad printed in 1551[1] is about a queen of Ireland who was to be beheaded on a charge of adultery; but at the last moment a man dressed in a monk's cowl arrived, asked permission to shrive the queen, and at once threw down his hood and revealed that he was a knight who had come to defend her honour. He vanquished both her accusers. We are not told his name, but only that he was of Catalan nationality, a statement which is of course significant with regard to the origin of the ballad. Other Spanish stories less certainly or less closely related to our type will be mentioned later (pp. 139–40).

The Spanish chronicles and also, to some extent, the English romance represent the older form of the tradition, characterized, for example, by having two accusers. This feature is lost in the later form of the story. The later versions fall into two subdivisions. The first group consists of two seventeenth-century Provençal chronicles, *L'Histoire et Chronique de Provence* by César de Nostradamus and *La Royalle Couronne des Roys d'Arles* by M. J. Bovis,[2] and a story told in 1640 by René de Cerisiers,[3] who says he took it from some historical records. The second subdivision is made up of a number of romantic stories in several languages (see pp. 134–5), which have the general plot and also many details in common with the older form of the tradition, particularly *The Earl of Toulouse*, but which have lost sight entirely of the historical background of the earlier versions.

Nearest to the older form are the two Provençal chronicles

[1] In the *Tercera Parte de la Silva de Romances*. Reprinted by Menéndez y Pelayo, op. cit., vol. ii, pp. 242–4.

[2] Both versions are reprinted, the former with certain omissions, by Lüdtke, pp. 179–81.

[3] It occurs in the preface to his book *Les Trois États de l'Innocence* (Paris, 1640). I have not seen this edition, but have used Sir William Lower's English translation (London, 1656).

and Cerisiers's story. Like the Spanish versions, but unlike *The Earl of Toulouse*, they call the queen's champion Raymond Berenguier, Comte de Barcellone (Nostradamus), Raymond Berenger, Comte de Provence et de Barcelonne (Arles chronicle), or Remond Teste d'estoupe, the last of the Berangers, Count of Barcelona and Provence (Cerisiers). It seems likely that on this point *The Earl of Toulouse* has preserved the original name, Bernard. As the Bernard whom Lüdtke considers to be the historical prototype was probably count of both Toulouse and Barcelona, it is but natural that legend on one side of the Pyrenees should know him as the count of Toulouse and on the other as the count of Barcelona. Nor is it strange that Spanish tradition should later ascribe the story to a different and better known count of Barcelona, whereas *The Earl of Toulouse*, which is based on French tradition, has kept the original name. The story as told in the Provençal chronicles and by Cerisiers must have been under Spanish influence.

Rubió thinks that since practically all the Catalan versions mention the gift of Provence as a reward to the rescuer, this feature, and perhaps this form of the story generally, may be due to an attempt to explain the historical fact of the joining of Provence to Catalonia. One of the Catalan chroniclers, the author of the *Flos Mundi*, is uncertain about the gift and suggests as an alternative explanation that Provence may have been acquired by inheritance. North of the Pyrenees this view is expressed by Cerisiers, who says that those who think the merit of Remond's defence of the empress earned him Provence have not read the records well: he acquired Provence by marrying Douce, 'one of its heiresses'. What these 'records' are to which Cerisiers refers we do not know; but his information is correct: the countship of Provence was acquired by Ramon Berenguer III by his marriage with Douce in 1112.

It is not merely in the matter of the champion's name that the Provençal chronicles are linked with Spanish tradition. Like the *Flos Mundi*, and like Beuter and other Spanish chroniclers, they have apparently been under the influence of the Gunhild legend. Beuter and Nostradamus say that the empress was an English princess Matilda, daughter of King Henry I of England; Cerisiers, too, calls her Matilda, but says that she was the daughter of Henry II of England; the Arles chronicle keeps the name Matilda, but says that she was 'fille de Camet qui avoit esté Roy de Dannemarc et estoit Roy d'Angleterre'. 'Camet' is obviously a mistake for 'Canut(e)'. The emperor to whom all these chronicles refer is Henry V (Cerisiers calls him Henry IV), who in 1114 married Matilda, daughter of Henry I of England. But how did the story come to be attached to her? As pointed out by Grundtvig (*DgF* i, p. 187), although Matilda's husband was Henry V of Germany, yet as king of Arles he was Henry III. Gunhild's husband, too, was a King Henry III (he never became emperor in her lifetime). Moreover, both Gunhild and Matilda were English princesses married to German emperors or kings. It is not difficult to see how the story usually attached to Gunhild could have become transferred to Matilda; and the Arles chronicle has only carried the prevailing confusion a little farther by calling Matilda Canute's daughter.[1] It may not even be necessary to assume an oral tradition on the Continent; indeed, 'Camet' for 'Canut' points to a written source.[2] The amazing thing is, however, that the Gunhild story in this modified form became mixed up with the story of the count of Barcelona and the empress of Germany. Most of the details in the Provençal versions belong unquestionably to the latter story; the single accuser may or may not be due to the influence of the Gunhild-Matilda legend.

[1] The height of confusion is reached when, as in the Danish Gunhild ballad, the story is attached to Duke Henry 'the Lion' (who was married to a Princess Matilda, daughter of Henry II of England: see p. 43), but his wife's name is said to be Gunhild and they live at Spire, i.e. Speyer, the favourite residence of the Salian emperors of Germany.

[2] The Gunhild legend was known on the Continent not only through the English chroniclers, but also through such continental writers as Helinandus (Migne's edition, col. 930) and Vincent of Beauvais (*Speculum Historiale*, bk. 25, ch. 17), who both quote William of Malmesbury's version of the story. Another chronicler, Alberic of Trois-Fontaines (p. 787), tells the story in a way clearly reminiscent of William of Malmesbury, although he does not quote him.

The origin of this confusion may have to be sought in the south of France, which was probably the cradle of the Earl of Toulouse legend.[1] Aquitaine in the ninth century formed part of the domains of Count Bernard, who successfully defended it against the Emperor Louis (cf. the war mentioned in *The Earl of Toulouse*). Legends tend to become transferred to the best known local figure; Gaston Paris (pp. 30–32) thinks that the fact that the Gundeberg legend was known in France, possibly in the form of a song (see p. 102), may have helped to create the Earl of Toulouse story out of the historical facts about Bernard and Judith: after all, Bernard never did fight a combat with his accusers. From Aquitaine, after a time, the story must have spread both southwards to Spain and northwards to Brittany and England; but in some of the later versions that issued from Aquitaine the story appears to have been confused with the Gunhild-Matilda legend. This second transfer may have been due partly to political circumstances. After her first husband's death in 1125 the Empress Matilda married Count Geoffrey of Anjou, and their son, the later Henry II of England, through his marriage with Eleanor of Aquitaine in 1152 extended his domains to the Pyrenees. The dynastic alliance may have opened the door to a similar merging of legends, Matilda taking the place of Judith, or the unnamed empress, in the Earl of Toulouse story.[2]

Grundtvig (*DgF* i, pp. 187–8) considers the Earl of Toulouse type to be a direct offshoot of the English Gunhild legend, which in his opinion wandered from England through Flanders and France to Spain. But, so far as I can see, apart from the confusion in the Provençal and Spanish chronicles just mentioned, the similarities on which Grundtvig's view is based are only the following: (1) both legends are about the wife of a German

---

[1] See Lüdtke, p. 125, and Rubió, p. 279.

[2] It is interesting to speculate whether some form of the Earl of Toulouse story could have had Matilda's daughter-in-law, Eleanor, for its heroine. The English Gunhild ballad as found in the Percy MS. is about a Queen Elinor, probably Eleanor of Aquitaine (see p. 17), and there is good reason to suppose that the ballad in its present form is in debt to the Earl of Toulouse story (see pp. 156–7).

prince; (2) she is to be burnt if nobody will defend her; (3) a messenger goes out to find a champion, who arrives at the last moment. No. 1 feature hardly proves anything, and certainly not that the continental Earl of Toulouse tradition borrowed its German setting from an English source. No. 2 is not confined to the Earl of Toulouse type and the English ballad alone, and thus cannot prove any direct relationship between the two. It occurs also in the Swan Knight story and in *Hirlande*, and traces of it are found in *Sibilla*, *Octavian*, and elsewhere.[1] No. 3, at least the first part of it, may be peculiar to these two traditions, but why assume that *The Earl of Toulouse* took it from the ballad? It is not found in the early English Gunhild tradition, but only in the later ballad, the manuscript of which dates from about 1650. In the Earl of Toulouse type, on the other hand, it is found in the earliest record, Desclot's chronicle of *c.* 1300. It would be more natural, therefore, to assume that the ballad had taken it from *The Earl of Toulouse*, which, as a matter of fact, I believe to be the case (see pp. 156–7).

It is stated expressly in *The Earl of Toulouse* that its source is a 'lay of Bretayn' (l. 1220).[2] This makes Grundtvig's theory of its origin extremely complicated. He himself realized this, as will be seen from the following quotation: 'After the English Gunhild legend had travelled to Spain, an echo of the legend found its way—goodness knows through what channels—back to its home country, England, where it occurs in a fifteenth-century romance, "The Erl of Tolous"' (*DgF* i, pp. 188–9). Compared with this view Lüdtke's theory is remarkably simple.

The second subdivision of late versions (cf. p. 130) consists of prose and verse renderings in French, German, Danish, Italian, and Latin. The oldest member of the group is a French miracle play, *Le Miracle de la Marquise de la Gaudine*, in a

---

[1] e.g. in Grimm's folk-tale No. 49, *The Six Swans*.

[2] This information is probably not to be taken too literally: cf. Paris, op. cit., p. 7, n. 2. The original was almost certainly in French. As pointed out by Lot, op. cit., p. 152, the queen's name in the English romance, *Dame Beulybon*, is obviously a corruption of the French phrase *dame belle et bonne*.

manuscript of *c.* 1400.[1] Next in age comes *Philopertus et Eugenia*, a story told in Latin by Jacob Wimpfeling, who heard it from a Count von Henneberg while travelling with him from Speyer to Strassburg. Wimpfeling turned the story from German into Latin and prefaced it by a letter to a friend in which he explained the special circumstances in which he heard the story. The letter is dated 1470.[2] Among other members of this group may be mentioned the Danish metrical romance *Den kyske Dronning* (1483) dealt with in an earlier chapter (§ 23), a German prose story by Wickram about a Scots knight Galmy and a duchess of Brittany (printed 1539), and an Italian story by Bandello[3] about a duchess of Savoy (1554). Later translations and imitations, especially of Bandello's story, are too numerous and widespread to be mentioned here.[4]

In this group of stories the original historical background has been abandoned; the action is set in various countries, England, Brittany, Burgundy, Poland, &c., and it is about purely fictitious characters. Other deviations from the old form of the story are: (1) there is only one accuser; (2) the accusation is made in revenge for despised love; (3) the king is absent during his seneschal's treacherous assault on the queen's virtue; (4) practical proof of the alleged adultery is supplied by smuggling somebody into the queen's bed. Now the last three of these points are shared by *The Earl of Toulouse*, which thus acts as a connecting link between the old and the new form of the story. Indeed it is possible that the versions in this group go back to the French original of *The Earl of Toulouse*.[5] All four points which distinguish them from the Spanish group have parallels in the Sibilla legend, from which they were probably borrowed.[6] The Sibilla type, too, is of French origin.

[1] Ed. Paris and Robert, *Miracles de Nostre Dame*, vol. ii, pp. 121 ff.
[2] See Schüddekopf, 'Eine unbekannte Erzählung Wimpfelings'.
[3] Summarized by Lüdtke, pp. 181–6.
[4] On this point see, e.g., Bolte's preface to his and Scheel's edition of Wickram, pp. viii–ix.
[5] This point has been contested by Lot, op. cit., pp. 153–4.
[6] The first three of these points are common to a large number of persecution stories. The fourth is found in the Sibilla, Earl of Toulouse, and

In a simplified form the filiation of the various versions of our story may be illustrated thus:

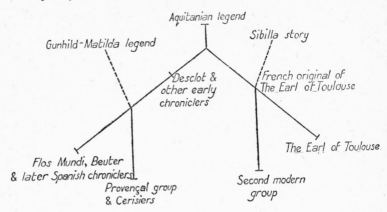

In reality, the relations are more involved than would appear from this table. Between the different branches there must have been a number of cross-currents which it is now difficult to trace. For instance, the disguise as a monk and the confession instead of a simple interview are found both north and south of the Pyrenees, but in Spain only in some of the later versions. Whence this feature came, and how it spread, we do not know.

Before closing this section we must mention yet a few stories. These are either of uncertain date or else less closely, sometimes only partially, related to the Earl of Toulouse type.

An eighteenth-century copy of a now lost Latin manuscript of the beginning of the sixteenth century tells a story which must undoubtedly be classed as a version of our type.[1] It is about Goufier de Lastours, the well-known warrior of the first crusade and the hero of numerous stories. When the queen of

Octavian types, and in the ballad of *Sir Aldingar*; cf. p. 126, n. 6. Hempel (p. 237) contends that the motif of the Pretended Lover was borrowed by the Sibilla type from the Earl of Toulouse story. This is connected with his theory (pp. 241–6) that the former type as a whole is chiefly descended from the latter. Hempel's theory creates enormous difficulties in the way of chronology, not to mention the fact that the Sibilla type with regard to denouement represents a much more primitive form of the motif than the Earl of Toulouse legend.

[1] See Thomas, 'Le Roman de Goufier de Lastours'.

France was accused of infidelity, he first disguised himself as a monk and heard her confession of innocence, and then appeared in the lists as her champion defeating her accuser. He would take no reward except the right to bear the royal fleur-de-lis. It is difficult to fit this version into our system of classification, especially as we do not know when it originated. Was the original story in Latin, French, or Provençal? Although there is only one accuser, the story makes a somewhat primitive impression.

A story in some respects similar to the Earl of Toulouse story, though possibly not related to it, is told in the Low German poem *Morant and Galia*. This poem, which is based on an unknown French source, must have been written between 1190 and 1210; it is embodied in the fourteenth-century story-cycle usually termed *Karl Meinet*.[1] The action is as follows.

The traitor Rohart and two accomplices accuse Morant de Rivers, Charlemagne's brave standard-bearer, of adultery with Queen Galia. To corroborate the accusation Rohart disguises himself as a pilgrim reporting fresh evidence of the alleged crime. Morant and the pilgrim fight a duel in which Morant is victorious. In the heat of the battle Rohart loses his false beard, and his treachery is thus revealed. The guilty persons are put to death, and Morant is indemnified. Charlemagne asks Galia's forgiveness.

This story is known from no other source, but an allusion to it occurs in the thirteenth-century Spanish work *La Gran Conquista de Ultramar*. This compilation of stories and legends has, by its author's own admission, been translated from the French.[2] In his reference to our story the author calls the heroine Sibilla, a name which, he says, Galia received when she was baptized (she was the daughter of a heathen king Galafer).[3]

[1] In addition to von Keller's *Karl Meinet* there is an edition of *Morant and Galia* alone by Kalisch. See also Bartsch, *Über Karlmeinet*; and Frings, 'Der Eingang von Morant und Galie'.

[2] See the edition by Pascual de Gayángos. Cf. also G. Paris, *Romania*, vol. xvii (1888), pp. 522 ff.

[3] See Paris, *Histoire Poétique de Charlemagne*, p. 388.

The only one, so far as I know, to class *Morant and Galia* as an offshoot of the Earl of Toulouse type[1] is Hempel (p. 254). Although the main outline is the same in both stories, concrete points of similarity are few. Hempel mentions three such points: (1) a genuine friendship between the queen and a famous knight is deliberately misrepresented by slanderous people; (2) the number of accusers is more than one (but *Morant and Galia* mentions three accusers, while our type has only two); (3) the motive for the accusation is envy or ambition, not thwarted love. The last point restricts the similarity to the Spanish group (cf. Lüdtke, pp. 114–15), and both 2 and 3 point to an early version of the Earl of Toulouse type. If there is a connexion, *Morant and Galia* must have been derived from an earlier version than any now extant, because unlike the Earl of Toulouse and his equivalents in the other versions, but like the historical prototype Bernard, Morant fights not merely from a sense of chivalric duty or a feeling of personal attachment to the queen, but in order to save his own life and honour. This fits in well with what we know of the date and origin of *Morant and Galia*. On the other hand, most of the specific characteristics of the Earl of Toulouse type are missing. The disguise as a pilgrim in *Morant and Galia* may have been suggested by the disguise as a confessor in the Earl of Toulouse type; but there is the important difference that in the one story the disguise is used by the traitor, in the other by the rescuer.[2] It may also be significant that Morant has a dream warning him of coming evil. In the Earl of Toulouse type, too, a dream occurs, but here it is either the husband or the accused lady who dreams (cf. p. 156).

The balance of evidence is perhaps on the whole slightly in favour of Hempel's theory. *Morant and Galia* gives the impression of being a free adaptation of a very early form of the Earl

---

[1] Various attempts have been made to establish a theory that the story belongs to the Sibilla type: see Bartsch, op. cit., pp. 28 ff. But *Morant and Galia* is obviously much closer in structure to the Earl of Toulouse type.

[2] A similar sort of disguise is found in the story of *Sainte Tryphine* (see p. 153).

of Toulouse story, shorn of most of the details typical of that group. The inclusion in the Charlemagne cycle may be due to influence from the story of Sibilla. The author of the *Gran Conquista* obviously confused the two stories.

Another somewhat doubtful version of the Earl of Toulouse story occurs in the *Crónica General* compiled by command of King Alfonso X of Castile.[1] The accused lady is here Queen Elvira, wife of Sancho the Great of Navarre (1000–35). The account differs considerably from the genuine Earl of Toulouse story: the two accusers are the lady's own sons, and although a confession occurs, it is the two sons who confess that their mother is innocent. What we have here seems to be an adaptation of our story to suit specific historical circumstances. According to Gaston Paris[2] the account can scarcely be later than the twelfth century.

Alfonso's nephew, the infante Juan Manuel, included as part of the forty-fourth tale of his *Libro de los Enxiemplos del Conde Lucanor* (c. 1235),[3] a story of a lady accused of adultery, but rescued from the stake by a stranger, Pero Nuñez, who arrived accidentally at the last moment. In an interview with him before the battle she confessed that, although she had not committed the crime of which she was accused, she had had the intention of doing so. Pero Nuñez therefore had misgivings about the justice of the cause, but nevertheless declared himself her champion. He vanquished her accuser, but lost an eye in the battle. Here, again, we have some of the details of the Earl of Toulouse story, the rescue at the last moment by a stranger and the lady's confession to her champion. It may also be significant that the event is said to have happened in *tierra de Tolosa*, probably, as the editors remark, the former county of Toulouse. The accuser, on the other hand, is the husband's brother as in the Crescentia type, and the lady's partial guilt is a feature entirely alien to our group of stories. Altogether, though there

[1] Ed. Menéndez Pidal, *Primera Crónica General de España*, ch. 791, pp. 474–5.
[2] 'Le Roman du Comte de Toulouse', p. 22.
[3] Knust and Birch-Hirschfeld's edition, pp. 197–8 and 401–3.

is doubtless some connexion with the Earl of Toulouse type, we hesitate to class the story as a direct descendant of that type.

Pérez de Hita in the first part of his historical novel *Las Guerras Civiles de Granada* (1595)[1] included a story obviously modelled on our type. As part of a general conspiracy the family of the Zegris accused the queen of Granada, whose name is not given, of adultery with Albinhamad, the chief of the Abencerrages. The latter was beheaded without trial, and the queen was sentenced to death at the stake unless she could find four champions to meet her four accusers. On the advice of a Christian captive she wrote to Don Juan Chacón, a knight of King Ferdinand of Castile, appealing for help, and he undertook her defence. On the day appointed for the battle the queen looked in vain for her champion, and she had almost given up hope when four men dressed in Turkish habits appeared and offered themselves as her defenders. They were her champion and three other Christian knights, though none but the queen suspected this. They were victorious, and after being magnificently entertained departed again without revealing their identity except to the queen. Their Turkish garments were later found in a wood, and it was surmised that they had been waylaid and killed. Many of the elements of this tale clearly belong to the Earl of Toulouse type, but they have been altered to suit the needs of the novel in which they are set.

Outside the field of actual versions of our story, faint echoes may be heard in some early French romances, which therefore have a certain value as testimony to the spread of the story. Gaston Paris (p. 23 n.) points out that two versions of *Floire et Blanchefleur* may have been under the influence of the Earl of Toulouse tradition. One of these versions dates from the twelfth century; but as the supposed parallelism is not at all certain, we must be careful in drawing inferences from it. Uncertain, too, is an incident in the Vulgate *Mort Artu*,[2] where

---

[1] Ed. Blanchard-Demouge. See especially chs. 13–15.

[2] See, e.g., J. D. Bruce's edition, pp. 63 ff. The incident is also incorporated in the English metrical romance *Morte Arthure* as well as in Malory's *Morte d'Arthur*.

Guinevere is falsely accused of having poisoned a knight and is granted forty days' respite to find a champion. On the last day Lancelot turns up in disguise, challenges her accuser, and conquers him, whereupon a recognition scene follows. In spite of the obvious similarity to the Earl of Toulouse story, we cannot on that evidence alone infer a direct borrowing. *Mort Artu* dates from the first half of the thirteenth century. From the same period dates *Le Roman de la Violette*, in which another possible loan occurs; a girl is accused of murder by a repulsed lover and is going to be burnt, but is rescued at the last moment by her true lover, who kills her accuser in single combat (see p. 150, n. 4).

More certain, in my opinion, is a story which is found in Chrétien de Troyes's *Yvain*:[1] the damsel Lunete is condemned to death on a false accusation, but at the last moment, when the fire is already blazing, Yvain turns up and challenges her accusers, three in number. He conquers them with the help of his faithful lion, and they have to take Lunete's place at the stake. Very much the same story occurs in the Welsh tale of *Owein and Lunet*.[2] We are here on debatable ground, but it is fairly certain that the latter story is derived from a French source,[3] though it does not seem to go back to Chrétien's *Yvain*. It is considered, at least by some, to be based on an earlier French romance now lost, possibly the same from which Chrétien drew his story. In our particular incident the main difference is that the Welsh story knows only two accusers. This, too, suggests an earlier form of the story than Chrétien's. As *Yvain* dates from the latter half of the twelfth century, the earlier romance cannot be much later than the middle of that century. While avoiding the general issue of the provenance of the *matière de Bretagne*, I venture to hold that this particular incident shares one of its ancestors with *The Earl of Toulouse*.[4]

[1] Foerster's edition, ll. 4313 ff.
[2] *The Mabinogion*, vol. ii, pp. 64–65.
[3] See, e.g., Zenker, *Forschungen zur Artusepik*, esp. pp. 287–9; Chambers, *Arthur of Britain*, ch. v; and Loomis, *Arthurian Tradition and Chrétien de Troyes*, pp. 32–38 and 317–19.
[4] At a later date we have an echo of our story in *Doon de Mayence*: Doon

When compared with the types previously mentioned, the Earl of Toulouse type seems very close to the Gunhild story in structure. The two have one important point in common: the single combat. The main difference is that the chivalric element is stronger in *The Earl of Toulouse* than in the ballad, with the exception of the Scottish version (see pp. 55 and 116).[1] The type about to be mentioned in the following section has also a single combat, but has at the same time stronger ties with folk-tales.

§ 44. *The Swan Knight Type*

This type presents a host of problems, which we cannot enter into here.[2] The central episode in the story is the arrival of an unknown knight in a boat drawn by a swan, just at the moment when a woman is being unjustly persecuted. The knight conquers her persecutor in single combat and marries her (in some versions her daughter), but he makes her promise never to question him about his name and origin. She later breaks this promise, whereupon he departs in the same mysterious way that he came.

One of the earliest references to this story that we have[3] dates from the end of the twelfth century and occurs in a Latin prose romance, or collection of romances, *Dolopathos*, by the monk Johannes de Alta Silva, i.e. of the Abbey of Haute-Seille in the diocese of Toul. This book belongs to the cycle of the Seven Wise Masters, in which each of the seven sages tells a story. Though Johannes has preserved the frame of the work as he

rescues his falsely accused mother from the stake by a fight with two opponents. While the latter detail is probably taken from the Earl of Toulouse type, the fact that the rescuer is the lady's own son is clearly reminiscent of the Swan Children story (see pp. 144–5). A similar combination of motifs is seen in *Valentine and Orson* (see p. 150, n. 4).

[1] The relation of the ballad to the Earl of Toulouse type will be further discussed in a later section (pp. 156–8).

[2] For literature on the subject see Hibbard, *Mediæval Romance in England*, pp. 251–2. Cf. also Chauvin, *Bibliographie des ouvrages arabes*, vol. viii, pp. 206–8.

[3] The earliest mention seems to be that found in a letter written by Guy of Bazoches soon after 1170. See G. Paris, *Romania*, vol. xxx (1901), p. 406, n. 3; and J. F. D. Blöte, *ZfdA*, vol. xlvii (1904), pp. 185 ff.

found it, he has substituted stories of his own for some of the original ones.[1] Among these new tales is the one that concerns us here.

The Swan Knight story is not told in full by Johannes, but is only alluded to very briefly. The allusion comes at the end of another of his stories, that of the Swan Children. A certain nobleman one day while hunting in the forest met a fair and mysterious lady, obviously a fairy. She was holding a golden necklace in her hand, but when he removed it, all her power had gone, and he carried her home and married her. His mother, however, hated her daughter-in-law, and when the young wife bore seven children at a birth, six boys and a girl, each with a golden chain round its neck, the husband's mother substituted seven puppies and ordered a servant to expose the children. The husband, believing his mother's accusation that his wife had given birth to puppies, had her buried up to her breasts in the middle of the palace, where she was left to share the food of the dogs. Meanwhile the children had been found by a hermit, who brought them up in the forest. Their grandmother heard of their existence and sent a man out to fetch their golden chains, emblems of their origin from a supernatural mother. He took six of the chains, but the girl escaped. Thenceforth the boys had to remain swans till the chains could be restored. The girl, however, vindicated her mother's innocence and restored her brothers to their human form. One child alone, whose chain had been damaged, had to remain a swan. And then comes the reference to the Swan Knight story (Hilka's edition, p. 86): 'Hic est cignus de quo fama in eternum perseuerat quod cathena aurea militem in nauicula traxit armatum.'

That this reference is to the Swan Knight story is confirmed by later French tradition, where the story of the Swan Children and that of the Swan Knight are nearly always linked together.[2]

[1] Cf. G. Paris, *Romania*, vol. ii (1873), pp. 481 ff.

[2] An exception is formed by the Berne MS. No. 627, which contains only the Swan Knight story. Cf. A. G. Krüger, *Romania*, vol. xxiii (1894), pp. 445 ff.; and H. A. Smith, ib., vol. xxxviii (1909), pp. 120 ff.

There are, or have been, at least three other French recensions of the combined Swan Children and Swan Knight stories, besides foreign translations and adaptations.[1] Presumably the reason why Johannes mentions the Swan Knight story so briefly is that he only wants an example of a wicked woman (the mother-in-law) and consequently has no use for the continuation of the story. The fusion of the two originally distinct stories must have taken place shortly before the composition of *Dolopathos*, probably in the latter half of the twelfth century. We can observe how in the later French versions the fusion becomes more complete.

The Swan Children story is obviously closely related to Grimm's folk-tale No. 49, *The Six Swans*.[2] Here a girl, to restore her six brothers to human form, has to remain silent for six years. A king finds her, falls in love with her, and marries her. His mother accuses her of having given birth to puppies, and she, not being able to protest her innocence, is to be burnt, but is rescued at the last moment by her brothers released from their spell at the expiry of the six years. As pointed out by Huet,[3] several details in Johannes' story also recall the tale of *The Envious Sisters*,[4] for example the way in which the young mother is punished. It may also be due to the influence of that story, or it may have been part of the original Swan Children story, that the persecuted lady is the mother, not the sister, of the Swan Children. It is undoubtedly an original trait that, just as

[1] G. Paris, *Romania*, vol. xix (1890), pp. 314 ff., names the recensions after their respective heroines, *Elioxe*, *Isomberte*, and *Beatrix*. The Beatrix recension is by far the best known. It is represented, e.g., by the versions published by Hippeau and Baron de Reiffenberg, and by several translations and adaptations. Among the latter may be mentioned the English prose version printed by Copland early in the sixteenth century and reprinted by Thoms in *Early English Prose Romances*, vol. iii. A late-fourteenth-century English romance in alliterative verse entitled *Cheuelere Assigne* contains (in spite of the name!) only the first part of the story, the Swan Children story.

[2] Cf. also Nos. 9 and 25 and Hans Andersen's story *The White Swans*. See Bolte and Polívka's *Anmerkungen*, vol. i, pp. 427 ff., esp. pp. 432–3.

[3] 'Sur quelques formes de la légende du Chevalier au Cygne', pp. 206–14.

[4] This tale is extremely common both in Europe and in Asia. It is told by Grimm as *The Three Little Birds* (No. 96). Cf. Bolte and Polívka's *Anmerkungen*, vol. ii, pp. 380 ff.

in *The Six Swans*, it is the sister of the Swan Children who brings about their deliverance. In some of the later French versions it is one of the boys, named Hélias, who escapes being turned into a swan, and he then vindicates his mother's innocence by a single combat. This feature is undoubtedly unoriginal, as shown, for example, by the fact that the same versions still talk of six boys and a girl. The combat is very likely due to the analogy of the Swan Knight story itself. In fact, it is the victorious defender of the mother who later becomes the celebrated 'Knight of the Swan', drawn in tow by his brother, who had to remain a swan.[1]

In German tradition we find the story of the Swan Knight without the usual introductory tale. The hero is here commonly called Lohengrin. This name, derived from Lothringen (= Lorraine), may have been introduced by Wolfram of Eschenbach, who tells the Swan Knight story as a sequel to his *Parzival*, Lohengrin being Parzival's son.[2] Among other German versions is that by Conrad of Würzburg;[3] here, as in certain French and Dutch forms of the tale, the action is set at Nijmegen in the time of Charlemagne, who himself appears in the story.

The origin of the Swan Knight legend has been much debated.[4] It has been thought by some to have a mythical meaning,[5] and it has most recently been explained as essentially the story of a demon lover.[6] Gaston Paris held it to be totemistic in

---

[1] One further difference between the older and the younger versions is that in the latter the accusation has become a charge of adultery. Cf. p. 113 and Schlauch, *Chaucer's Constance*, pp. 78 ff. The bearing of several children at one birth, according to a widespread superstition, was a sign of adultery. Traces of that belief are met with elsewhere in medieval literature, for example in *Octavian*. See Hibbard, op. cit., pp. 242 and 295–6; and Krappe, 'Florent et Octavien', p. 362.

[2] For a summary of the story see Grimm's *Deutsche Sagen*, No. 536.

[3] Summarized ib., No. 538.　　　[4] See Hibbard, op. cit., pp. 248 ff.

[5] See von der Hagen, 'Die Schwanensage'; Möller, 'Die Sage vom Schwanritter'; Blöte, 'Der zweite Teil der Schwanrittersage'; Poisson, 'L'Origine celtique de la légende de Lohengrin'; Zenker, *Forschungen zur Artusepik*, pp. 174–5; R. S. Loomis, *Celtic Myth and Arthurian Legend*, ch. 31; and Krüger, *Die Quellen der Schwanritterdichtungen*.

[6] See Krogmann, 'Die Grundform der Schwanenrittersage' and the same author's 'Die Schwanenrittersage'.

its origin.[1] Blöte, after first advancing a mythological theory, abandoned this in favour of an hypothesis that the Swan Knight was an historical personage, and that popular imagination created the story out of certain events in his life.[2] Whether or not that is true, it is certainly true that some of the French versions are attached to Godfrey of Bouillon's family; they are obviously attempts to celebrate the greatness of the hero of the first crusade by making him a descendant of the Swan Knight.

The truth may be a compromise between the mythological theory and the view that the story is a simple ancestor legend. There is some ground for believing that the original version of the Swan Knight legend contained no judicial combat at all, but merely told of the arrival of a mysterious, probably supernatural knight, who married a native of the country, became the progenitor of a celebrated noble family, and disappeared as miraculously as he had come.[3] In that form the story is strikingly like the tale of Skjöld (Scyld) in Danish and Anglo-Saxon legend, and there is very likely a connexion, the two being ultimately one and the same story. 'In general, the legend of the progenitor arriving on a ship seems to be known among a number of people inhabiting the coasts of the North Sea, as well as among the Danes, and to have attached itself to various names according to the necessity of the case.'[4]

If this theory is correct, the Swan Knight story was originally quite distinct from the kind of tale we are here trying to trace, that of the persecuted lady. The story of the Swan Children, on the other hand, certainly represents a form of our theme; it is possibly an amalgamation of two different types of the folk-tale

[1] *Romania*, vol. xxiii (1894), p. 484, and vol. xxvi (1897), p. 581.

[2] See Blöte, 'Der historische Schwanritter'; 'Der clevische Schwanritter'; 'Die Sage vom Schwanritter in der Brogner Chronik'; and 'Das Aufkommen der Sage von Brabon Silvius'.

[3] Cf. G. Paris, *Romania*, vol. xxiii (1894), p. 484, and vol. xxx (1901), p. 408. This view has been contested by J. F. D. Blöte, *ZfrPh*, vol. xxvii (1903), pp. 12–14; and by Krogmann, 'Die Grundform', &c.

[4] Olrik, *The Heroic Legends of Denmark*, p. 399. Cf. also Klaeber's *Beowulf* (3rd ed.), p. 122, n. 1. G. Schütte, *Oldsagn om Godtjod* (Copenhagen, 1907), p. 138, goes much farther, adducing supposed Lombard, Frisian, and other parallels.

of the Persecuted Lady (cf. above, pp. 144–5). The introduction of the Persecuted Lady motif into the Swan Knight story, and of the judicial combat into both the Swan Knight and the Swan Children story, are later developments which we cannot here attempt to investigate further. It is conceivable that the idea of a duel was borrowed from some story like *The Earl of Toulouse*, to which the Swan Children and Swan Knight stories show a certain likeness, for instance in the feature of the rescuer arriving from afar at the last moment.

On one point we seem to have a direct borrowing from some other legend. In the Beatrix redaction of our story (cf. p. 144, n. 1), the traitor against whom the boy (the later Swan Knight) has to fight is called Macaire or some similar name. Thus in Copland's English version mentioned above his name is Makayre, and in *Cheuelere Assigne* it is Mauquarre. Baron de Reiffenberg is perhaps right when he suggests (p. xcvi of his edition) that the name goes back to the story of Sibilla; but we cannot be sure, since the *chansons de geste* borrowed names of characters from each other to an extent which is not always realized. Not only do we find a traitor named Macaire in *Sibilla*, *Florence of Rome*, and *The Swan Knight*, but also in several romances where the Persecuted Lady theme is entirely absent.[1]

Although the Swan Knight legend may owe but little to other stories of accused ladies, it appears to have influenced some of those other stories, chiefly *Hirlande*. Before we go into that question it will be expedient to mention two other medieval romances, *Octavian* and *Valentine and Orson*.

§ 45. 'Octavian'

In an earlier section (§ 17) the story of Octavian was summarized from the mid-fourteenth-century southern English version. There exists also a very similar northern English version, dating from about the same period. Both these versions

---

[1] See Langlois, *Table des noms propres dans les chansons de geste*. Cf. also Sauerland, *Ganelon und sein Geschlecht*, esp. pp. 36–38. A parallel to Macaire is the name Miles (Milon), which is a common name for a traitor both in our particular type of tale (*Florence of Rome*, *Olif*) and outside.

go back to a French source, which is related to, perhaps even identical with, a metrical romance preserved in a manuscript in the Bodleian Library. This manuscript was written about 1300 by an Anglo-Norman scribe, and the poem itself is probably not much older.[1] An unpublished poem of the fourteenth century, *Florent et Octavien*,[2] tells in the main the same story, though the latter part probably contains a good deal of imported matter. We have evidence, also, of a now lost thirteenth-century Dutch *Roman van Octaviaen* in verse.[3] Finally, from the fifteenth century onwards the story is found in prose versions in Italian, French, German, Dutch, Danish, and Swedish folkbooks.[4]

It is not possible here to enter into the question of the relationship and history of the various versions of the tale.[5] Vollmöller (p. xviii) and Krappe (p. 359) assume a twelfth-century *chanson de geste* as the ultimate source of the various redactions of the poem.[6] Vollmöller believes that the poem edited by him reproduces the original more faithfully than the fourteenth-century version, but that point has been challenged by G. Paris.[7] For our purpose, however, what chiefly matters is the relation of the

---

[1] Vollmöller, the editor, thinks (p. iv) that it dates from the former half of the thirteenth century. Cf., however, G. Paris, *Romania*, vol. xi (1882), p. 610.

[2] For a list of the MSS. of *Florent et Octavien* see Vollmöller, pp. xvi–xviii. A summary of the story is given by Paulin Paris in the *Histoire littéraire de la France*, vol. xxvi (1873), pp. 303 ff.

[3] Cf. Jan te Winkel in Paul's *Grundriss*, 2nd ed., vol. ii (Strassburg, 1901), p. 425.

[4] See Streve, *Die Octavian-Sage*; Schlauch, *Chaucer's Constance*, pp. 86 ff.; and Kessler, *Der Prosaroman vom Kaiser Oktavian*. There are two Italian versions: (1) *Il Libro delle Storie di Fioravante* and (2) bk. ii, chs. 42–52, of the *Reali di Francia*. See Rajna and Vandelli's edition of the *Reali*, vols. i and iii. The Danish folk-book (not mentioned by Schlauch) was first printed in 1597 and has been republished (from the 2nd ed., 1658) by Jacobsen, Olrik, and Paulli, *Danske Folkebøger*, vol. iv.

[5] See Krappe, 'Florent et Octavien'.

[6] I do not know the particular reasons for this assumption. J. Olrik in his introduction to the Danish folk-book, p. vi, repeats the assumption and adduces as evidence a passage from the Elioxe version of the Swan Children (ed. H. A. Todd, *PMLA*, 1889, l. 3099), where there is probably an allusion to our story. *Elioxe* dates from the end of the twelfth century; cf. G. Paris, *Romania*, vol. xix (1890), p. 320.

[7] *Romania*, vol. xi (1882), p. 611.

story to the motif in general and to other story types in particular. *Octavian* contains a mixture of old and new elements; for
example, the accuser is the mother-in-law, but the charge is
one of adultery, not of animal birth. The condemnation to
death by fire and the subsequent pardon and exile remind one
of the Sibilla type and are very likely borrowed from that story.
There can be no doubt that the episode of the Pretended Lover
is a loan from the story of Sibilla.[1] The two stories differ in that
Sibilla bears a child in her exile, while the queen in *Octavian*[2]
is accompanied into exile by her previously born twins Florent
and Octavien. The motif of the twins and their kidnapping by
wild beasts is paralleled in the Eustace legend, from which it
was probably borrowed.[3] In both *Octavian* and *Sibilla* the
children help to vindicate their mother's innocence. In *Florent
et Octavien* Octavien openly accuses his grandmother and fights a
duel with her champion, just as Hélias in the Swan Children
story defends his mother's honour. This episode, however, is
told quite incidentally and near the end of the poem; it appears
to be a late addition. The ending of *Florent et Octavien* forms a
transition to the story of *Florence de Rome*, which in one of the
manuscripts is appended as a continuation of the Octavian
story: Florent's son Othon is Florence's father.[4] This part of
the story is undoubtedly unoriginal.

§ 46. '*Valentine and Orson*'

This story[5] has twice spread from France over the rest
of Europe. In its early form, as it appeared in a now lost or

---

[1] Cf. Nyrop, *Storia dell' Epopea Francese*, p. 78.

[2] Her name differs in the various versions. The southern English version
calls her Floraunce; in *Florent et Octavien* her name is Florimonde; and
in the Italian versions she is called Drugiolina and Drusolina. In the French
Octavian and in the northern English version she has no name at all.

[3] Cf. G. H. Gerould, *PMLA*, vol. xix (1904), pp. 437–8; and L. Jordan,
Archiv, vol. cxxi (1908), pp. 345–6.

[4] This ending is not peculiar to the MS. mentioned, Bibliothèque
Nationale, F.Fr. 24384. Similar allusions to *Florence de Rome* are found in
two MSS. which do not contain the latter poem. See Wallensköld's edition
of *Florence de Rome*, vol. i, pp. 3–6.

[5] The latest treatments of the subject are Dickson, *Valentine and Orson*,

unknown French poem, it was taken over by Dutch, German, and Swedish literature.[1] In its later form as a prose folk-book it passed through more than a hundred editions in France, England, the Netherlands, Germany, and Italy.[2] The story has also been dramatized in England, France, Spain and Germany.[3] Externally, the two phases in the evolution of the story are distinguished (*a*) by different names (the former is called *Valentine and Nameless* and the latter *Valentine and Orson*), and (*b*) by the former being usually in verse and the latter in prose. In content, too, there are considerable divergencies.

The later redaction has been summarized in a previous chapter (§ 19) from the English sixteenth-century version. The earlier redaction is distinguished by several primitive features. The mother-in-law appears as accuser, though assisted by a bishop. The accusation is of child-murder, and an attempt is made to substantiate the charge by exposing the queen's newly born twins. The queen is banished from the country. In her exile she is persecuted a second time by a repulsed lover, who accuses her of murder in much the same way that Constance and Crescentia are accused.[4]

A Study in Late Medieval Romance; and Dieperink, *Studien zum Valentin und Namelos*. See also Krappe, '*Valentine and Orson*'.

[1] See Schlauch, *Chaucer's Constance*, pp. 89–93. The latest edition of the Swedish version is Wolf, *Namnlös och Valentin*.

[2] See the bibliography in Seelmann, *Valentin und Namelos*, pp. xxx ff.

[3] See Klemming, *Namnlös och Valentin*, pp. xiii, xv, xvii; Seelmann, op. cit., p. ix; and Dickson's edition (not his study mentioned above), p. li. A Breton play on the subject is mentioned by Luzel, *Sainte Tryphine et le Roi Arthur*, p. xxiv.

[4] See pp. 117 and 119. For a detailed discussion of this episode and its sources see Dickson, *Valentine and Orson, A Study in Late Medieval Romance*, pp. 70–80, 128–30, 153. The idea of an accusation of child-murder is undoubtedly of folk-tale origin; cf. Dickson, op. cit., p. 73, where further references will be found. In the literature of romance it seems to have been first introduced in tales of the Constance or Crescentia type. In later romances this motif is combined with a rescue from the stake at the last moment, probably taken from the Earl of Toulouse type. This combination is first met with in Gerbert de Montreuil's *Roman de la Violette*, ll. 3950 ff.: Meliatir makes love to Euriant. She refuses him, and when he tries to force her, she defends herself and knocks out some of his teeth. In revenge, he murders Ysmain, the daughter of the duke with whom Euriant is staying, and puts the bloody knife in Euriant's hand. She is to be burnt, but at the last moment

This second accusation, which has undoubtedly been taken from one of the two types mentioned, is typical of the story as a whole. The romance is a late composite of elements borrowed from elsewhere. The oldest manuscript of the early redaction, a fragment of a Dutch version, dates from the fourteenth century; the rest of the manuscripts are fifteenth century or later. Presumably the poem is not much older than the oldest extant version. The feature of the twins has probably been taken from *Octavian* and thus ultimately from the Eustace legend. In the later redaction of the story they are born in exile, which recalls the Sibilla type. Altogether, the later redaction seems to have been influenced more by the story of Sibilla. For example, the archbishop's pursuit of the exiled queen and her knight has undoubtedly been modelled on Macaire's pursuit of Sibilla. With these few remarks we must leave this question, which has been dealt with much more thoroughly by Dr. Dickson.

§ 47. *'Hirlande'*

This story is commonly referred to as the Hirlande or Hirlanda legend after the name of the heroine of the oldest, though perhaps not the most original, of the versions. It is found in a book by the Jesuit father René de Cerisiers entitled *Les Trois États de l'Innocence* (Paris, 1640),[1] which recounts the lives of Joan of Arc, Geneviève of Brabant, and Hirlande.

The king of England was suffering from leprosy and, according to a Jewish doctor, could only be cured by washing in the blood and eating the heart of an unbaptized infant of noble birth. Gérard, brother of Duke Artus of Brittany, was anxious to further his fortunes and decided to attempt a cure. His sister-in-law, Hirlande, was expecting a child, and while her

---

Gerart, her lover, arrives and vanquishes Meliatir in single combat.—Both Dickson and Buffum (pp. xlvi f.) seem to have overlooked the parallelism with the Earl of Toulouse type. In the case of *Valentine and Nameless* there is undoubtedly a secondary influence from the Swan Knight type: the rescue is not by the accused woman's lover (husband, &c,), but by her son.

[1] I have not seen this book, but have used Sir William Lower's English translation (London, 1656). Hirlande's story is summarized, from the French edition of 1706, by Koehler in 'Sainte Tryphine et Hirlande'.

husband was away at the wars, Gérard bribed the nurse to steal
the infant and to make the mother believe that she had given
birth to a still-born child. The nurse was dispatched to England
with the child, but was intercepted by an Abbot Bernard of St.
Malo, who had been commanded by an angel to save the child.
Gérard, meanwhile, accused Hirlande of child-murder, and
fearing her husband's vengeance she fled away and took service
as a maid at a neighbouring castle. After several years she
was discovered by chance and was reunited with her husband.
They lived happily together until she gave birth to another
child. Gérard, wishing to secure for himself the succession to
the dukedom, decided to throw suspicion on the legitimacy of
the child. He accused Hirlande of adultery. The accusation was
believed and she was condemned to be burnt, but at the last
moment a boy appeared as her champion, challenged her accuser
and overcame him. Gérard confessed his crime and was put to
death. The boy turned out to be Hirlande's own son, whose
foster-father, the abbot, had been commanded by an angel to
arm the boy and send him to the defence of his mother.

Cerisiers's book came to enjoy great popularity and was
translated into English, Dutch, German, and Italian. Folkbooks based on these translations were circulated in Germany,
Holland, and Flanders.[1]

Two other versions of the legend are known, both of Breton
origin. One is a mystery play in verse, *Sainte Tryphine et le
Roi Arthur*, published in the nineteenth century on the basis
of three manuscripts which the editor, F. M. Luzel, had succeeded in tracking down. The manuscripts themselves, says
Luzel, are relatively modern, but the play is traditional, and the
text must have been copied and recopied by generation after
generation, often no doubt with many alterations. We know
nothing of the author, nor the exact date of the play; but it is
probably of the fifteenth century, and Luzel (p. xxxv) suggests
that the author may have been a priest or cleric 'with a light

---

[1] See Koehler, op. cit., and 'Die deutschen Volksbücher von der Pfalzgräfin Genovefa und von der Herzogin Hirlanda'.

ballast of history, mythology and legend'. Mystery plays continued to be performed in Brittany well into the nineteenth century, and as *Sainte Tryphine* was one of the most popular of the plays, its plot and action must have been familiar to a large number of people. This is perhaps the way in which to account for the third version of our story, a folk-tale, *Sainte Tryphine et Saint Mélar*, taken down by A. Le Braz in the latter half of the nineteenth century. It resembles the play closely, while at the same time both versions differ in certain details from Cerisiers's story.

In the first place, the name of the heroine is Tryphine, while the accuser is called Kervoura (in the folk-tale Kervouron). Secondly, the accuser is the heroine's brother, not brother-in-law. Thirdly, Tryphine's husband is king, not duke, of Brittany. Fourthly, he is not at the wars, but on a visit to the English court, at the time of his wife's confinement. Fifthly, practical proof of the accusation of adultery is attempted by means of two soldiers, who have been bribed by Kervoura to importune the queen with love-proposals, while the king hidden watches the scene. The mystery play adds a further detail: Kervoura persuades an accomplice to disguise himself as a priest and to tell the king that Tryphine has confessed to him that the child was conceived in adultery. A minor point in which all three versions differ is the boy's foster-parentage. In the play the boy is brought up by the bishop of St. Malo, and in the folk-tale by the Pope (who at that time was living in London!). A comparatively small detail of some interest is that, in the play, Kervoura greets his tiny opponent with the words (in Luzel's French translation), 'Cent de ton espèce, je n'en ferais nul cas dans un combat!' These words, as has been pointed out by Hempel (see below), bear a striking likeness to Aldingar's remark in Child's version A.

Cerisiers says that he took the story from a manuscript in the town of Autun, but Steinberger, who investigated the legend, was unable to discover any such document.[1] What Cerisiers saw

---

[1] *Untersuchungen zur Entstehung der Sage von Hirlanda von Bretagne*, p. 10.

may have been one of those manuscripts that Luzel mentions as being kept by Breton families as heirlooms at the bottom of their oak chests, whence they are brought out to be recited on special occasions. These are not, however, very old documents, since they are copied afresh from time to time. Cerisiers may have been shown such a manuscript; but it is extremely likely that at the same time he drew on oral tradition. He was born at Nantes and may have heard the story or seen the play performed there. Several of the differences between his and the other versions can be explained as having arisen in the course of oral transmission. One such point is worth noting: the name *Hirlande*, as pointed out by Koehler, is no other than the geographical name Ireland (Irlande) misheard as the name of the heroine; the mystery play says that she was an Irish princess. The name *Tryphine*, incidentally, is equally unoriginal; it is taken from the Breton legend of Sainte Tréfine (Trifine), who is said to have been cruelly done to death by her husband, though without any accusation.[1]

Most of the details of the Hirlande legend are familiar to us from other stories; the legend as a whole appears to have been composed of elements taken from elsewhere. Its indebtedness to other stories of persecuted ladies has been discussed by Steinberger and Hempel.[2] Steinberger thinks that the Gunhild story spread from England to Brittany and formed the basis of the Hirlande legend, which received its present shape through later influence from the Swan Children story. Hempel lays greater stress on supposed influence from the Earl of Toulouse type, which he thinks is responsible for all those features which cannot be traced back to the Swan Children story. He points out the following correspondences with the Earl of Toulouse type: (1) practical proof of the accusation is attempted (in mystery and folk-tale); (2) Hirlande is to be burnt (in mystery and folk-

---

[1] A mystery play about this saint, *Cognomerus et Sainte Tryphine*, has been published by A. Le Braz. It has little more than the name of the heroine in common with our story. See also C. Grant Loomis, 'King Arthur and the Saints', p. 480, n. 4; and Margaret Schlauch, 'Saints Tryphine and Hirlanda'.

[2] *Nibelungenstudien*, pp. 251-2.

tale: beheaded) if nobody will defend her; (3) a youthful champion comes from afar at the last moment. The last two points, Hempel admits, are also to be found in the Swan Children story, whence the feature of the heroine's son acting as her defender has definitely been taken. The idea of the supposititious lover is not, as Hempel seems to think, confined to the Earl of Toulouse type, in which it is certainly unoriginal (see p. 126, n. 6); nor is feature No. 2 confined merely to the types that Hempel mentions (see p. 134). Other correspondences with the Earl of Toulouse type are, according to Hempel: (4) there are two accusers, and their motive is envy and ambition (this is a mistake; I fail to see how Hempel could come to make such a statement: there is only one accuser, Gérard (Kervoura), but he makes use of accomplices); (5) the duke has a dream foreboding evil. Finally, Hempel mentions two not very convincing parallels, one of them with the German translation of *Hirlande*, in which, Hempel thinks, certain details were borrowed direct from the Earl of Toulouse type. Since they do not occur in the French original, they are of no interest to us in this connexion.

Hempel attaches great importance to two parallels which, in his opinion, prove the existence of a direct connexion between the Hirlande story and the modern British Gunhild ballad: (1) the preparations for the execution are described in a somewhat similar way in *Sir Hugh le Blond* and in *Hirlande* (Cerisiers's version): on the scaffold a chair covered with black velvet is placed for the queen (duchess); (2) in the mystery play, as in *Sir Aldingar*, the opponents before beginning their fight exchange some contemptuous remarks, and there is a verbal coincidence at this point in the stories.[1] On the basis of these details Hempel (p. 252) goes so far as to suggest that the British ballad and the Hirlande group together form a sub-group under the Earl of Toulouse type.

Let us deal with the latter theory first. It is a flimsy structure built on most insecure foundations. The mention of a black

---

[1] Or almost: *Sir Aldingar* has 'halfe a hundred', *Tryphine* 'cent'.

velvet chair can no more prove kinship than can, shall we say, reference to armour in connexion with a tournament. There were certain conventions regarding executions of people of noble birth, which were doubtless widely known. For instance, in Pérez de Hita's *Guerras Civiles de Granada* (cf. p. 140) the preparations for the queen's execution are very similar: the scaffold and the chair are covered with black cloth. As regards the second point, it is important to realize that 'flytings before battle' belong to the commonplaces of medieval literature (see p. 51, n. 3). To class the Gunhild ballad as a descendant of the Earl of Toulouse type is entirely unjustified. The ballad, in its later development, may have been influenced by that type, but its origin lies elsewhere. The Hirlande story, too, may have been influenced by the Earl of Toulouse type, although the arguments that Hempel brings forward are far from convincing; the influence must at any rate have come from a variant no longer extant. It is even arguable that both the ballad and the Hirlande story came under the influence of the same model, or of versions nearly alike, thus receiving an occasional superficial likeness, but that is as far as we can safely go.

Even in this last admission we have perhaps gone farther than the facts allow. Certain features of the Hirlande legend may, or may not, have been borrowed from the Earl of Toulouse story. Certain later accretions to the ballad story (see p. 110) must have been taken from elsewhere and may have come from the Earl of Toulouse story, but hardly from the same version that influenced, if it did influence, the Hirlande story. To mention only two points: (1) both the ballad and the Hirlande story have a practical proof of the accusation, but there is not the slightest similarity in the details of this feature; (2) both the ballad and the Hirlande story contain an ominous dream, but in Hirlande, as in the romance of *The Earl of Toulouse*, it is the emperor who dreams, while in the ballad it is the queen.

While the relationship of the Hirlande story to the Earl of Toulouse type remain somewhat doubtful, there is good ground for supposing that the later accretions to the ballad came from some version of the Earl of Toulouse story. In an earlier chapter four points were mentioned which must be considered later additions to the original story. These were: (1) the supposititious lover; (2) the queen's dream; (3) the queen is to be burnt if she cannot prove her innocence; and (4) messengers are sent out to find a champion, who comes riding from afar at the last moment. Now these four points belong to the characteristics of the later versions of the Earl of Toulouse story. It is true that some, at least, of the points can be paralleled separately elsewhere, but the fact that all four occur together in the Earl of Toulouse type suggests borrowing from that source as the simplest solution. No one version now known combines them all in exactly the form in which they occur in the ballad, but it is extremely probable that there once existed a version that did combine them. With regard to the form of point 1 most of the versions differ: the lover is a noble youth (*The Earl of Toulouse*, Bandello) or a scullion (*Galmy*) or a dwarf (*Miracle de la Marquise*) but never a leper as in the ballad. A close parallel to point 2 is found in *Galmy*,[1] where it is the queen who dreams, while in *The Earl of Toulouse* itself it is the emperor who has a strange dream; moreover, his dream contains no prophecy of a happy ending.

It is obvious that these details in the ballad story cannot have come from the English romance of *The Earl of Toulouse* in the form in which we know it. Neither, of course, can they have been taken from the Hirlande story, which in none of the points in question offers a particularly close parallel. It seems safe, therefore, to conjecture the existence of a now lost or unknown version of the Earl of Toulouse story containing the details in a form similar to the English ballad. On the question of what was the form of that version, whether verse or prose, written or oral, it is impossible to say anything with certainty. It is worth recalling, however, the way in which Jacob Wimpfeling heard his version of the story in Germany in the fifteenth century

[1] Bolte's edition, p. 73; cf. his Introduction, p. xi, n. 2.

(see p. 135). The story may have travelled to England in some similar way, as an oral prose tale.

One of the four points in which we assumed that the British ballad had been influenced from without is found only in the English version; the Scottish version knows nothing of the queen's dream. This may be due to a later loss; on the other hand, the fact that the two versions differ in other respects, also, may not be without significance. While in *Sir Aldingar*, as in the ancient English versions, the champion is a dwarf, in the Scottish version he appears as a normal human being. The romantic, chivalric element has become predominant. Is this due to influence from the Earl of Toulouse type, or is it an independent development? *Sir Aldingar* obviously presents a more original form of the story, and yet it, too, has been influenced by the Earl of Toulouse story. Has the Scottish version undergone a second revision? It may be significant in this respect that the two British versions show no verbal similarity at all (see pp. 109–10; cf. also p. 11 n, and p. 93, n. 2).

§ 48. *'Joufrois'*

This story occurs in a single version, contained in a French *roman d'aventure* about the eventful life of one Joufroi. It is only the opening of the poem that concerns us here (ll. 91–631). Joufroi, we are told, was the son of a Count Richier of Poitiers and his wife Alienor. One day the boy asked his father to send him to England to learn the noble art of chivalry at the English court. Joufroi was well received by King Henry. The seneschal of the court tried in vain to win Queen Alice's love. In revenge for his rebuff he accused her of adultery with a kitchen-boy. The king wanted to have her hanged or burnt, but Joufroi offered to defend her honour in single combat if the king would make him a knight. Everyone thought him mad to undertake the fight since he was so young (ll. 302–3: 'li biaus vaslet de Poitiers Estoit enfens'), but contrary to all expectations Joufroi was victorious and cut off the seneschal's head.

The poem, of which only a fragment survives (4,611 lines),

appears to have been written in the first half of the thirteenth century somewhere in the east or south-east of France.[1] Nothing is known of its author apart from what little the poem tells us. He appears to have belonged to the nobility and to have been a man of the world rather than a professional poet. He says that he based his poem on a Latin prose book which he found at Saint-Pierre-de-Maguelonne (near Montpellier), but it is doubtful how much truth there is in this statement. The many historical names that we find in the poem have no doubt been thrown in merely to give the account a more plausible appearance. The king may have been Henry I (1100–35), whose second wife was Alice of Louvain. On the other hand, the fact that the troubadour Marcabrun appears in the poem would seem to point to Henry II's reign (1154–89). Count Richier and Countess Alienor are probably fictitious characters.

The author seems to have drawn his material from the conventional stock of stories current in the Middle Ages.[2] The poem consists of a long string of episodes, mostly of an amorous kind, all showing Joufroi in the part of champion and lover of fair ladies, and the author has adapted his material to serve this purpose. Thus our episode, from being a story of a persecuted lady, has become a story of a gallant knight. The central character is Joufroi; we hear nothing about the queen's distress, but a great deal about Joufroi's gallantry. Typically enough, later in the poem, when Joufroi revisits England, the queen grants him that which she denied the treacherous seneschal.

Notwithstanding the difference in tone and tenor, and despite deviations in some of the details such as the setting of the story, the resemblance of the Joufroi episode to the Gundeberg-Gunhild tradition is remarkably close. It cannot be a mere coincidence; but where did the author get the story from? It seems that there are three possibilities. Firstly, he may have heard the English ballad. This would presuppose that he had been to

---

[1] Opinions differ regarding the dialect of the poem. See, e.g., G. Paris, *Romania*, vol. x (1881), pp. 411 ff.; and P. B. Fay, ib., vol. lviii (1932), pp. 114 ff.

[2] See Jordan, 'Zum altfranzösischen Joufrois'.

England, and since we know nothing about his life, the theory must remain a pure hypothesis. Several of the adventures in the poem are set in England, but the description does not show any particularly intimate knowledge of the country. Secondly, he may have heard a continental ballad or folk-tale, which may have been either the Flemish predecessor of the English ballad or some continuation of the old French poem on Queen Gunde-berg (see p. 133), with the setting changed from Lombardy to England. Thirdly, he may have derived the story from a manu-script source, perhaps some chronicle based partly on Paul the Deacon and his predecessors and partly on some account of the Gunhild story.

None of these solutions is entirely satisfactory, and none can be proved to be correct. The origin of the Joufroi story remains a mystery. Its importance to us lies in the testimony that it bears to the currency of our motif in the early thirteenth century.

§ 49. *Summary and Conclusion*

We have seen in a previous chapter (ch. vii) that the English Gunhild tradition can be traced back to the seventh century, to a story about Queen Gundeberg of Lombardy. This story, like that of the Gunhild ballad, ends with a judicial combat. Another infidelity story, possibly of independent origin, was current in Germany about the year 900. It was about the Empress Richardis, wife of Charles the Fat. It differed from the story of Gundeberg by having an ordeal instead of a judicial combat for its solution. Very much the same story was later told of the Empress Cunegund (d. 1033). The Richardis-Cunegund legend must be considered one of the ancestors of the English Gunhild story, which represents an amalgamation of the Lombard and German legends. The Scandinavian Gunhild tradition, on the other hand, seems to have originated in the German tradition alone and to have ended with an ordeal, until it was later, in the thirteenth century, influenced by the English form.

The motif of the Falsely Accused Wife is not confined to this fairly simple family of stories. It is a widely popular theme in both oriental and occidental tales. It is not possible, at least in the present state of our knowledge, to trace them all back to a common ancestor, although we can sometimes in particular cases prove derivation and borrowing. The earliest treatment of the theme that I know is the Bible story of *Susanna*, which goes back to about 100 B.C. After that date there appears to be a wide gap: I have come across no examples of the motif in classical literature. The theme does not emerge again till the seventh century of our era, when we meet it in Lombardy, in the story of Queen Gundeberg. There may be a connexion between the two earliest occurrences of the motif, perhaps through the undercurrent of folk-tale, but we have no means of ascertaining that. Nor is it possible for us to prove that the Gundeberg story is related to the Richardis-Cunegund legend, or to the many other medieval stories of accused queens, with the exception of the English Gunhild story.

Most of those medieval infidelity stories which do not form part of the Gundeberg-Gunhild pedigree can be grouped together under certain main types: the Crescentia type, the Sibilla type, the Earl of Toulouse type, &c. Both the Crescentia and the Sibilla type, and particularly the former, differ quite considerably from the Gunhild story. They contain neither a judicial combat nor an ordeal, but only a long-drawn-out denouement with a final recognition scene. Considerably closer to our ballad in structure is the Earl of Toulouse type. We find here, as in the Gundeberg-Gunhild tradition, a single combat. The Earl of Toulouse story may in a sense be an offshoot of the Gundeberg story (see p. 133), though we cannot be sure of that. It seems certain, however, that the English Gunhild ballad was later influenced by some version of the Earl of Toulouse story, from which it borrowed several minor details (see pp. 156–8).

The Scandinavian ballad in its modern form can be explained as being on the whole a continuation of the German Gunhild tradition mixed with the English form of the story. One feature, however, does not seem to have come from either of those sources, nor from an earlier Scandinavian substratum (cf. pp. 110–11): at the beginning of the ballad the king goes away to the wars, leaving Raadengaard in charge. Now this detail occurs in numerous medieval persecution stories, such as *Crescentia*, *Geneviève*, and *Sisibe*, and is also frequent in folk-tales on the same theme. The possibility of borrowing is therefore almost unlimited, but the most likely source appears to be the romance *Den kyske Dronning* (§ 23), either in its present or, perhaps, in some earlier redaction.

While it is certainly not possible, as Grundtvig would have it (*DgF* i, p. 203), to claim Teutonic origin for the motif as such, the particular type of story which ends with a *judicium Dei*, whether a single combat or an ordeal of ploughshares, may be Teutonic in its origin. The stories of that type are confined chiefly to our ballad and its immediate ancestors. Outside that tradition we find the feature in the Earl of Toulouse type, where it may be due to influence from the Gundeberg story (cf. p. 133), and in the Swan Children and Swan Knight stories, which may owe it to the Earl of Toulouse type (p. 147). The other medieval stories containing the feature, such as *Hirlande* and *Joufrois*, have certainly taken it from one or other of the stories already mentioned.

The number of historical and legendary figures to whom infidelity stories have been ascribed is truly amazing: *Gundeberg*, *Richardis*, *Cunegund*, *Gunhild*, *Judith*, *Elvira*, *Emma*, *Eleanor*, *Alice*, *Matilda*, *Galia*, *Sibilla*, *Hildegard*, *Geneviève*, *Attila*, *Theodoric of Bern*, *Henry the Lion*, &c. The reason for the transfer was probably in most cases a desire to give the story added interest by telling it about a person better known to the hearers or readers. In one or two cases the change of name may not have been deliberate, but may have been due to a mistake. The similarity of names like *Gund*eberg and *Gun*hild, and perhaps also Cune*gund* (cf. p. 95) and *Gud*ilinda (p. 91, n. 1), may be significant. In the case of such a well-known hero of history and legend as Charlemagne we find our motif used not once but repeatedly: *Galia*, *Sibilla*, and *Hildegard* are all said to have been married to Charlemagne. To the Charlemagne cycle belongs also the story of *Olif*, who is said to be a sister of Charlemagne (Scandinavian versions) or of Pippin (French and Spanish versions). In the late romance of *Valentine and Nameless* (second redaction: *Valentine and Orson*), the heroine, Phila (= *Belyssant* in *Valentine and Orson*), is said to be King Pippin's sister.[1]

Grundtvig's efforts (*DgF* i, pp. 193 ff.) to demonstrate an early association of our motif with the Theodoric legend have not been entirely successful. The evidence remains very slender. Theodoric is involved in an accusation story in *Guðrúnarkviða III* and is himself the husband of an accused wife in the Icelandic and Faroese versions of our ballad, but it is doubtful how far back these stories go. The rest of the evidence consists of the accusation story in the *Wolfdietrich Saga* mentioned above (p. 126)[2] and of the occurrence of the name Theodoric in *Crescentia*, where it belongs both to the accused wife's husband and to the latter's brother, Crescentia's persecutor. Grundtvig also attaches some importance to the occurrence of the name Thierry in *Florence of Rome* (the English version summarized in § 18 has Tyrry), and finally he mentions a French miracle play about a King Thierry and his wife Osanne.[3]

[1] In this connexion a story not strictly within our purview might also be mentioned, namely that of *Berthe au grand pied*, the heroine of which, Pippin's wife, is falsely accused, though not of adultery. See, e.g., Hempel, *Nibelungenstudien*, pp. 192 and 254 ff.

[2] Wolfdietrich is neither husband nor lover, but the child supposed to have been born in adultery.

[3] Ed. Paris and Robert, *Miracles de Nostre Dame*, vol. v, pp. 257 ff. Cf. also L. Petit de Julleville, *Les Mystères*, vol. ii, pp. 306 ff. It is sufficient here to quote the summary given in the manuscript before the play begins: 'Cy commence un miracle de Nostre Dame du roy Thierry, a qui sa mére fist entendant que Osanne, sa femme, avoit eu trois chiens, et elle avoit eu trois filz, dont il la condampna a mort, et ceulx qui la dorent pugnir la mirent en mer; et depuis trouva le roy ses enfans et sa femme.' The tale does not fit into any of the types described above. The accusation is the primitive one of animal birth, not adultery, and the punishment that of exposure in a boat. The play has obviously no direct connexion with any of the other stories cited by Grundtvig. It is in some respects like the Constance type (§ 40), where a similar accusation and punishment occurs. The story is most likely based directly on a folk-tale, and the choice of Thierry as the name of the king is possibly entirely arbitrary.

Grundtvig further points out that the names Raadengaard, Memering, and Adelring (the sword mentioned in A) belong to the Theodoric legend. Adelring, however, is probably a late accretion to the Danish ballad, since it only occurs in that one version, and that Memering did not originally belong to the Theodoric legend has been demonstrated in a previous chapter (§ 29). On Raadengaard see § 28.

The Gunhild ballad is a relatively late development; it can scarcely go farther back than the end of the eleventh century, when the Gunhild legend as we know it seems to have been formed in Flanders and brought over to England. The legend had very likely from the beginning the form of a ballad: at any rate, we know that early in the twelfth century there existed in England a ballad about Gunhild. At a later date, some time between *c.* 1300 and 1650 and probably nearer to the latter date, the Gunhild ballad was entirely revised and modelled on some version of the Earl of Toulouse story, from which several details were taken. Scandinavia received the Gunhild story in a different form from that in the English ballad, with an ordeal instead of a single combat. We do not know when the story first reached Scandinavia, but it must have been before *c.* 1250. Presumably it had from the first the form of a ballad, though we have no certain evidence of that. In the thirteenth century the English Gunhild ballad became known in Norway, where it influenced the local ballad, and the revised form then spread to Denmark. The Faroes were only partially and Iceland not at all influenced by the English tradition.

Owing to the later revision of the English ballad, the surviving Scandinavian versions show much closer likeness to the early English form of the story, as it has come down to us in the summaries given by the chroniclers. There is no verbal similarity between the surviving British and Scandinavian ballads. Yet the peculiar phrase which occurs in several Scandinavian versions, '. . . Mimmer-Tand (*or* Mimring-Tand), han var den mindste kristne Mand', is probably a translation of the lines underlying Matthew Paris's words *propter corporis parvitatem*

Mimecan dicebatur. The Middle English form may have been something like this:

> He was ycleped Mimecan,
> For þat he was þe leste man.

The necessity of the rhyme explains why the ending *Tand* (from *-can*, the diminutive meaning of which was not understood in Scandinavia) was kept even when the lines were translated into Norwegian, and was later faithfully preserved in Scandinavia.

APPENDIX

TEXTS

with translations of the Scandinavian versions

I. BRITISH VERSIONS

A

Child, *English and Scottish Popular Ballads*, vol. ii, pp. 44–46. From the Percy MS. of *c.* 1650. A few obvious mistakes have been corrected; they are noted by Child, p. 48.

1. Our king he kept a ffalse steward,
      Men called him Sir Aldingar

   . . . .

   . . . .

2. He wold haue layen by our comely queene,
      Her deere worshipp to haue betraide;
   Our queene shee was a good woman,
      And euer more said him nay.

3. Aldingar was offended in his mind,
      With her hee was neuer content,
   But he sought what meanes he cold find out,
      In a fyer to haue her brent.

4. There came a lame lazer to the kings gates,
      A lazar was blind and lame;
   He tooke the lazar vpon his backe,
      Vpon the queenes bed he did him lay.

5. He said, Lye still, lazar, wheras thou lyest;
      Looke thou goe not away;
   Ile make thee a whole man and a sound
      In two howres of a day.

6. And then went forth Sir Aldingar,
      Our queene for to betray,
   And then he mett with our comlye king,
      Saies, God you saue and see!

7. 'If I had space, as I haue grace,
     A message I wold say to thee:'
   'Say on, say on, Sir Aldingar,
     Say thou on and vnto me.'

8. 'I can let you now see one of the greiuosest sights
     That euer Christen king did see;
   Our queene hath chosen a new, new loue,
     She will haue none of thee.

9. 'If shee had chosen a right good knight,
     The lesse had beene her shame;
   But she hath chosen a lazar man,
     Which is both blinde and lame.'

10. 'If this be true, thou Aldingar,
      That thou dost tell to me,
    Then will I make thee a rich knight
      Both of gold and fee.

11. 'But if it be false, Sir Aldingar,
      That thou doest tell to me,
    Then looke for noe other death
      But to be hangd on a tree.
    Goe with me,' saide our comly king,
      'This lazar for to see.'

12. When the king he came into the queenes chamber,
      Standing her bed befor,
    'There is a lodly lome,' says Harry King,
      'For our dame Queene Elinor!

13. 'If thou were a man, as thou art none,
      Here thou sholdest be slaine;
    But a paire of new gallowes shall be built,
      Thoust hang on them soe hye.

14. 'And a fayre fyer there shalbe bett,
      And brent our queene shalbee:'
    Fforth then walked our comlye king,
      And mett with our comly queene.

15. Saies, God you saue, our queene, Madam,
      And Christ you saue and see!
    Heere you haue chosen a new, new loue,
      And you will haue none of mee.

16. 'If you had chosen a right good knight,
    The lesse had beene your shame;
  But you haue chosen a lazar man,
    That is both blind and lame.'

17. 'Euer alacke!' said our comly queene,
    'Sir Aldingar is false to mee;
  But euer alacke!' said our comly queene,
    'Euer alas, and woe is mee!

18. 'I had thought sweuens had neuer been true;
    I haue prooued them true at the last;
  I dreamed in my sweauen on Thursday at eueninge,
    In my bed wheras I lay,

19. 'I dreamed a grype and a grimlie beast
    Had carryed my crowne away,
  My gorgett and my kirtle of golde,
    And all my faire heade-geere.

20. 'How he wold haue worryed me with his tush,
    And borne me into his nest,
  Saving there came a little hawk,
    Flying out of the east.

21. 'Saving there came a little hawke,
    Which men call a merlion;
  Vntill the ground he stroke him downe,
    That dead he did fall downe.

22. 'Giffe I were a man, as I am none,
    A battell I would proue;
  I wold fight with that false traitor;
    Att him I cast my gloue!

23. 'Seeing I am able noe battell to make,
    You must grant me, my leege, a knight,
  To fight with that traitor, Sir Aldingar,
    To maintaine me in my right.'

24. 'I 'le giue thee forty dayes,' said our king,
    'To seeke thee a man therin;
  If thou find not a man in forty dayes,
    In a hott fyer thou shall brenn.'

25. Our queene sent forth a messenger;
    He rode fast into the south;
    He rode the countryes through and through,
    Soe ffar vnto Portsmouth.

26. .   .   .   .

    .   .   .   .
    He cold find never a man in the south country
    That wold fight with the knight soe keene.

27. The second messenger the queen forth sent
    Rode far into the east;
    But, blessed be God made sunn and moone!
    He sped then all of the best.

28. As he rode then by one riuer side,
    There he mett with a little child;
    He seemed noe more in a mans likenesse
    Then a child of four yeeres old.

29. He askt the queenes messenger how far he rode;
    Loth he was him to tell;
    The little one was offended att him,
    Bid him adew, farwell.

30. Said, Turne thou againe, thou messenger,
    Greete our queene well from me;
    When bale is att hyest, boote is att next;
    Helpe enough there may bee.

31. 'Bid our queene remember what she did dreame
    In her bedd wheras shee lay;
    She dreamed the grype and the grimly beast
    Had carryed her crowne away;

32. 'Her gorgett and her kirtle of gold,
    Alsoe her faire head-geere;
    He would haue werryed her with his tushe,
    And borne her into his nest.

33. 'Saving there came a little hawke,
    Men call him a merlyon;
    Vntill the ground he did strike him downe,
    That dead he did ffall downe.

34. 'Bidd the queene be merry att her hart,
      Euermore light and glad;
  When bale is att hyest, boote is at next,
      Helpe enoughe there shalbe.'

35. Then the queenes messenger rode backe,
      A gladed man then was hee;
  When he came before our queene,
      A gladd woman then was shee.

36. Shee gaue the messenger twenty pound,
      O lord, in gold and ffee;
  Saies, Spend and spare not while this doth last,
      Then feitch thou more of me.

37. Our queene was put in a tunne to burne,
      She thought no thing but death;
  Thé were ware of the little one
      Came ryding forth of the east.

38. With a mu   .   .   .   .
      A louelie child was hee;
  When he came to that fier,
      He light the queene full nigh.

39. Said, Draw away these brands of fire
      Lie burning before our queene,
  And feitch me hither Sir Aldingar,
      That is a knight soe keene.

40. When Aldingar see that little one,
      Ffull litle of him hee thought;
  If there had beene halfe a hundred such,
      Of them he wold not haue wrought.

41. Hee sayd, Come hither, Sir Aldingar;
      Thou seemust as bigge as a ffooder;
  I trust to God, ere I haue done with thee,
      God will send to vs an auger.

42. Saies, The first stroke that's giuen, Sir Aldingar,
      I will giue vnto thee,
  And if the second giue thou may,
      Looke then thou spare not mee.

43. The litle one pulld forth a well good sword,
      I-wis itt was all of guilt;
    It cast light there over that feild,
      It shone soe all of guilt.

44. He stroke the first stroke att Aldingar,
      He stroke away his leggs by his knee;

   .   .   .   .

     .   .   .   .

45. Sayes, Stand vp, stand vp, thou false traitor,
      And fight vpon thy feete;
    For and thou thriue as thou begins,
      Of a height wee shalbe meete.

46. 'A preist, a preist,' sayes Aldingar,
      'Me for to houzle and shriue!
    A preist, a preist,' sayes Aldingar,
      'While I am a man liuing a-liue!

47. 'I wold haue laine by our comlie queene;
      To it shee wold neuer consent;
    I thought to haue betrayd her to our king,
      In a fyer to haue had her brent.

48. 'There came a lame lazar to the kings gates,
      A lazar both blind and lame;
    I tooke the lazar vpon my backe,
      In the Queenes bed I did him lay.

49. 'I bad him, Lie still, lazar, where he lay,
      Looke he went not away;
    I wold make him a whole man and a sound
      In two houres of a day.

50. .   .   .   .

     .   .   .   .

  'Euer alacke!' sayes Sir Aldingar,
      'Falsing neuer doth well;

51. 'Forgiue, forgiue me, queene, Madam!
      For Christs loue forgiue me!'
    'God forgaue his death, Aldingar,
      And freely I forgiue thee.'

52. 'Now take thy wife, thou King Harry,
     And loue her as thou shold;
   Thy wiffe shee is as true to thee
     As stone that lies on the castle wall.'

53. The lazar vnder the gallow tree
     Was a pretty man and small;
   The lazar vnder the gallow tree
     Was made steward in King Henerys hall.

B

Child, vol. ii, pp. 46–48. From Scott's *Minstrelsy of the Scottish
Border*. The ballad was communicated to Scott by K. Williamson Burnet,
of Monboddo, as written down from the recitation of an old woman, long
in the service of the Arbuthnot family.

1. The birds sang sweet as ony bell,
     The world had not their make;
   The queen she's gone to her chamber,
     With Rodingham to talk.

2. 'I love you well, my queen, my dame,
     Bove land and rents so clear,
   And for the love of you, my queen,
     Would thole pain most severe.'

3. 'If well you love me, Rodingham,
     I'm sure so do I thee;
   I love you well as any man,
     Save the king's fair bodye.'

4. 'I love you well, my queen, my dame,
     'T is truth that I do tell;
   And for to lye a night with you,
     The salt seas I would sail.'

5. 'Away, away, O Rodingham!
     You are both stark and stoor;
   Would you defile the king's own bed,
     And make his queen a whore?

6. 'To-morrow you'd be taken sure,
     And like a traitor slain,
   And I'd be burned at a stake,
     Altho I be the queen.'

7. He then steppd out at her room-door,
     All in an angry mood,
   Untill he met a leper-man,
     Just by the hard way-side.

8. He intoxicate the leper-man,
     With liquors very sweet,
   And gave him more and more to drink,
     Until he fell asleep.

9. He took him in his arms two,
     And carried him along,
   Till he came to the queen's own bed,
     And there he laid him down.

10. He then steppd out of the queen's bower,
      As swift as any roe,
    Till he came to the very place
      Where the king himself did go.

11. The king said unto Rodingham,
      What news have you to me?
    He said, Your queen's a false woman,
      As I did plainly see.

12. He hastend to the queen's chamber,
      So costly and so fine,
    Until he came to the queen's own bed,
      Where the leper-man was lain.

13. He looked on the leper-man,
      Who lay on his queen's bed;
    He lifted up the snaw-white sheets,
      And thus he to him said.

14. 'Plooky, plooky are your cheeks,
      And plooky is your chin,
    And plooky are your armis twa,
      My bonny queen's layne in.

15. 'Since she has lain into your arms,
    She shall not lye in mine;
  Since she has kissd your ugsome mouth,
    She never shall kiss mine.'

16. In anger he went to the queen,
    Who fell upon her knee;
  He said, You false, unchaste woman,
    What's this you've done to me?

17. The queen then turnd herself about,
    The tear blinded her ee:
  'There's not a knight in a' your court
    Dare give that name to me.'

18. He said, 'T is true that I do say
    For I a proof did make;
  You shall be taken from my bower,
    And burned at a stake.

19. 'Perhaps I 'll take my word again,
    And may repent the same,
  If that you'll get a Christian man
    To fight that Rodingham.'

20. 'Alass! alass!' then cried our queen,
    'Alas and woe to me!
  There's not a man in all Scotland
    Will fight with him for me.'

21. She breathed unto her messengers,
    Sent them south, east, and west;
  They could find none to fight with him,
    Nor enter the contest.

22. She breathed on her messengers,
    She sent them to the north;
  And there they found Sir Hugh le Blond,
    To fight him he came forth.

23. When unto him they did unfold
    The circumstance all right,
  He bade them go and tell the queen
    That for her he would fight.

24. The day came on that was to do
      That dreadful tragedy;
    Sir Hugh le Blond was not come up,
      To fight for our lady.

25. 'Put on the fire,' the monster said,
      'It is twelve on the bell;'
    ''T is scarcely ten, now,' said the king,
      'I heard the clock mysell.'

26. Before the hour the queen is brought,
      The burning to proceed;
    In a black velvet chair she's set,
      A token for the dead.

27. She saw the flames ascending high,
      The tears blinded her ee:
    'Where is the worthy knight,' she said,
      'Who is to fight for me?'

28. Then up and spak the king himsell:
      'My dearest, have no doubt,
    For yonder comes the man himsel,
      As bold as eer set out.'

29. They then advanced to fight the duel,
      With swords of temperd steel;
    Till down the blood of Rodingham
      Came running to his heel.

30. Sir Hugh took out a lusty sword,
      'T was of the metal clear,
    And he has pierced Rodingham
      Till 's heart-blood did appear.

31. 'Confess your treachery, now,' he said,
      'This day before you die;'
    'I do confess my treachery,
      I shall no longer lye.

32. 'I like to wicked Haman am,
      This day I shall be slain:'
    The queen was brought to her chamber,
      A good woman again.

33. The queen then said unto the king,
    Arbattle's near the sea;
    Give it unto the northern knight,
      That this day fought for me.

34. Then said the king, Come here, Sir Knight,
    And drink a glass of wine,
    And, if Arbattle's not enough,
      To it we'll Fordoun join.

C

Child, vol. ii, p. 48. From Dr. Joseph Robertson's Note-Book, 1 January
1830.

1. They've putten her into prison strang,
    A twalmon lang and mair,
    Until the mice and wild rattens
      Did tear her yallow hair.

   .   .   .   .

2. 'One shake o your han,' said Rodingham,
    'One shak o your han gie me:'
    'I cam na here for shaking hans,
      But to fight maist desperatelie.'

3. 'It's nae ten strucken on the clock,
    Nor eleven on the bell:'
    'We'll doe ill deeds anew ere night,
      Tho it were strucken twall.'

II. DANISH VERSIONS[1]

A

DgF (i.e. Grundtvig, *Danmarks gamle Folkeviser*) i, pp. 204–6. From the Karen Brahe MS. of *c.* 1550. A few obvious mistakes have been corrected; they are noted in *DgF* i, p. 213.

1. Frw Guner seeder y Spirre,
   hynder beedis beeggle saa dyre.
   ' Hynnde frw Gundder.

2. Hyndder beedder bieegle aff synndenn
   thy rigest och thy yngist.
   Hyndis beedis beeglle aff weestenn,
   dy riggest och thy beste.

3. Hyndder bieedes till aff nuordenn
   alle thy beedde thuorde.
   Hyndir beedder till aff østenn
   thy rigest och thi thrøste.

4. Hynndder baad hertug Heenddrick
   saa krancke skieebbenn thi saamell fieeck.
   Hand hynd bad, och hand hynd fiennge,
   Storum och strid der-efter ginge.

5. Tthend herre skulde y lieedinng faarre,
   Raffuenngaard hand skulde hieeme werre:
   'Wogtte thu weell Bronsuig,
   och halle-beeddere Slesuig.

6. Wogtte thu fuld weell y Spirre,
   och miest frw Gunder hynnd dyrre.'
   Haartugenn styrrer synn sneecke fraa land,
   Raffuengaard rider synn gaanger paa sannd.

7. Raffuenngaard axller skaarlagenn-skieend,
   hand gaar i lofftt forr droningen ind:
   'Y skall faa meg suer Aaddellring
   saa bad Henddrick herre mynn.'

---

[1] In the modern Danish versions a few minor changes in spelling and punctuation have been introduced for the sake of greater consistency.

A

(*Translation*)

1. Lady Gunder sits at Spirre;
   Suitors try for her hand so dear (?).

2. Suitors come from the south,
   The richest and the youngest;
   Suitors come from the west,
   The richest and the best.

3. Suitors come from the north,
   All that dare to woo her;
   Suitors come from the east,
   The richest and the bold(est).

4. Duke Hendrik sued for her hand:
   An evil fate they dreed together.
   He wooed her and he wedded her:
   Storm and strife there followed.

5. The lord must go to the wars,
   Ravengaard must bide at home:
   'Ward thou Brunswick well,
   And ward thou Slesvig better.

6. 'Full well ward thou at Spirre,
   And best of all Lady Gunder, the dear one.'
   The duke steers his ship from land,
   Ravengaard rides his steed on the sand.

7. Ravengaard busks him in scarlet,
   Goes to the queen's bower aloft:
   'Ye must give me the sword Adelring,
   So said Hendrik my lord.'

8. 'Icke saagde mynn herre meg saa
   thett sidste synde hand skildis meg fraa.'
   'Kand ieg icke Aadellring faa,
   daa skaall ieg eedder lygge opaa.'

9. 'Daa lyff och lyuff, thett thu faar skaam,
   ind er herre Gud langtt beder ind graam.'
   Heerttugenn kaam fraa lieeding hieem,
   Raffuengaard gaar hanom vd igenn.

10. 'Huor staar thett y Spyrre?
    huor lydder frw Guneld hynn dyre?'
    'Edders landde staar som dy stuode,
    frw Gunild haffuer saa ilde giortt.'

11. 'Och icke weell ieg dynn ord nu thro,
    ieg aldrig vthroskaab til hind suo.'
    'Ieg thett med mynn øggen suo,
    att erricke-bieespen huoss hynd luo.'

12. 'Tthaa skaal ieg hynndder saa byrrig och slaa,
    dett ingenn mand hynd hiellpe maa.'
    Hertug Henddrik axller skaarlagenn-skyeend,
    hand gaar y lofftt for droningenn ind.

13. Harttugenn innd aff dørrenn threend,
    droningenn stuod hanom op igenn:
    'Weell-komenn, eddellig haare myn,
    huor haffuer eedder y lieeddinng lidd?'

14. 'Weell haffdde meg lydd y lieedding y aar,
    haffde dw icke saa ildde giortt.'
    'Mynn naaddige herre, y sygger icke saa,
    rett aldrig ieg der thengtte opaa.'

15. 'Saa weeslig du der thengtte paa,
    der errkee-bespenn huosz deg luo.'
    Saa sluo hand hynndder saa saarre,
    slett ingenn hynder hieelpe thuordde.

16. Tther waar heelder ingenn indde,
    for-vden thuo høffske quinde.
    For-vddenn thuo høffske wyffue,
    dy bad thend frw y lyffue.

8. 'In sooth my lord said not so
   When last he departed me fro.'
   'If Adelring I cannot have,
   Falsely shall I lie of you.'

9. 'Then lie and lie till thou art shamed,
   Yet greater is God than the grim one (?).'
   The duke came home from the wars,
   Ravengaard goes forth to greet him.

10. 'How stands it at Spirre?
    How fares Lady Gunild, the dear one?'
    'Your lands stand as they did,
    Lady Gunild has done you great wrong.'

11. 'Thy word I will not trow;
    Ne'er did I see her false to me.'
    'I saw with mine own eyes,
    The archbishop lay with her.'

12. 'Then will I so beat and baste her
    That no man shall bring her help.'
    Duke Hendrik busks him in scarlet,
    Goes to the queen's bower aloft.

13. The duke stepped in at the door,
    The queen rose up to greet him.
    'Welcome, my noble lord!
    How has the war gone with you?'

14. 'Well had the war gone with me this year,
    Hadst thou not done me such wrong.'
    'My gracious lord, scold me not so;
    Never thought I to do you wrong.'

15. 'In sooth thou thoughtst to do me wrong
    When the archbishop lay with thee.'
    So sorely then he beat her,
    No man dared to help her.

16. Nor was there any witness
    Save only two ladies of the court,
    Save only two women of the court,
    They begged the queen's life.

17. 'Mynn eddellig herre, y skaal thett icke thro,
    Raffuengaard haffuer hynd løggenn paa.'
    'Thaa skaal hun nu fly seg denn mand,
    y krinnsenn thør med Raffuengaard staande.'

18. Offuen-hoffuett och baarre-fuod,
    saa vseell kaam hun aff dørrenn vd.
    Hun gick seeg till heelde,
    som kieemper dy drak sneelde.

19. Droninggenn ind aff dørrenn thrennd,
    alle stuod kieemper hynd op igenn.
    'Er her nu ingenn inde,
    som feegtt weell for quinndde?'

20. Alle stuod kieemper och thuaffued
    for-vddenn Miemerinng, suaridtt:
    'Ieg thientte y edders faaders gaard
    weell y fulde femttenn aar.

21. Ieeg suo edder aldrig saa vseell,
    saa baar om edders axell.
    Ieg suo edder aldrig baare-fuod
    paa den grøne greese-rod.

22. Some daa gaff hand giøbbind guld,
    och suome daa gaff hand skoller fuld.
    Raffuenn-gaard gaff han allder-mieest,
    men hand haffuer sueegenn edder alder-først.

23. Allttyd suod ieeg weed ennde,
    som alle guodde gaaffuer weendde.
    Nu weell ieg for edder y kreendsenn gaa,
    om y weell meg suerd Aadellring faa.'

24. 'Alltt om du welltt y krindsenn gaa,
    saa weell skall thu suerd Addellring faa.'
    Tthi skreff krindsenn paa denn moold,
    thy gick der-y meed suerd och skiold.

25. 'Nu skalltt thu saa suere meg,
    att thu weedst icke suerd Aadellrinng.'
    'Saa hiellp meg Gud paa mynn thro:
    ieg weed icke vddenn grebb for-offuen iiordt.

17. 'My noble lord, believe it not;
Ravengaard has belied her.'
'Then she shall get her a man
Will enter the lists with Ravengaard.'

18. Bareheaded and barefooted,
Piteous she stepped out at the door.
She went her to the hall (?)
Where bold knights were drinking.

19. The queen stepped in at the door,
All the knights rose up to greet her.
'Is there no one here
Will fight for a woman?'

20. The knights stood silent all
Save only Memering, said,
'I served in your father's court
For full fifteen years.

21. 'I never saw you so piteous,
With shoulders bare.
I never saw you barefooted,
Treading the green grass.

22. 'To some he gave great store (?) of gold
And to others he gave goblets full.
To Ravengaard he gave most of all;
Yet he has forsaken you first of all.

23. 'Always I sat at the table-end
Where no good gifts came.
Now I will enter the lists for you
If ye will get me the sword Adelring.'

24. 'If thou wilt enter the lists,
I' faith thou shalt have the sword Adelring.'
They traced a circle on the ground,
They entered it with sword and shield.

25. 'Now thou must swear before me
That thou knowst not the sword Adelring.'
'So help me God, on my troth
I know but the hilt above ground.

26. Nu skaalltt thu saa suerre iggenn
att thu west icke suerd Saaderinng.'
'Saa hieellpe meg Gud foroffuenn,
som ieg weed icke suerd Swdde-wynndtt.'

27. Tthett første huog, der Raffuengaard huog,
daa huog hand Meemerings suerdtt y thuo.
Thett melltte heertugenn som hand stuod:
'Nu matte thu siee denn gierning dw giordde.'

28. Hun suaridtt: 'Ieg haffuer icke deenn gierning giortt,
ind-dog mynn sølligge keemppe saa fuor.'
Thett første huog, ther Mømering huog,
tha hog hand Raffuengaards suerd y thuo.

29. 'Du holltt op, Mymerring, hog icke meeg,
men ieg kaand myn skuo tuing.'
Raffuengaard nedder ad iorddenn løb,
suerd Swd-wynnd hand for seg skøød.

30. 'Du haffuer nu dieeg om mieen suoritt,
dynn søllig seell hun er forlorenn.'
Dett første huog, der Raffuengaard huog,
daa huog hand Memerings suerd y thuo.

31. 'Hollt op, Raffuengaard, huog icke meeg,
men ieg kaand myn skoo tuing.'
Miemering needer till iorrdenn leebb,
suerd Aadellring han for seeg skøød.

32. 'Nu haffuer du dieg on myeen suorenn,
dynn søllig seel hun er forlorenn.'
'Ieg haffuer meg icke om mieenn suorit:
ieg west icke vdden greff for-offuen iordtt.'

33. Tthett første huog, der Miemering huog,
daa huog hand Raffuengards suerd y thuo.
Thett anditt huog, der Miemerring huog,
da huog hand Raffuengaards hallss y thuo.

34. 'Sie nu, kieer herre mynn,
huor hand fuor med keempen dynn.
Myn eddellig herre, weell y throff,
att Raffuengaard haffuer meg løffuett paa?'

26. 'Now thou must swear in return
That thou knowst not the sword Sudwynd.'
'So help me God in heaven,
I know not the sword Sudwynd.'

27. At the first blow that Ravengaard struck
He cut Memering's sword in two.
Up spoke the duke where as he stood:
'Now mayst thou see the deed thou didst.'

28. She answered, 'I have not done that deed,
Though my poor champion fared thus ill.'
At the first blow that Memering struck
He cut Ravengaard's sword in two.

29. 'Hold thy hand, Memering: strike not
While I tie my shoe-latchet.'
Ravengaard bent him down to the ground,
Seized the sword Sudwynd.

30. 'Now thou hast forsworn thyself,
And thy poor soul is lost.'
At the first blow that Ravengaard struck
He cut Memring's sword in two.

31. 'Hold thy hand, Ravengaard: strike not
While I tie my shoe-latchet.'
Memering bent him down to the ground,
Seized the sword Adelring.

32. 'Now thou hast forsworn thyself,
And thy poor soul is lost.'
'I have not forsworn myself:
I knew but the hilt above ground.'

33. At the first blow that Memering struck
He cut Ravengaard's sword in two.
At the second blow that Memering struck
He cut Ravengaard's neck in two.

34. 'Look now, dear my lord,
How he used thy champion.
My noble lord, will ye now believe
That Ravengaard has lied of me?'

35. Herr Heennddrick klaper hynder weed huiden kinnd:
    'Forlaad meg thett, allerkieereste mynn.'
    Miemerring kaam der staalkeenn hiem
    med blodig hoffued och brøden bienn.

36. 'Frw Guner, giør for edders faadders sieell:
    gyff meg brød, men ieg maa løffue.'
    'Hørdu, Miemering, huad ieg sigger dieeg,
    dinn saard skall ieg laadde leege deeg.

37. Alle dynn dage ieg giffuer dieg brød,
    seelliff skallt thu slidde skaarlagenn rød.'
    Sagde frw Gundder.

B

DgF i, pp. 206–7. Recorded in 1844 on the island of Fur in the Lim Fjord
by Pastor Fischer. Grundtvig changed the spelling from Gunhild to Gunild
to accord better with present-day Jutland pronunciation.

1. Hendrik han vilde sejle fra Land
   og forlade sin Liljevand.
       Det saa vilde han Hendrik,
       sejle fra Land
       og forlade sin Liljevand.

2. 'Og hør du, Ravnlil fager of fiin,
   du skal nu vogte Allerkjæresten min.
       Det saa sagde han Hendrik,
       fager og fiin, etc.

3. Ja, du skal hende vogte og gjem',
   ret ligesom hendes Herre var hjem'.'
       Det saa sagde han Hendrik,
       vogte og gjem', etc.

4. Hendrik han styrer sin Snekke fra Land,
   Ravnlil han vender sin Ganger fra Strand.

5. Ravnlil han reed til Fru Gunilds Gaard,
   ud' stod Fru Gunild, var svøbt udi Maar.

6. 'Og hør du, Gunild fager og fiin,
   Vil du nu gjøre Vilje min?

7. Vil du ej gjøre Vilje mod mig,
   saa stor en Løgn skal jeg lyve paa dig.'

35. Sir Hendrik strokes her white cheek:
    'Forgive me, my dearest love.'
    Memering came staggering home
    With bloody head and broken bones.

36. 'Lady Gunder, for your father's soul
    Give me bread while as I live.'
    'Harken, Memering, to what I say:
    Thy wounds will I heal.

37. 'All thy days will I give thee bread,
    And in scarlet will I clothe thee.'

B

(*Translation*)

1. Hendrik he would sail from land
   And leave behind his lily-wand.

2. 'Harken, Ravnlil fair and fine,
   Thou must ward my dearest love.

3. 'Thou must watch and ward her,
   Right as were her lord at home.'

4. Hendrik steers his ship from land,
   Ravnlil turns his steed from the strand.

5. Ravnlil rode to Lady Gunild's hall;
   At the gate stood Lady Gunild, wrapped in vair.

6. 'Harken, Gunild fair and fine,
   Wilt thou do my will?

7. 'If thou wilt not do my will,
   So falsely shall I lie of thee.'

8. 'Ja lyv, ja lyv, til du faaer Skam:
   Sandhed for Løgn det gaaer vel fram.'

9. Hendrik han styrer sin Snekke til Land,
   Ravnlil han vender sin Ganger mod Strand.

10. 'Og hør du, Ravnlil fager og fiin,
    hvordan lever Fru Gunild, Allerkjæresten min?'

11. 'Fru Gunild det er ret et Horebæst,
    hun skaaner hverken Munk eller Præst.'

12. 'Og hør du, Ravnlil fager og fiin,
    vil du bytte Ganger med Snekke min?'

13. Hendrik han reed til Fru Gunilds Gaard,
    ud' stod Fru Gunild med udslagne Haar.

14. Han greb hende ved hendes fagre Guldhaar
    og slog hende mod den sorteste Jord.

15. 'Saa længe skal du nu slaaes og slids,
    til du faaer en Kæmpe, som vil Dysten rid'.'

16. Fru Gunild tog over sig Kappen saa blaa,
    og hen til Kæmpehuus monne hun gaae.

17. 'Og hør I, Kæmper, er I her ind':
    er her ikke een, der vil slaaes for en Kvind'?'

18. De Kæmper de talte ikke et Ord,
    men Memering sprang over breden Bord.

19. Den første Dyst, de sammen reed,
    gik Memerings Ganger i Knæene ned.

20. 'Saae du det, min Vive:
    min stolte Ravn kunde flyve.'

21. Den anden Dyst, de sammen reed,
    da gik Ravnlil hans Hoved af Led.

22. 'Saae du det, min guddydige Mand:
    den lille han den store overvandt.'

23. 'Tolv Tønder af det rødeste Guld
    giver jeg dig, for du vandt hende huld.'

8. 'Lie and lie till thou art shamed;
    Truth over falsehood shall prevail.'

9. Hendrik steers his ship to land,
    Ravnlil turns his steed to the strand.

10. 'Harken, Ravnlil fair and fine,
    How does Lady Gunild, my dearest love?'

11. 'Lady Gunild she is a whore,
    She spares neither monk nor priest.'

12. 'Harken, Ravnlil fair and fine,
    Change thy steed for this ship of mine.'

13. Hendrik rode to Lady Gunild's hall;
    At the gate stood Lady Gunild with waving hair.

14. He seized her by her fair golden hair
    And flung her down on blackest earth.

15. 'So long shalt thou be drubbed and drummed,
    Till thou get a knight will fight for thee.'

16. Lady Gunild wrapped her in mantle of blue;
    To the knights' hall she wended her way.

17. 'Harken, knights in the hall:
    Is there not one will do battle for a woman?'

18. The knights spoke never a word,
    But Memering sprang over the broad board.

19. At the first joust that they rode
    Memering's charger sank on its knee.

20. 'Sawst thou that, my wife!
    My proud Rav(e)n could fly.'

21. At the second joust they rode,
    Ravnlil's neck was broken.

22. 'Sawst thou that, my God-pious man:
    The little one slew the big one.'

23. 'Twelve barrels of the red, red gold
    I offer thee, for thou won her fair.'

24. 'Tolv Tønder Guld det er vel godt,
    men Skam faae den, der sælger hende bort.'

25. Memering og Gunild af Gaarden reed,
    tilbage stod Hendrik, han Hænderne vreed.

C

DgF i, pp. 207–9. Recorded in 1852 on the island of Mors in the Lim Fjord
by P. C. Sørensen, schoolmaster in the village of Tæbring.

1. Ja, Henrik reed til Valle,
   hvor Kæmperne drikke alle.
        Gjorde Henrik.
        Ja, Valle,
        hvor Kæmperne drikke alle.
        Gjorde Henrik.

2. 'Og hør du, Rundkrud Hagensgaard,
   og vil du nu passe paa min Gaard?
        Sagde Henrik.
        Ja, Hagensgaard, etc.

3. Du passe vel paa Sudselille,
   du passe vel paa Strudselille,
   du passe vel paa Spyre,
   og mest paa Fru Gunild den dyre.'
        Sagde Henrik.
        Ja, Spyre, etc.

4. Ja, Rundkrud reed til Henriks Gaard,
   udenfor Fru Gunild for ham monne staae.

5. 'Og hør du, Gunild favr og fiin,
   og vil du nu føje Viljen min?'

6. 'Den sidste Gang, jeg min Herre saae,
   da sagde han, jeg det ej gjøre maa.'

7. 'Ja, vil du ej føje Viljen min,
   saa stor en Løgn skal jeg lægge paa dig.'

8. 'Ja, lyv du, mens du lyve maa,
   saa stor en Ulykke skal du faae.'

9. Ja, Rundkrud reed til Valle,
   hvor Kæmperne drikke alle.

24. 'Twelve barrels of gold is a goodly boon,
    But shame on him that sells her away.'

25. Memering and Gunild rode from the hall;
    Hendrik stood behind, he wrung his hands.

C

(*Translation*)

1. Henrik rode to Valle,
   Where all the knights sit drinking.

2. 'Harken, Rundkrud Hagensgaard,
   Wilt thou ward my land?

3. 'Full well ward thou Sudselille,
   Full well ward thou Strudselille,
   Full well ward thou Spyre,
   And best of all Lady Gunild, the dear one.'

4. Rundkrud rode to Henrik's hall;
   At the gate stood Lady Gunild to greet him.

5. 'Harken, Gunild fair and fine,
   And wilt thou grant my will?'

6. 'When last I saw my lord,
   He said I may not so.'

7. 'If thou wilt not grant my will,
   So falsely shall I lie of thee.'

8. 'Lie, while lie thou mayst,
   A great ill shall betide thee.'

9. Rundkrud rode to Valle,
   Where all the knights sit drinking.

10. 'Og hør du, Rundkrud Hagensgaard,
    hvorledes staaer det til udi min Gaard?'

11. 'Det staaer sig vel med Sudselille,
    det staaer sig vel med Strudselille,
    det staaer sig vel med Spyre,
    Fru Gunild hun er en Hore.'
       Sagde Rundkrud.
       Ja, Spyre, etc.

12. 'Og hør du, Rundkrud Hagensgaard,
    der er saa mange, du har løjet paa.'

13. 'Jeg siger ej andet, end hvad jeg saae:
    Erkebispen hos hende laae.'

14. Ja, Henrik reed nu til sin Gaard,
    udenfor Fru Gunild for ham monne staae.

15. 'Jeg kan vel paa min Herre see,
    hvad enten han er drukken eller vred.'

At this place there is a gap of one or more stanzas, which the singer
was unable to remember. They recorded the conversation that ensued,
and that Henrik *slog hende paa hviden Kind.*

16. Ja, Memring reed til Henriks Gaard,
    udenfor Fru Gunild for ham monne staae.

17. 'Og hør du, Gunild favr og fiin,
    hvi fælder du saa modig Taare paa Kind?'

18. 'Jeg haver vel Aarsag at fælde Taare paa Kind,
    thi Rundkrud haver løjet paa mig.'

19. 'Du laane mig din Faders Hest,
    saa strider jeg Dysten allerbedst.'

20. 'Ja, Hest og Harnisk skal du faae,
    det bedste, Guldsværdet ej bide kan paa.'

21. Ja, Memring reed til Valle,
    hvor Kæmperne drikke alle.

22. 'Og hør du nu, Rundkrud Hagensgaard,
    og vil du nu Dysten med mig slaae?'

10. 'Harken, Rundkrud Hagensgaard,
    How stands it at home?'

11. 'Well stands it at Sudselille,
    Well stands it at Strudselille,
    Well stands it at Spyre;
    Lady Gunild she is a whore.'

12. 'Harken, Rundkrud Hagensgaard,
    So many hast thou belied.'

13. 'I say not aught but what I saw:
    The archbishop lay with her.'

14. Henrik rode to his hall;
    At the gate stood Lady Gunild to greet him.

15. 'Well can I see from my lord:
    Either he is drunk or angry.'

At this place there is a gap of one or more stanzas recording their
conversation and that Henrik 'struck her on her white cheek'.

16. Memring rode to Henrik's hall;
    At the gate stood Lady Gunild to greet him.

17. 'Harken, Gunild fair and fine,
    Why dost thou weep so sorely?'

18. 'Well have I cause to weep,
    For Rundkrud has belied me.'

19. 'Lend thou me thy father's horse,
    Then will I fight thy battle best.'

20. 'Horse and armour shalt thou have,
    Which no sword of gold shall bite.'

21. Memring rode to Valle,
    Where all the knights sit drinking.

22. 'Harken, Rundkrud Hagensgaard,
    And wilt thou fight a battle with me?'

O

23. 'Jeg ta'r dig med min venstre Haand,
kaster dig saa langt fra Land.'

24. 'Jeg tager dig med min mindste Finger,
knuser alle dine Lemmer isønder.'

25. Den første Dyst, de sammen reed,
Memrings Hest den faldt paa Knæ.

26. Den anden Dyst, de sammen reed,
Memring hug Rundkruds Hoved af.

27. Ja, Memring reed til Henriks Gaard,
udenfor Fru Gunild for ham monne staae.

28. 'Og hør du, Gunild favr og fiin,
der har du det Hoved, der har løjet paa dig.'

29. Fru Gunild gneed hendes Hoved i Skind,
saa ganger hun sig for Henrik ind.

30. 'Og hør du, Henrik favr og fiin,
der seer du det Hoved, der har løjet paa mig.'

31. 'Ak, hvem udi mit ganske Land
har hugget Rundkrud, den store Mand?'

32. 'Ja, Memring, den mindste Mand,
har hugget Rundkrud, den store Mand.'

33. 'Jeg giver ham Sudselille,
jeg giver ham Strudselille,
jeg giver ham min Spyre,
Fru Gunild vil jeg beholde, den dyre.'
    Sagde Henrik.
    Ja, Spyre, etc.

34. 'Behold du selv din Sudselille,
behold du selv din Strudselille,
behold du selv din Spyre:
Fru Gunild har jeg vundet, den dyre.'
    Sagde Memring.
    Ja, Spyre,
    Fru Gunild har jeg vundet, den dyre.
    Sagde Memring.

23. 'I'll take thee with my left hand,
    Fling thee far from out this land.

24. 'I'll take thee with my smallest finger,
    Break all thy limbs in sunder.'

25. At the first joust that they rode
    Memring's steed fell on its knee.

26. At the second joust that they rode
    Memring cut off Rundkrud's head.

27. Memring rode to Henrik's hall;
    At the gate stood Lady Gunild to greet him.

28. 'Harken, Gunild fair and fine,
    Here is the head has lied of thee.'

29. Lady Gunild lapped her head in fur,
    Goes to Henrik's chamber.

30. 'Harken, Henrik fair and fine,
    Here seest thou the head has lied of me.'

31. 'Alack! Who in all my land
    Has slain Rundkrud, the big man?'

32. 'Memring, the smallest man,
    Has slain Rundkrud, the big man.'

33. 'I offer him my Sudselille,
    I offer him my Strudselille,
    I offer him my Spyre;
    I will keep Lady Gunild, the dear one.'

34. 'Keep thou thy Sudselille,
    Keep thou thy Strudselille,
    Keep thou thy Spyre;
    I have won Lady Gunild, the dear one.'

G[1]

DgF ii, pp. 641–2. Taken down in 1855 by A. C. Paulsen, schoolmaster in the village of Dalby, from the recitation of widow Karen Marie Sørens-datter of Refs in the district of Thy, north of the Lim Fjord.

1. 'Hørst du, Ravnlil favr og fin:
   og vilst du vogte Allerkjæresten min?'
      Og det saa sagde han Henrik,
      favr og fin,
      og vilst du vogte Allerkjæresten min?

2. 'Og jeg skal hende baade vogte og gjem',
   ret ligesom du selv var hjem'.'
      Og det saa sagde han Ravnlil,
      vogte og gjem', etc.

3. 'Hørst du, Gunni baade favr og fin:
   og vilst du gjøre Vilje min?'

4. 'Du lovede, du vilde mig vogte og gjem',
   ret ligesom min Kjærest var hjem'.'

5. 'Og vilst du ej gjøre Vilje med mig,
   saa stor en Løgn skal jeg lyve paa dig.'

6. 'Ja lyv, ja lyv, til du faar Skam!
   Sandhed og Ret det gaar vel fram.'

7. Ravnlil han red ned paa Strand:
   kom saa kom da Henrik i Land.

8. 'Hørst du, Ravnlil favr og fin:
   hvorledes lever Allerkjæresten min?'

9. 'Hun lever jo, som hun kan bedst:
   hun sparer hverken Munk eller Præst.'

10. Henrik han kom ridend' i Gaard:
    ude stod Fru Gunni, var svøbt i Maar.

11. Han greb hende ved hendes favre Guldhaar:
    kastede hende mod den sorteste Jord.

12. 'Saadan skal du daglig stride,
    til du skaffer mig en Kæmpe, der kan Dysten ride.'

13. Gunni hun tog paa sin Kappe saa blaa:
    hen til Kæmpehus saa vilde hun gaa.

---

[1] The classification is that used by Grundtvig, in which the letters D–F are reserved for the Faroese and Icelandic versions (see pp. 222–35).

G

(*Translation*)

1. 'Harken, Ravnlil fair and fine,
   Wilt thou ward my dearest love?'

2. 'I will both watch and ward her,
   Right as though thou wert at home.'

3. 'Harken, Gunni both fair and fine,
   And wilt thou do my will?'

4. 'Thou promised to watch and ward me,
   Right as were my sweetheart at home.'

5. 'If thou wilt not do my will,
   So falsely shall I lie of thee.'

6. 'Lie and lie till thou art shamed;
   Truth and right shall yet prevail.'

7. Ravnlil rode down to the strand;
   Then came Henrik to land.

8. 'Harken, Ravnlil fair and fine,
   How does my dearest love?'

9. 'She lives as she may best,
   She spares neither monk nor priest.'

10. Henrik came riding to his hall;
    At the gate stood Lady Gunni, wrapped in vair.

11. He seized her by her fair golden hair,
    Threw her down on blackest earth.

12. 'Such usage shalt thou daily dree,
    Till thou get a knight can fight for thee.'

13. Gunni clad her in mantle of blue;
    To the knights' hall she would wend her way.

14. 'Goddag, I Venner, som sidder her ind'!
er der ingen, som vil stride for en Kvind'?'

15. Da hørtes der Tale, da svartes der jo:
Mimring han sprang over breden Bord.

16. 'Jeg skal daglig stride for dig,
saa længe som Blodet er varmt udi mig.'

17. Mimring og Ravnlil skulde Dysten rid':
Henrik og Gunni skulde derpaa se.

18. Den første Dyst, de sammen red,
da gik Hr. Mimrings Hest udi Knæ.

19. 'Saast du det, min udydige Mø!
strax paa Stedet skal Mimring dø.'

20. Den anden Dyst, de sammen red,
da gik Hr. Ravnlils Hoved af Led.

21. 'Saast du det, min udydige Mand!
han veed ikke det store, han vandt.'

22. 'Og jeg vil give dig ti Tønder Guld,
fordi du har vundet min Kjærest saa huld.'

23. 'Nu har jeg vunden hende baade liden og stor:
Skam skuld' de faa, som sælger hende bort!'

24. Mimring han spændt' Sværdet ved Sid'.
'Kom nu, Fru Gunni, saa ville vi rid'!'

25. Mimring og Gunni af Gaarden red:
Henrik det saae, han Hænder vred.

H

DgF ii, pp. 642–4, and x, p. 4. Taken down in 1854 by J. L. Knudsen,
teacher at Rødding Folk High School, from the recitation of a 64-year-old
woman, Kirsten Marie Helvegs, of Agerskov, Haderslev County, South
Jutland. H. Grüner Nielsen in 1909 made a phonograph recording of the
first two stanzas as sung by an 80-year-old man, Laurids Top, who had learnt
it from Kirsten Marie Helvegs.

1. Hans Hendrik skuld' a Landet far':
Röngård skuld' vær' hjemm' å ta Landet var'.
De skuld' Hans Hendrik,
a Landet far',
Röngård skuld' vær' hjemm' å ta Landet var'.

14. 'Hail, my friends here in the hall,
    Is there no one will fight for a woman?'

15. Up spoke one and answered yea,
    Mimring sprang over the broad board.

16. 'I will daily fight for thee,
    While the blood runs warm in me.'

17. Mimring and Ravnlil must to the battle;
    Henrik and Gunni must look thereon.

18. At the first joust that they rode
    Sir Mimring's steed sank on its knee.

19. 'Sawest thou that, my unchaste maid!
    On the spot must Mimring die.'

20. At the second joust that they rode
    Sir Ravnlil's neck was broken.

21. 'Sawest thou that, my unchaste man!
    Little he knows the big boon he won.'

22. 'I offer thee ten barrels of gold,
    For that thou won my sweetheart fair.'

23. 'Now I have won her both little and big,
    Shame on them that sell her away.'

24. Mimring girt his sword by his side:
    'Come, Lady Gunni, and let us ride.'

25. Mimring and Gunni rode from the hall;
    Henrik looked on, he wrung his hands.

H

(*Translation*)

1. Hans Hendrik must fare abroad,
   Röngård must stay and guard the land.

2. 'Du vogt mig Borg å Brönsvig!
du vogt mig Borg å Slesvig!
Du vogt mig Spir'
og lidel Fru Gunder den dyr'!'

3. Hans Hendrik skyder Guldsnekke fra Land:
Röngård spaserer i hviden Sand.
De gjör Hans Hendrik,
Guldsnekke fra Land, etc.

4. Röngård han svøver sæ Hôj i Skind:
så gær han i Lowt for Fru Gunder ind.

5. 'Å hør du, Fru Gunder bå fawr å fin:
å vil du gjöre Villen min?'

6. 'De vild' æ ikk' gjör for ti Tynder Guld:
å vær' min Herr' så svigefuld.'

7. 'Ja, vil du ej gjör' Villen min,
så skal æ lyw' om Æren din.'

8. 'Lyw du, Röngård, te du fær Skam!
vor Herr' er möje riger, end du est gram.'

9. Hans Hendrik skyder sin Guldsnekke til Land:
Röngård spaserer i hviden Sand.

10. 'Ja, hvudden stær Borg å Brönsvig?
ja, hvudden stær Borg å Slesvig?
Ja, hvudden stær Spir'
å lidel Fru Gunder den dyr'?'

11. 'Ja, vel stær Borg å Brönsvig,
ja, vel stær Borg å Slesvig.
Ja, vel stær Spir':
Fru Gunder hun er en Hor'.'

12. Hans Hendrik han kom rijend' i Gård:
Fru Gunder hun ud a Vindvet så.

13. 'Æ kan de mæ min Öjen se:
hvad enten er min Herre syg hæ vre?'

14. Hans Hendrik ind a Dören tren:
Fru Gunder stander ham op te-re'.

15. Han slow hind' under Øre:
'Få du Skam, din Hore!'

2. 'Ward thou my castle in Brunswick,
   Ward thou my castle in Slesvig,
   Ward thou Spire
   And little Lady Gunder, the dear one.'

3. Hans Hendrik urges his golden ship from land,
   Röngård walks on the white sand.

4. Röngård enfolds his head in fur,
   Goes to Lady Gunder's bower aloft.

5. 'Harken, Lady Gunder both fair and fine,
   And wilt thou grant my will?'

6. 'I would not do that for ten barrels of gold
   And be so false to my lord.'

7. 'If thou wilt not grant my will,
   Then shall I belie thine honour.'

8. 'Lie then, Röngård, till thou art shamed;
   The Lord is much greater than thou art grim.'

9. Hans Hendrik urges his golden ship to land,
   Röngård walks on the white sand.

10. 'How stands my castle in Brunswick?
    How stands my castle in Slesvig?
    How stands Spire
    And little Lady Gunder, the dear one?'

11. 'Well stands thy castle in Brunswick,
    Well stands thy castle in Slesvig,
    Well stands Spire:
    Lady Gunder she is a whore.'

12. Hans Hendrik came riding to his hall,
    Lady Gunder looked forth from the window.

13. 'I can see with mine eyes:
    Either my lord is sick or angry.'

14. Hans Hendrik stepped in at the door,
    Lady Gunder rises to greet him.

15. He struck her under the ear:
    'Shame on thee, thou whore!'

16. 'Nej, æ er ingen Hore,
    ikk' heller vil æ vor'e.'

17. Fru Gunder hun svøver sæ Hôj i Skind:
    så gær hun i Lowt for Nimmering ind.

18. 'Er her nogen inde,
    te der vil strij' for Kvinder?'

19. 'Er der nogen, der tör vove:
    te der vil strij' for Horer?'

20. De svar' den lille Nimmering Tant:
    'Så vel hjælper æ dæ, om æ kan.'

21. Nimmering han svøver sæ Hôj i Skind:
    så gær han i Lowt for Röngård ind.

22. Den første Dyst, di sammen rej:
    da jow han Röngårds Hat a.

23. Den anden Dyst, di sammen rej:
    da jow han Röngårds Hôj a.

24. Nimmering stikker hans Sværd ve Sij':
    'Kom nu, Fru Gunder, så vil vi rij'!'

25. 'Nej, ikk' så vil æ mæ dæ rij':
    för æ fær Höwn ör Hans Hendrik.

I

DgF iii, pp. 779–80, and x, p. 4. Taken down on 24 February 1857, by
A. H. Schade, of Nykøbing on the island of Mors in the Lim Fjord, from
the recitation of a 57-year-old man, Jens Tinstøber, who had learnt it from
his father. The singer was only gradually able to reconstruct the ballad.
Minor emendations have been made; they are noted in *DgF*.

1. 'Og hørst du, Ravnhild favr og fin!
   og du skal jo vogte Allerkjæresten min.'
       Og det saa sagde han Henrik,
       favr og fin,
       og du skal jo vogte Allerkjæresten min.

2. 'Ja, du skal hende baade vogte og gjemm',
   ret ligesom jeg selv var hjemm'.'
       Og det saa sagde han Henrik,
       vogte og gjemm', etc.

16. 'Nay, I am not a whore,
    Nor will I ever be one.'

17. Lady Gunder enfolds her head in fur,
    Goes to Nimmering's chamber aloft.

18. 'Is there any one here
    Will fight for women?

19. 'Is there any one dares
    To fight for whores?'

20. Answer made little Nimmering Tant,
    'I will help thee if I can.'

21. Nimmering enfolds his head in fur,
    Goes to Röngård's chamber aloft.

22. At the first joust that they rode
    He knocked off Röngård's hat.

23. At the second joust that they rode
    He knocked off Röngård's head.

24. Nimmering puts up his sword by his side:
    'Come, Lady Gunder, and let us ride.'

25. 'Nay, I will not ride with thee
    Till I am revenged on Hans Hendrik.'

I

(*Translation*)

1. 'Harken, Ravnhild fair and fine,
   Thou must ward my dearest love.

2. 'Thou must watch and ward her,
   Right as though I were at home.'

3. 'Ja, jeg skal hende baade vogte og gjemm',
ret ligesom du selv var hjemm'.'

4. 'Og vilst du nu ej gjøre Villig med mig,
saa stor en Løgn skal jeg lyve paa dig.'

5. 'Ja, lyv, ja, lyv kun, til du faar Skam!
Sandhed og Ret de gaar vel fram.'

6. Ravnhild han red sin Ganger paa Strand,
og saa kom da Henrik i Land.

7. 'Og hørst du, Ravnhild favr og fin!
hvordan lever Gunni, Allerkjæresten min?'

8. 'Ja, hun lever, som hun kan bedst:
hun sparer hverken Munk eller Præst.'

9. Henrik han kom ridendes i Gaard,
ud' stod Fru Gunni, var svøbt i Maar.

10. 'Velkommen, min Kjærest, af Leding hjem!
hvorledes haver Rejsen gangen med dig?'

11. 'Ja, Rejsen den haver gangen mig vel;
hvordan lever du med din Ungersvend?'

12. Han greb hende ved hendes favre Guldhaar,
og kastede hende mod den sorteste Jord.

13. 'Slig Kamp og Dyst skal du daglig lid',
til du skaffer mig en Kæmp', der kan Dysten rid'.'

14. Gunni trækker om sig sin Kaabe saa blaa,
til Kæmpehuset saa vilde hun gaa.

15. 'Og hører, I Mænd, som sidder her ind':
er der nogen af eder, som vil stride for en Kvind'?'

16. Da hørtes den Tale, da hørtes de Ord,
Memring han sprang over breden Bord.

17. 'Og jeg skal daglig stride for dig,
saa længe Blodet rinder varmt udi mig.'

18. Ja, Memring og Ravnhild skuld' Dysten rid',
Henrik og Gunni skuld' derpaa se.

19. Den første Dyst, de sammen red,
da gik Herr Memring hans Hest udi Knæ.

3. 'Ay, sure, I will watch and ward her,
   Right as though thou wert at home.'

4. 'If thou wilt not do my will,
   So falsely shall I lie of thee.'

5. 'Lie and lie till thou art shamed;
   Truth and right shall yet prevail.'

6. Ravnhild rode his steed on the strand,
   And then came Henrik to land.

7. 'Harken, Ravnhild fair and fine,
   How does Gunni, my dearest love?'

8. 'She lives as she may best,
   She spares neither monk nor priest.'

9. Henrik came riding to his hall;
   At the gate stood Lady Gunni, wrapped in vair.

10. 'Welcome, my sweetheart, home from the wars!
    How has the journey gone with thee?'

11. 'The journey has gone well with me:
    How dost thou with thy young swain?'

12. He seized her by her fair golden hair
    And threw her down on blackest earth.

13. Such battling and bruising shalt daily dree,
    Till thou get a knight can fight for thee.

14. Gunni robes her in cloak so blue,
    To the knights' hall she would wend her way.

15. 'Harken, men in the hall,
    Is there any of you will fight for a woman?'

16. Up spoke one and answered her,
    Memring sprang over the broad board.

17. 'I will daily fight for thee,
    While the blood runs warm in me.'

18. Memring and Ravnhild must to the battle;
    Henrik and Gunni must look thereon.

19. At the first joust that they rode
    Sir Memring's steed sank on its knee.

20. 'Ja, saast du det, du udydige Mø!
    strax her paa Stedet skal Herr Memring dø.'

21. Den anden Dyst, de sammen red,
    da gik Herr Ravnhild hans Hoved af Led.

22. 'Saast du det, min udydige Mand!
    om den lille ikke den store overvand.'

23. 'Ja, nu vil jeg give dig to Tønder Guld,
    fordi du har vunden min Kjærest saa huld.'

24. 'Nej, nu har jeg vunden hende liden og stor,
    men Skam skal de faa, der sælger hende bort!'

25. Memring han spændte Sværdet ved Sid':
    'Kom nu saa, Gunni! saa ville vi rid'.'

26. Saa Memring og Gunni af Gaarden red,
    Henrik, saa saare hans Hænder han vred.

K

DgF iv, pp. 722–7, and x, p. 4. A composite version made up from recitations in the years 1869–74 by eleven men and women of the district of Hammerum, Ringkøbing County. Individual variants are noted in *DgF*.

1. Gunder hun sidder paa Spire,
    og hende bad Bejle rige.
        Det gjord' hun Gunder.
        Paa Spire,
    og hende bad Bejle rige.

2. Der kom Bejle af Sønder,
    de rige Mænd og Bønder.
        De bad hend' Gunder, etc.

3. Og der kom Bejle af Vester,
    de rige Mænd og Præster.

4. Og der kom Bejle af Norden,
    de rige Mænd og store.

5. Og der kom Bejle af Øster,
    de rige Mænd og første.

6. Saa kom Hendrik, favr og fin,
    han fort' hend' Gunder hjem til sin.

20. 'Sawest thou that, thou unchaste maid!
On the spot Sir Memring must die.'

21. At the second joust that they rode
Sir Ravnhild's neck was broken.

22. 'Sawest thou that, my unchaste man,
That the little one slew the big one!'

23. 'Now I will offer thee two barrels of gold,
For that thou won my sweetheart fair.'

24. 'Nay, I have won her little and big,
But shame on them that sell her away.'

25. Memring girt his sword by his side:
'Come now, Gunni, and let us ride.'

26. Memring and Gunni rode from the hall,
So sorely did Henrik wring his hands.

K

(*Translation*)

1. Gunder she sits at Spire;
To her came suitors rich.

2. Suitors came from the south,
The rich men and the yeomen.

3. Suitors came from the west,
The rich men and the priests.

4. Suitors came from the north,
The rich men and the great.

5. Suitors came from the east.
The rich men and the first.

6. Then came Hendrik fair and fine,
He brought Gunder home to his hall.

7. Hendrik skuld' i Leding far',
   Ravnlil skuld' vær' hjemm' og ta' Landet var'.

8. 'Hør du, Ravnlil favr og fin!
   vil du vogt' mig Gunder min?'

9. 'Ja, jeg skal hend' baad' vogt' og gjemm',
   ret som min Herre selv var hjemm'.'

10. Hendrik han styrer hans Snække fra Land,
    Ravnlil staar efter paa hviden Sand.

11. Ravnlil svøber hans Hoved i Skind,
    saa gaar han i Loft for Gunder ind.

12. 'Og hør du, Gunder baad' favr og fin!
    og vil du nu gjør' Villi min?'

13. 'Nej, jeg vil ej gjør' Villi din,
    om du mig røver end Livet min.

14. Jeg ment', du skuld' mig vogt' og gjemm',
    ret som min Herre selv var hjemm'.'

15. 'Vil du ej gjør' Villi min,
    saa stor en Løgn skal jeg sætt' aa dig.'

16. 'Ja, lyv og lyv, til du faar Skam!
    Ret og Sanden gaar vel fram.'

17. Hendrik han styrer hans Snække for Land,
    Ravnlil rider hans Ganger paa Sand.

18. 'Velkommen, Hendrik, Herre min!
    hvordan har du lidet paa Rejsen din?'

19. 'Vel har jeg lidet paa Rejsen min,
    hvordan lever Gunder, Allerkjærest' min?'

20. 'Ja, hun lever saadan her hjemme
    alt med hendes Munkedrenge.

21. Hun spar sig ej for Præster,
    ej for de Munkegjæster.'

22. Og Hendrik sprang til Hesten høj,
    han red langt faster', end Fuglen fløj.

23. Hendrik han kom ridend' i Gaard,
    ud' stod Gunder med hendes udslagen Haar.

7. Hendrik must go to the wars,
   Ravnlil must stay and guard the land.

8. 'Harken, Ravnlil fair and fine,
   Wilt thou ward my Gunder?'

9. 'I will both watch and ward her,
   Right as were my lord at home.'

10. Hendrik steers his ship from land,
    Ravnlil stays behind on the white sand.

11. Ravnlil enfolds his head in fur,
    Goes to Gunder's bower aloft.

12. 'Harken, Gunder both fair and fine,
    And wilt thou grant my will?'

13. 'Nay, I will not grant thy will
    Even though thou take my life.

14. 'I thought thou shouldst me watch and ward,
    Right as were my lord at home.'

15. 'If thou wilt not grant my will,
    So falsely shall I lie of thee.'

16. 'Lie and lie till thou art shamed;
    Right and truth shall yet prevail.'

17. Hendrik steers his ship to land,
    Ravnlil rides his steed on the sand.

18. 'Welcome, Hendrik, my lord,
    How hast thou fared on thy journey?'

19. 'Well have I fared on my journey,
    How does Gunder, my dearest love?'

20. 'She lives here at home
    All with her swains, the monks.

21. 'She spares not herself for the priests,
    Nor for the monks, her guests.'

22. Hendrik sprang on his horse so high,
    He rode faster than bird could fly.

23. Hendrik came riding to his hall;
    At the gate stood Gunder with waving hair.

24. 'Velkommen, Hendrik, Herren min!
hvordan har du lidet paa Rejsen din?'

25. 'Ja, vel har jeg lidet paa Rejsen min,
hvordan lever du med Munkedreng' din'?'

26. Han tog hend' i hendes favre Haar,
han slog hend' ned imod sorten Jord.

27. 'Ja, jeg skal ej levne Liv i dig,
uden du faar en Kæmpe, vil for dig strid'.'

28. Gunder slog over sig Kaabe blaa,
ad Kæmpehus saa lader hun staa.

29. Gunderlil ind ad Døren tren,
[med aabent Hoved og bare Ben].[1]

30. 'Er her ingen inde,
der tør strid' for en Kvinde?'

31. 'Er her nu ingen her ude,
som vil strid' for en Hore?'

32. De tej' alle stille,
foruden Mimmering lille.

33. Mimmering han sad nederst ved Bord,
han svar' hend' Gunder et Ord.

34. 'Ja, jeg vil sandelig strid' for dig,
saa læng' der er varm Blod i mig.

35. Jeg har tjent din Fader i elleve Aar,
men aldrig saa' jeg din bare Taa.'

36. Mimmering og Ravnlil skuld' Dysten ri',
Hendrik og Gunder skuld' derpaa si.

37. Den første Dyst, de sammen red,
Mimmerings Hest i Knæen' skred.

38. 'Saa' du det, min udydige Kvind'!
min Kæmp' han skal nok Sejren vind''

39. 'Det var slet ingen Dyst at øv',
det var ikkuns, djer Hest' at prøv'.'

40. Den anden Dyst, de sammen red,
Ravnlils Hoved ad Heden skred.

[1] Reconstructed from version A, st. 18.

24. 'Welcome, Hendrik, my lord!
    How hast thou fared on thy journey?'

25. 'Well have I fared on my journey.
    How dost thou with thy swains, the monks?'

26. He caught her by her fair hair,
    He flung her down on the black earth.

27. 'No life will I leave in thee,
    But an thou get a knight will fight for thee.'

28. Gunder donned her cloak so blue,
    To the knights' hall she bends her course.

29. Gunderlil stepped in at the door
    Bareheaded and barefooted.

30. 'Is there no one within
    Dares to fight for a woman?

31. 'Is there no one without
    Will fight for a whore?'

32. They were silent all
    Save only little Mimmering.

33. Mimmering sat at the low end of the board,
    He answered Gunder a word.

34. 'Verily will I fight for thee,
    While the blood runs warm in me.

35. 'I served thy father for eleven years
    But never did I see thy bare toe.'

36. Mimmering and Ravnlil must to the battle;
    Hendrik and Gunder must look thereon.

37. At the first joust that they rode
    Mimmering's steed fell on its knee.

38. 'Sawest thou that, my unchaste woman!
    My champion will surely win.'

39. 'That was not a joust they rode,
    That was only to prove the horse.'

40. At the second joust they rode
    Ravnlil's head fell on the heath.

41. 'Saa' du det, min udydige Mand!
    min Kæmp' han vandt den Lillivand.'

42. Mimmering sprang til højen Hest,
    han satt' Fru Gunder for hans Bryst.

43. Mimmering ud af Krinsen red,
    Hendrik gik efter, hans Hænder han vred.

44. 'Syv Tønder af det hvide Sølv
    dem giver jeg dig for Gunder hendes Skyld.

45. Syv Tønder af det røde Guld
    dem giver jeg dig for Gunder huld.'

46. 'Med Æren har jeg hende vunden og faa't,
    og gid de faa Skam, der sælger hend' bort!'

47. Mimmering red sig ud af Gaard,
    Hendrik han græd, hans Hænder han slog.

L

DgF iv, pp. 728–9. Recorded in 1859 by Jens Christiansen Berg of Hammerlund, Skanderborg (now Aarhus) County.

1. Hendrik han vilde af Landet uddrag',
   og Gunde skuld' bliv' hjemm' og tag' Huset var'.
   Og det gjorde han Hendrik,
   af Landet uddrag',
   og Gunde skuld' bliv' hjemm' og tag' Huset var'.

2. Han sagde til Ravnlil favr og fin:
   'Du vogter mig Gunde, Allerkjæresten min!'

3. 'Ja, jeg skal hende vogt', og jeg skal hende gjemm',
   lige som min Herre var hjemm'.'

4. Ja, Hendrik gik sig ned til den Strand,
   da opkom en Sejler og tog ham fra Land.

5. 'Vil du nu ej gjøre Vilje mod mig,
   saa stor en Løgn skal jeg lyve paa dig.'

6. 'Ja, lyver du, til du faar Skam!
   thi Ret og Sandhed gaar vel fram.'

7. Nu Ravnlil gik da ned til den Strand,
   da opkom nu Hendrik fra fremmede Land.

41. 'Sawest thou that, my unchaste man!
    My champion won the lily-wand.'

42. Mimmering sprang on high horseback,
    Set Lady Gunder him before.

43. Mimmering rode from the lists;
    Hendrik came after, he wrung his hands.

44. 'Seven barrels of the silver white
    I offer thee for Gunder's sake.

45. 'Seven barrels of the gold so red
    I offer thee for Gunder fair.'

46. 'With honour have I won and ta'en her,
    And shame be on them that sell her away.'

47. Mimmering rode from the hall;
    Hendrik wept, he beat his hands.

L

(*Translation*)

1. Hendrik he would fare abroad,
   And Gunde must stay and guard the house.

2. Said he to Ravnlil fair and fine:
   'Ward thou Gunde, my dearest love.'

3. 'Ay, sure, I will watch her and I will ward her,
   Even as were my lord at home.'

4. Hendrik went him down to the strand,
   Up came a ship and took him from land.

5. 'If thou wilt not do my will,
   So falsely shall I lie of thee.'

6. 'Lie thou then till thou art shamed,
   For right and truth shall yet prevail.'

7. Ravnlil he went down to the strand,
   Up came Hendrik from foreign land.

8. 'Velkommen, min Herre, kommen velgaaen hjem!
   hvorledes har Rejsen ganget med Dem?'

9. 'Ja, vel er jeg kommen velgaaen hjem,
   hvordan lever Gunde, Allerkjæresten min?'

10. 'Ja, hun sparer ikke Naboer bedst,
    ja, hun sparer hverken Munk eller Præst.'

11. Nu Hendrik han kom da ridend' i Gaard,
    da ud' stod Fru Gunde, var vel svøbt i Maard.

12. 'Velkommen, min Herre, kommen ridendes hjem!
    hvordan haver Rejsen standen med Dem?'

13. 'Ja, vel er jeg kommen ridendes hjem,
    hvordan lever du med din' unge Svend'?'

14. Han tog da Fru Gunde i sit favre Guldhaar,
    og saa slog han hende imod sorteste Jord.

15. Fru Gunde tog over sig Kaaben blaa,
    til Kæmpehuset saa vilde hun gaa.

16. 'Og er der ikke en Mand her inde,
    som der kunde stride vel for en Kvinde?'

17. Nu Mimmering han strax fra Bordet opsprang,
    han rækked Fru Gunde snehvidendes Haand.

18. Nu Mimmering og Ravnlil skuld' Dysten rid',
    og Hendrik og Gunde skal derpaa si.

19. Den første Dyst, de da sammen red,
    Ravnlil slog Mimmerings Hest udi Knæ.

20. Den anden Dyst, de sammen red,
    Mimmering slog Ravnlil Hovedet fra.

21. 'Ti Tønder udaf det rødeste Guld
    dem giver jeg dig, for du vandt hende huld.'

22. 'Ja, vel haver jeg hende vunden og faa't,
    men skam faar den, som der sælger hende bort.'

23. Nu Mimmering og Gunde af Gaarden de red,
    og Hendrik stod ude, hans Hænder han vred.

8. 'Welcome, my lord, safely home again!
   How has the journey gone with you?'

9. 'Ay, sure, I am safely home again.
   How does Gunde, my dearest love?'

10. 'She spares not her neighbours best,
    She spares neither monk nor priest.'

11. Hendrik came riding to his hall;
    At the gate stood Lady Gunde, well wrapped in vair.

12. 'Welcome, my lord, riding home again!
    How have ye fared on your journey?'

13. 'Ay, sure, I came riding home again.
    How dost thou with thy young swains?'

14. He caught Lady Gunde by her fair golden hair
    And flung her down on blackest earth.

15. Lady Gunde donned her cloak so blue,
    To the knights' hall she would wend her way.

16. 'Is there not a man in the hall
    Will fight a battle for a woman?'

17. Mimmering straightway sprang from the board,
    Stretched forth to Lady Gunde a snow-white hand.

18. Mimmering and Ravnlil must to the battle,
    And Hendrik and Gunde must look thereon.

19. At the first joust that they rode
    Ravnlil drove Mimmering's steed on its knee.

20. At the second joust that they rode,
    Mimmering smote off Ravnlil's head.

21. 'Ten barrels of the red, red gold
    I offer thee, for thou won her fair.'

22. 'Ay, sure, I have won and taken her,
    But shame on him that sells her away.'

23. Mimmering and Gunde rode from the hall;
    Henrik stood at the gate, he wrung his hands.

M

DgF x, pp. 5–6. Taken down in 1879 or 1880 by Maren Hansen of Rands, from the recitation of Maren Kristjans of Gaarslev, Vejle County.

1. Gunne hun boede nede ved Ro,
   og hende kom Bejlere til og fraa.
      Nede ved Ro,
      og hende kom Bejlere til og fraa.
      Og de bad Gunne.

2. Og der kom Bejlere af Øster:
   de rige Mænd og Fyrster.
   Og der kom Bejlere af Norden:
   de rige Mænd og Storden.

3. Og der kom Bejlere af Vester:
   de rige Mænd og Præster.
   Og der kom Bejlere af Sønder:
   de rige Mænd og Bønder.

4. Hr. Henrik bad Drengen sadle sin Hest:
   'I Aften vil a Fru Gunne gæst'.'
      Sadle sin Hest:
      'I Aften vil a Fru Gunne gæst'.'
      Og det sagde Henrik.

5. Ja, Henrik kom ridend' i Gaard,
   ude stod Fru Gunn' med udslagen Haar.
      Ridend' i Gaard, etc.

6. 'Og hør du, Gunnelil favr og fin,
   og vil du nu vær' Allerkæresten min?'

7. Ja, Henrik han skuld' te Lejren faar',
   Ravnlil skuld' bliv' hjem' aa ta' Gunne vaar'.

8. Ja, Ravnlil han klæder sit Hoved i Skind,
   saa gik han ad Loftet til Fru Gunnelil ind.

9. 'Og hør du, Gunnelil favr og fin,
   og vil du nu gør' Viljen min?

10. Og vil du ej gøre Viljen min,
    saa stor en Løgn sætter jeg paa dig.'

11. 'Ja lyv, og lyv te du faar Skam,
    Rett' og Sand' go val fram.'

M

(*Translation*)

1. Gunne she dwelt down at Ro;
   Her came suitors to and fro.

2. Suitors came from the east,
   The rich men and the princes.
   Suitors came from the north,
   The rich men and the great (?).

3. Suitors came from the west,
   The rich men and the priests.
   Suitors came from the south,
   The rich men and the yeomen.

4. Sir Henrik bade the boy saddle his steed:
   'To-night will I visit Lady Gunne.'

5. Henrik came riding to the hall;
   At the gate stood Lady Gunne with waving hair.

6. 'Harken, Gunnelil fair and fine,
   Wilt thou be my dearest love?'

7. Henrik must go to the battle-camp,
   Ravnlil must stay and guard Gunne.

8. Ravnlil wraps his head in fur,
   Goes to Lady Gunnelil's bower aloft.

9. 'Harken, Gunnelil fair and fine,
   And wilt thou grant my will?

10. 'If thou wilt not grant my will,
    So falsely shall I lie of thee.'

11. 'Lie and lie till thou art shamed;
    Right and truth shall yet prevail.'

12. Ravnlil spaserede paa hviden Sand,
    da kom Hr. Henrik der i Land.

13. 'Hvordan lever Folkene hjemme,
    hvordan lever Gunne, min Hjertenskær?'

14. 'Hun spared sig ikke for Præster,
    langt mindre for Munkegæster.'

15. Ja, Henrik han kom ridend' i Gaard,
    ud' stod Fru Gunne med udslagen Haar.

16. 'Ja, velkommen, Henrik, hjem til mig,
    hvordan har du lidt paa Rejsen din?'

17. 'Ja, vel har jeg lidt paa Rejsen min,
    hvordan har du lidt med Munkedreng' din'?'

18. Han tog hende i hendes favre Haar,
    han slog hende mod sorten Jord.

19. Ja, Gunne slog over sig Kaaben blaa,
    ad Kæmpehus saa lod hun staa.

20. 'Og er her nogen herinde,
    som tør stride for en Kvinde?'

21. Ja, alle ti stille, ved Bordet sad,
    saanær lille Immerik, nederst ved Bordet sad.

22. 'Jeg tjente hendes Fader i elleve Aar,
    men aldrig saa jeg hendes bare Fod.

23. Ja, jeg skal Dysten rid' for dig,
    saalæng' der er varmt Blod i mig.'

24. Ja, Immerik og Ravnlil skuld' Dysten rid',
    og Gunne og Henrik skuld' derpaa se.

25. Den første Dyst, de sammen red,
    Immeriks Hest i Knæ nedskred.

26. 'Og saa du det, min udydige Kvinde,
    min Kæmpe kan den Sejr vinde.'

27. Den anden Dyst, de sammen red,
    Ravnlils Hoved af Hesten skred.

28. 'Og saa du det, min udydige Mand,
    min Kæmpe han den Sejr vandt.'

12. Ravnlil walks on the white sand,
    Then came Sir Henrik to land.

13. 'How fare the folk at home,
    How fares Gunne, my dear heart?'

14. 'She spares not herself for the priests,
    Still less for the monks, her guests.'

15. Henrik came riding to his hall;
    At the gate stood Lady Gunne with waving hair.

16. 'Welcome, Henrik, home to me!
    How hast thou fared on thy journey?'

17. 'Well have I fared on my journey.
    How hast thou fared with thy swains, the monks?'

18. He caught her by her fair hair,
    Flung her down on the black earth.

19. Gunne donned her cloak so blue,
    To the knights' hall she bent her course.

20. 'Is there any one in the hall
    Dares to fight for a woman?'

21. All were silent at the board,
    Save little Immerik, sat at the end.

22. 'I served her father for eleven years,
    But never did I see her bare foot.

23. 'I will fight the battle for thee,
    While the blood runs warm in me.'

24. Immerik and Ravnlil must to the battle,
    And Gunne and Henrik must look thereon.

25. At the first joust that they rode
    Immerik's steed fell on its knee.

26. 'Sawest thou that, my unchaste woman!
    My champion can win the day.'

27. At the second joust that they rode
    Ravnlil's head fell from the horse.

28. 'Sawest thou that, my unchaste man!
    My champion has won the day.'

29. Immerik han af Kredsen red,
    Henrik han bagefter sine Hænder vred.

30. 'Syv Tønder af det rødeste Guld,
    det giver jeg dig for Gunne huld.'

31. 'Nu har jeg hende baade vunden og faaet,
    gid de faa Skam, som sælge hende bort.'

N

DgF x, p. 6. Taken down in 1866 by E. T. Kristensen from the recitation of Jes Smidt of Københoved, Haderslev County, South Jutland. First printed in E. T. Kristensen's *Gamle Viser i Folkemunde* (Copenhagen, 1891).

1. Fru Gunder hun sidder o Hæjler,
   hun haaj di manne Bæjler.
   De haaj Fru Gunder,
   Hæjler,
   hun haaj di manne Bæjler.

2. Hun haaj dem aa æ Østen,
   aa hun haaj dem aa æ Væsten.
   De haaj Fru Gunder, etc.

3. . . . han skuld' a Landet far',
   Fru Gunder skuld' blyw hjemm' aa ta' Landet var'.
   De skuld' han . . .,
   aa Landet far',
   Fru Gunder skuld' blyw hjemm' aa ta' Landet var'.

O

DgF x, p. 6. Taken down in 1909 by H. Nutzhorn, Folk High School teacher, from the recitation of Jens Arnum, bookseller in Askov, who had learnt it from his father, Lavst Arnum, born in 1835 at Landeby, near Løgumkloster, South Jutland.

Hans Hendrik vild' af Landet far',
og Ravnhild skuld' vær hjem' aa ta Landet i Var'.
    Det vild' Hans Hendrik,
    af Landet far',
    og Ravnhild skuld' vær' hjemm' aa ta Landet i Var'.

29. Immerik rode from the lists;
    Henrik stood behind, he wrung his hands.

30. 'Seven barrels of the red, red gold,
    I offer thee for Gunne fair.'

31. 'Now I have won and taken her,
    Shame be on them that sell her away.'

N

(Translation)

1. Lady Gunder sits at Hæjler;
   She had so many suitors.

2. She had them from the east,
   And she had them from the west.

3. . . . he must fare abroad,
   Lady Gunder must stay and guard the land.

O

(Translation)

Hans Hendrik would fare abroad,
And Ravnhild must stay and guard the land.

III. FAROESE VERSIONS

D

DgF i, pp. 209–10, and x, p. 4. Taken down in 1848 by V. U. Hammers-haimb from the recitation of Bílla Sofía of Famjen, Suðuroy. Some lines (printed in italics) are in Danish. A few emendations and corrections have been made; they are noted in *DgF* i, p. 213.

1. Tíðrikur reið sàr undir oy,
   — *Roser, ville I mig love?*—
   festi hàna Gunhild, væna moy.
   — *Mens de andre sove,*
   de legte alt om en Aften.

2. Hann festi hàna moy og førði hàna heim,
   kongur og vor erkibisp riðu við teim.

3. Tíðrikur skuldi í leiðinga fàra,
   Roysningur skuldi eftir vera.

4. '*Du vogte vel Riger, du vogte vel Land,*
   allerbedst Gunhild, den Liljevand.

5. *Du vogte vel Guldet, der ligger i Skriin,*
   allerbedst Gunhild, allerkjæreste min.'

6. *Roysningur svøber sit Hoved i Skind,*
   saa gaaer han i Loft for Gunhild ind.

7. 'Hoyrtú, Gunhild væna,
   viltú vera mín kæra?'

8. 'Eg verði ikki títt slegfredsvív:
   Tíðriks kongs ektavív.'

9. 'Viltú ikki trúlovast màr,
   so stóru lign skàl eg ljúgva á teg.'

10. 'Gud làti teg so ljúgva á meg,
    at sannur Gud skàl vitna teg.'

11. Tíðrikur stígur àv sín snekkju for land,
    Roysningur rennir sín gangara á sand.

12. 'Hoyrtú, Roysningur undir oy:
    og hvussu livir folkið undir oy?

13. Og hvussu livir folkið undir oy?
    og hvussu livir Gunhild, væna moy?

D

(*Translation*)

1. Tiðrik he did ride abroad,
   Wedded Gunhild, a maiden fair.

2. He wedded her and carried her home;
   The King and our archbishop rode in the train.

3. Tiðrik must go to the wars,
   Roysning must bide behind.

4. 'Ward thou well the realms, ward thou well the land,
   Best of all Gunhild, the lily-wand.

5. 'Ward thou well the gold, stored in the coffer,
   Best of all Gunhild, my dearest love.'

6. Roysning enfolds his head in fur,
   Goes to Gunhild's bower aloft.

7. 'Harken now, fair Gunhild,
   Wilt thou be my sweetheart?'

8. 'I will not be thy leman,
   King Tiðrik's wedded wife.'

9. 'If thou wilt not be my love,
   So falsely shall I lie of thee.'

10. 'God let thee so belie me
    That He shall witness (against?) thee.

11. Tiðrik steps from his ship to the land,
    Roysning rides his steed on the sand.

12. 'Harken, Roysning, to what I say:
    How fare the folk in my land?

13. 'How fare the folk in my land,
    And how fares Gunhild, the maiden fair?

14. Hvussu livir folk á Spírum?
    og hvussu livir Gunhild dýra?'

15. 'Vàl livir folkið undir oy,
    illa stolts Gunhild, væna moy.

16. Vàl livir folk á Spírum,
    illa stolts Gunhild dýra.

17. Eg tàð við mínum eygum sá,
    at erkibispur hjá henni lá.'

18. 'Hoyrtú, Roysningur undir oy:
    tú být grá gangar for gillina floy.'

19. Tíðrikur reið og rendi,
    sín góða gangara spreingdi.

20. Tíðrikur heim í gàrðin fór,
    úti stolts Gunhild firi honum stóð.

21. 'Tàð síggi eg á mín herras reið:
    antin er hann drukkin ella vreið.

22. Antin er hann drukkin ella vreið,
    ella hevir hann hitt so harða reið.'

23. Hann tekur í Gunhilds ljósu hand
    og leiðir hàna so í loftið fram.

24. Hann sló hàna eitt, hann sló hàna tvá,
    eingin stolts Gunhild hjálpa má.

25. Á golvinum gingu börnini tvey,
    Tíðrikur kongur átti tey.

26. 'Mín kæri fàðir, tú slá hàna ei so,
    men làt hàna Gunhild bera stál.'

27. *Gunhild gaaer ned til den Strand,*
    mødte hende liden Mimmering Tand.

28. *Mødte hende liden Mimmering Tand,*
    han var den eneste christen Mand.

29. '*Jeg tjente din Fader i otte Aar,*
    men ikke saae jeg dig saa jammerlig gaae.'

30. Gunhild gongur á onnur lond,
    tá sprungu àv henni sterka jarnbond.

14. 'How fare the folk at Spire,
    And how fares Gunhild, the dear one?'

15. 'Well fare the folk in thy land,
    Ill fares proud Gunhild, the maiden fair.

16. 'Well fare the folk at Spire,
    Ill fares proud Gunhild, the dear one.

17. 'I saw with mine own eyes,
    The archbishop lay with her.'

18. 'Harken, Roysning, to what I say:
    Change thy grey steed for my golden galley.'

19. Tiðrik rode amain,
    His good horse made he gallop.

20. Tiðrik sped to his hall;
    At the gate stood proud Gunhild to greet him.

21. 'I can see from my lord's riding:
    Either he is drunk or angry.

22. 'Either he is drunk or angry,
    Or else he has had so hard a ride.'

23. He takes Gunhild by the hand
    And leads her forth into the loft.

24. He struck her once, he struck her twice;
    No man can bring proud Gunhild help.

25. Forth on the floor stepped children two;
    Heirs they were to Tiðrik the King.

26. 'My dear father, beat her not so,
    But let Gunhild carry steel.'

27. Gunhild goes down to the strand;
    She met little Mimmering Tand.

28. She met little Mimmering Tand,
    He was the only Christian man.

29. 'I served thy father for eight years,
    But I ne'er saw thee wander so full of woe.'

30. Gunhild goes to foreign lands;
    Then fell from her strong iron bands.

31. Gunhild gár í kirkju inn,
    tá sprungu àv henni jarnbond fimm.

32. Tàð vàr um ein jóladàg,
    Gunhild góðar gàvur gàv.

33. Summum gàv hon reyðargull,
    summum gàv hon skálir full.

34. Men Roysningi gàv hon tan reyða ring,
    hann vàr allur við gull umkring.

35. Hann vàr allur við gull umkring,
    — *Roser, ville I mig love?*—
    hann voldi, hansara hjarta mátti springa.
    — *Mens de andre sove,*
    de legte alt om en Aften.

E

DgF i, pp. 210–11, and x, p. 4. Recorded by J. H. Schrøter, rector of
Suðuroy in the early nineteenth century, in two slightly different forms.
Variant readings are noted in *DgF* x.

1. Tíðrikur reið sàr undir oy,
   — Dansar I væl, mítt skönna unga lív —
   festi stolt Gunild, væna moy.
   — So mátti hon vorda mín.

2. Tíðrikur skuldi í leiðinga fàra,
   heima skuldi Roysning tàka londini vàra.

3. 'Tú vokta væl ríki, tú vokta væl land,
   allarmest Gunild, tà liljuvand.'

4. Tíðrikur dró í leiðinga hen,
   Roysningur hann vàr heima ígen.

5. 'Hoyr I, stolt Gunild undir oy,
   vila I vera mín væna moy?'

6. 'Eg verði ei títt skøkjulív,
   eg eri kong Tíðriks ektavív.'

7. 'Vil I ikki lovast meg,
   stóra lign skàl eg ljúgva pá teg.'

8. 'Gud gevi teg so ljúgva,
   til tíni eygum fljúgva.

31. Gunhild wends into a church;
     Then fell from her iron bands five.

32. It was on a Yule Day,
     Gunhild she gave goodly gifts.

33. To some she gave the gold so red,
     To others she gave goblets full.

34. But to Roysning she gave the red ring,
     It was made with gold about.

35. It was made with gold about;
     It caused his heart to break.

E

(*Translation*)

1. Tiðrik he did ride abroad,
    Wedded proud Gunild, a maiden fair.

2. Tiðrik must go to the wars,
    Roysning must stay and guard the land.

3. 'Ward thou well the realm, ward thou well the land,
    Best of all Gunild, the lily-wand.'

4. Tiðrik fared forth to the wars,
    Roysning bided at home.

5. 'Harken, proud Gunild, to what I say:
    Will ye be mine own fair love?'

6. 'I will not be thy paramour;
    I am King Tiðrik's wedded wife.'

7. 'If ye will not love me,
    So falsely shall I lie of thee.'

8. 'God grant thee so to lie
    Till thine eyes fly out.

9. Eg hirði ei, tú lýgur um meg,
   sannur Gud skàl løna teg.

10. Ljúgv og ljúgv, tó tú fært skamm,
    enn er Kristus mætari mann.'

11. Roysningur gár á sandi,
    Tíðrikur stýrir snekkju til landi.

12. 'Hoyr I, Roysningur undir oy:
    hvussu livir stolt Gunild, væna moy?'

13. 'Eg tàð við mínum eygum sá:
    biskups bróðir hos henni lá.

14. Ikki hann aleina,
    men allir hansara sveinar.'

15. 'Hoyr I, Roysning undir oy,
    tú byt [sic] grá gangar for gillini floy.'

16. Tíðrikur reið og rendi,
    so snart sum eldurin brendi.

17. Tíðrikur heim í gàrðin fór,
    úti stolt Gunild firi honum stóð.

18. 'Tàð síggi eg á mín herras reið,
    antin er hann drukkin, ella er han vreið.'

19. Hann tekur í Gunildu ljósu hand,
    leiðir hàna so í loftið fram.

20. Hann slær hàna í dàgar og dàgar tvá,
    eingin íð stolt Gunild hjálpa má.

21. Eingin torði tàla, uttan börnini tvey,
    og Tíðrikur kongur átti tey.

22. 'Mín kæri fàðir, slá ikki so,
    tú làt hàna Gunildu bera stál.

23. Tú làt hàna Gunild bera stál,
    tí henni bítur eingin eldur á.'

24. Gunild gengur eftir streti,
    allt við so jammerliga leti.

25. Hàr møtti henni Mimmaring Tann,
    hann vàr tann minsti kristin mann.

9. 'I reck not though thou lie of me;
   God shall give thee due reward.

10. 'Lie and lie till thou art shamed,
    Yet is Christ a greater man.'

11. Roysning walks on the sand,
    Tiðrik steers his ship to land.

12. 'Harken, Roysning, to what I say:
    How does proud Gunild, the maiden fair?'

13. 'I saw with mine own eyes,
    The bishop's brother lay with her.

14. 'And not he alone,
    But his merry men all.'

15. 'Harken, Roysning, to what I say:
    Change thy grey steed for my golden galley.'

16. Tiðrik rode amain,
    Swift as wild-fire spreads.

17. Tiðrik sped to his hall;
    At the gate stood proud Gunild to greet him.

18. 'I can see from my lord's riding:
    Either he is drunk or he is angry.'

19. He takes Gunild by the hand,
    Leads her forth into the loft.

20. He beats her for days, he beats her for two;
    No man can bring proud Gunild help.

21. No man durst speak save children two,
    And heirs they were to Tiðrik the King.

22. 'My dear father, beat her not so;
    Let thou Gunild carry steel.

23. 'Let thou Gunild carry steel,
    For her no fire will harm.'

24. Gunild walks in the street
    Moaning so woefully.

25. There she met Mimmaring Tann,
    He was the smallest Christian man.

26. 'Eg tanti tínum fàðir í átti ár,
     aldrig eg teg so jammerliga sá.'

27. Hann førdi hàna àv heiðið land,
     àv henni sprungu jarnband.

28. Gunild gár sàr í kirkju inn,
     àv henni sprungu jarnbond fimm.

29. Gunild gár sàr á kirkjugolv,
     àv henni sprungu jarnbond tolv.

30. Tàð vàr um ein jóladàg,
     Gunild góðar gàvur gàv.

31. Summum gàv hon spunnið gull,
     summum gàv hon skálir full.

32. Roysningi gàv hon reyðan ring,
     hann vàr allur við gulli kring.

33. Hann vàr allur við gulli kring,
     — Dansar I væl, mítt skønna unga lív —
     voldi tàð, hennar hjarta mundi springa.
     — So mátti hon vorda mín.

IV. ICELANDIC VERSION

F

DgF i, pp. 211–12. From a seventeenth-century manuscript in the Royal Library, Copenhagen. Variant readings from other manuscripts are noted in *DgF* i, p. 213.

1. Það var einn so blíðan dag,
    hún Gunnhildr öllum gjafir gaf.
    Sumum gaf hún malið gull,
    sumum gaf hún kerin full.
    Vel vilda eg við veröldina skilja.

2. Malið gull,
    sumum gaf hún kerin full.
    Rögnvaldi gaf hún rauðan skjöld,
    hann var ofinn með gull margföld.

3. 'Heyrðu það, Gunnhildr væna,
    þú skalt vera mín kvæna.

26. 'I served thy father for eight years;
    Ne'er did I see thee so full of woe.'

27. He led her out of heathen land;
    From her fell iron bands.

28. Gunild wends her into a church;
    From her fell iron bands five.

29. Gunild wends her up the aisle;
    From her fell iron bands twelve.

30. It was on a Yule Day,
    Gunild she gave goodly gifts.

31. To some she gave the twisted gold,
    To others she gave goblets full.

32. To Roysning she gave a red ring,
    It was made with gold about.

33. It was made with gold about;
    It caused her [*sic*] heart to break.

F

(*Translation*)

1. It fell upon a merry day,
   Gunhild she gave gifts to all.
   To some she gave the gold so fine,
   To others she gave goblets full.

2. To Rögnvald she gave a red shield,
   The top was decked with plenteous gold.

3. 'Harken now, fair Gunhild,
   Thou shalt be my sweetheart.

4. Eina nótt eða allar tvær,
   þó ekki viljir þú leingr enn þær.'

5. 'Hversu má það verða
   af oss hèr á jörðu.

6. Að eg sè þín frillan fríð,
   Þiðriks kóngsins eigið víf.'

7. 'So skal eg á þig ljúga,
   að hver mann skal því trúa.'

8. 'Hirði eg ei þótt þú ljúgir,
   so augu þín út fljúgi.'

9. Rögnvaldr stóð á sandi,
   þar Þiðrik sigldi að landi.

10. 'Heyrðu það, Rögnvaldr, bróðir minn:
    hversu má fólk í rikjum min?'

11. 'Vel má fólk i [sic] Spýru,
    en illa má Gunnhildr dýra.

12. Hún hefir látið lokka sig,
    haldið illa trú við þig.

13. Eg með mínum augum sá:
    erkibiskup hjá henni lá.

14. Það sá eg í annað sinn:
    hjá henni láu riddarar fimm.'

15. Þiðrik stè á hvítan hest,
    allra manna reið han mest.

16. Hann kom þá til Spýru,
    er Gunnhildr lá í hvílu.

17. Hann tók í hennar gula lokk,
    dró hana fram à sængurstokk.

18. Hann barði hana daginn, hann barði hana tvo,
    þriðja fram til middags so.

19. Einginn þorði að spyrja
    Þiðrik kónginn dýra.

20. Utan hans ýngstu börnin tvau,
    Þiðrik, föður sinn, spurðu þau.

4. 'A single night or two,
   Though more thou may not grant.'

5. 'How may that befall
   To us here on earth,

6. 'That I should be thy leman,
   Þiðrik the king's own wife.'

7. 'Then will I so belie thee
   That every man shall trow it.'

8. 'I reck not though thou lie
   Till thine eyes fly out.'

9. Rögnvald stood on the sand,
   As Þiðrik sailed to land.

10. 'Harken, Rögnvald, my brother,
    How fare the folk in my land?'

11. 'Well fare the folk at Spire,
    But ill fares Gunhild, the dear one.

12. 'She has done amiss,
    Kept ill faith with thee.

13. 'I saw with mine own eyes,
    The archbishop lay with her.

14. 'I saw another time,
    Five knights lay with her.'

15. Þiðrik mounted his white steed,
    Of all men rode he swiftest.

16. He came then to Spire,
    Where Gunhild lay at rest.

17. He caught her by her yellow lock,
    Pulled her over the bedpost.

18. He beat her for one day, he beat her for two,
    Till midday on the third.

19. No man durst to plead
    With King Þiðrik, the gentle.

20. Save only his youngest children two,
    They pleaded with Þiðrik, their father.

21. 'Heyrðu það, Þiðrik, faðir minn:
    hvað hefir hún Gunnhildr gjört til þín?'

22. 'Hún hefir látið lokka sig,
    haldið illa trú við mig.'

23. 'Láttu hana bera járn,
    láttu hana troða stál.'

24. Níu sinnum bar hún járn,
    tíu sinnum trað hún stál.

25. Þegar hún kom á önnur lönd,
    af henni stukku öll járnbönd.

26. Rögnvaldr varð að hundi,
    en Gunnhildr varð að sprundi.

27. Rögnvaldr ofan til vítis sè,
    en Gunnhildr upp til himna stè.

28. Til vítis sè,
    en Gunnhildr upp til himna stè.
    Vendi eg mínu kvæði í kross,
    sjalfur Guð han veri með oss.
        Vel vilda eg við veröldina skilja.

21. 'Harken, Þiðrik, my father,
    What has Gunhild done to thee?'

22. 'She has done amiss,
    Kept ill faith with me.'

23. 'Let her carry iron,
    Let her walk on steel.'

24. Nine times she carried iron,
    Ten times she walked on steel.

25. Soon as she came to foreign lands,
    From her fell all iron bands.

26. Rögnvald waxed a dog,
    But Gunhild waxed a woman.

27. Rögnvald sank to his doom,
    But Gunhild rose up to heaven.

28. I end my song with the sign of the cross:
    May God Himself be with us.

V. NORWEGIAN VERSION

(Translation only)

P

Hans Strøm, 'Anmærkninger til Søndmørs Beskrivelse' [= Notes for a
Topography of Søndmør (district of Norway)]. *Kongelige Norske Viden-
skabers Selskabs Skrifter*, New Ser., vol. i (Copenhagen, 1784), pp. 167–8.
The passage is quoted by Grundtvig, *DgF* ii, pp. 644–5.

Rundøe . . . In the matter of past events on this island I know not
what credence can be given to that which is related in the so-called
Runda Ballad, which for a long time I sought in vain, until at length
I contrived to have it written down from the recitation of divers old
people, who still remember (albeit imperfectly) how to sing it. In
reality, it is a popular ballad, which recounts an event alleged to have
occurred on this island in the olden days, and all the verses of which
end with the burden *In* or *on Runda*. It should be remarked that this
is still the pronunciation used by the peasants when talking of this
island: they call it *Runda*, not *Rundøe*. The story is principally this,

that a certain woman, whose name was *Lady* [Fru] *Gunhild*, stepped with a golden crown on her head into the knights' hall and demanded of the knights that were there assembled whether they durst fight for a woman against a certain grim champion named *big* [store] *Ronnegaar*. Of the knights there present *Iselgrim*, *Thore-Kar* with his hammer, and *Hercules Grey* [Graa], are mentioned by name; but as they all remained silent and durst not answer a word, one *Mimmer-Tand* offered to fight with Ronnegaar, notwithstanding he was the smallest and hence known as *the smallest Christian man on Runda* ['den mindste kristne Mand paa Runda']. Lady Gunhild, to be sure, despised him for his low stature and cast a golden comb in his hair, saying he had better stay at home and tend his sheep; but he, losing no time, ran to the stable, saddled his horse and rode with Ronnegaar to the *hill-side* [liede], where they fought for the space of three days, until at length Ronnegaar was slain; whereupon Mimmer-Tand cut off his head, tied it to his saddle-bow, and rode thus in triumph back to the hall. Finally we hear of *Lady Gunhild at Dire* (this Dire appears to have been the name of the hall at which she lived), item, of the *wedding at Spire*; all of which I pass over as incomprehensible. Let it merely be observed, in conclusion, that the ballad is clearly perceived to be compounded of P. Syv's *Ballads* [Kæmpe-Viser], in particular Nos. 7, 8, and 18, about *Lady Grimild* and *Mimmering Tand*, and thus to be but fables made out of fables, albeit this or that detail may have had some historical foundation.

BIBLIOGRAPHY
LIST OF THE PRINCIPAL BOOKS AND PAPERS CITED

Note: The letters þ and ð are classed as *th*, ø and ö as *oe*, æ and ä as *ae*, and ü as *ue*.

AARNE, A., and THOMPSON, S., *Types of the Folk-Tale*. FF Communications, No. 74. Helsinki, 1928.

ADALBERT, *Vita Heinrici Imperatoris*. Ed. G. H. Pertz, Mon. Germ. Hist., Scriptores, vol. iv (1841).

Additamentum, Vitæ Sancti Heinrici. Ed. G. H. Pertz, Mon. Germ. Hist., Scriptores, vol. iv (1841).

AIMOINUS, *Historia Francorum*. Migne, vol. cxxxix.

ALBERIC OF TROIS-FONTAINES (Trium Fontium), *Chronicon*. Ed. P. Scheffer-Boichorst, Mon. Germ. Hist., Scriptores, vol. xxiii (1874).

AMOURS, F. J. *See* HUCHOWN.

Annales Palidenses. Ed. G. H. Pertz, Mon. Germ. Hist., Scriptores, vol. xvi (1859).

ANSTRUTHER, R. *See* RALPH NIGER.

ARNOLD, T. *See* HENRY OF HUNTINGDON.

ARWIDSSON, A. I. (ed.), *Svenska Fornsånger*. 3 vols. Stockholm, 1834–42.

BABINGTON, C. *See* HIGDEN, RANULPH.

BAKER, A. T., 'Nouveaux fragments de la chanson de la Reine Sibile'. *Romania*, vol. xliv (1915–17).

BARTSCH, K., *Über Karlmeinet*. Nuremberg, 1861.

BAUMGARTNER, W., 'Susanna'. *Archiv für Religionswissenschaft*, vol. xxiv (1926). See also vol. xxvii (1929), pp. 187–8.

BEAUJEU. *See* RENAUD DE BEAUJEU.

BECHSTEIN, R. *See* EBERNAND OF ERFURT.

BENSE, J. F., *Anglo-Dutch Relations*. Oxford and The Hague, 1925.

—— *A Dictionary of the Low Dutch Element in the English Vocabulary*. Oxford, 1926–38.

BERNHEIM, E., 'Die sagenhafte sächsische Kaiserchronik aus dem 12. Jahrhundert'. *NAGG*, vol. xx (1894).

BERTELSEN, H. See *Piðriks Saga af Bern*.

BIRCH-HIRSCHFELD, A. *See* JUAN MANUEL, DON.

BJÖRKMAN, E., *Nordische Personennamen in England*. Halle, 1910.

BLANCHARD-DEMOUGE, PAULA. *See* PÉREZ DE HITA, G.

BLÖTE, J. F. D., 'Das Aufkommen der Sage von Brabon Silvius, dem brabantischen Schwanritter'. *Verhandelingen der koninklijke Akademie van Wetenschappen te Amsterdam, Afdeeling Letterkunde*, New Ser., pt. v, No. 4 (1904).

BLÖTE, J. F. D., 'Der clevische Schwanritter'. *ZfdA*, vol. xlii (1898).
—— 'Der historische Schwanritter'. *ZfrPh*, vols. xxi (1897) and xxv (1901).
—— 'Der zweite Teil der Schwanrittersage'. *ZfdA*, vol. xxxviii (1894).
—— 'Die Sage vom Schwanritter in der Brogner Chronik'. *ZfdA*, vol. xliv (1900).

BOER, R. C., *Die Sagen von Ermanarich und Dietrich von Bern*. Halle, 1910.
—— See also *Edda*.

BOLTE, J., and POLÍVKA, G., *Anmerkungen zu den Kinder- und Hausmärchen der Brüder Grimm*. 5 vols. Leipzig, 1913–32.
—— *See also* WICKRAM, G.

BONILLA Y SAN MARTÍN, A. (ed.), *Libros de Caballerías*, pt. i. Madrid, 1907.

BOUQUET, M. See *Chroniques de St. Denis*.

BRADY, CAROLINE, *The Legends of Ermanaric*. University of California Press, 1943.

BRANDT, C. J. (ed.), *Romantisk Digtning fra Middelalderen*. 3 vols. Copenhagen, 1869–77.

BRESSLAU, H., 'Die Chroniken des Frutolf von Bamberg und des Ekkehard von Aura'. *NAGG*, vol. xxi (1896).
—— *Jahrbücher des deutschen Reichs unter Heinrich II*, vol. iii. Leipzig, 1875.
—— *Jahrbücher des deutschen Reichs unter Konrad II*, vol. ii. Leipzig, 1884.

BRØNDUM-NIELSEN, J., *Gammeldansk Grammatik*, vol. i (2nd ed.), Copenhagen, 1950; vol. ii (1st ed.), ibid., 1932.

BRUCE, J. D. See *Mort Artu*.

BRYANT, F. E., *A History of English Balladry*. Boston, 1913.

BUCHON, J. A. C. (ed.), *Chroniques Étrangères relatives aux Expéditions Françaises pendant le 13ᵉ Siècle*. Paris, 1840.

BUFFUM, D. L. *See* GERBERT DE MONTREUIL.

BUGGE, A., 'Handelen mellem England og Norge'. *Historisk Tidsskrift* (published by the Norwegian Historical Society), 3rd Ser., vol. iv (1898).

BUGGE, S., *Helgedigtene i den ældre Edda*. Copenhagen, 1896.

CEDERSCHIÖLD, G. See *Erex Saga*.

CERIZIERS, RENÉ DE, *The Triumphant Lady: or, The Crowned Innocence*. Translated into English, out of the original French, by Sir William Lower, Knight. London, 1656.

CERISIERS. *See* CERIZIERS, RENÉ DE.

CHAMBERS, SIR E. K., *Arthur of Britain*. London, 1927.
—— *English Literature at the Close of the Middle Ages*. Oxford, 1945.

CHAMBERS, R. W. See *Widsith*.

CHAUVIN, V., *Bibliographie des Ouvrages Arabes*, vol. viii. Liége, 1904.

Cheuelere Assigne. Ed. H. H. Gibbs. EETS, 1868.

CHILD, F. J. (ed.), *English and Scottish Popular Ballads*. 5 vols. Boston, 1882–98.
CHRÉTIEN DE TROYES, *Erec*. Ed. W. Foerster. Halle, 1896.
—— *Yvain*. Ed. W. Foerster. Halle, 1902.
—— See also *Erex Saga*.
Chroniques de St. Denis. Ed. M. Bouquet, *Recueil des Historiens des Gaules et de la France*, vol. iii. Paris, 1741.
CLOUSTON, W. A., *Popular Tales and Fiction*. 2 vols. Edinburgh, 1887.

DAHLERUP, V., and others, *Ordbog over det danske Sprog* (in progress). Copenhagen, 1918 ff.
DICKSON, A., *Valentine and Orson, A Study in Late Medieval Romance*. New York, 1929.
—— See also *Valentine and Orson*.
DIEPERINK, G. J., *Studien zum Valentin und Namelos*. Haarlem, 1933.
Doon de la Roche. Ed. P. Meyer and G. Huet. SATF, 1921.
Doon de Mayence. Ed. A. Pey. Paris, 1859.
DÜMMLER, E., *Geschichte des ostfränkischen Reichs*, vol. ii. Berlin, 1865.
DURÁN, A. (ed.), *Romancero General*. 2 vols. Madrid, 1851.

EBERNAND OF ERFURT, *Heinrich und Kunegunde*. Ed. R. Bechstein. Leipzig, 1860.
(Die) Edda. Ed. R. C. Boer. 2 vols. Haarlem, 1922.
Edda. See also SIJMONS, B., and GERING, H.
Edward the Confessor, Lives of. See LUARD, H. R.
EIKE OF REPGOW, *Sächsische Weltchronik*. Ed. L. Weiland, Mon. Germ. Hist., Deutsche Chroniken, vol. ii (1877).
EISSFELDT, O., *Einleitung in das Alte Testament*. Tübingen, 1934.
EKKEHARD OF AURA. *See* FRUTOLF.
ELLIS, SIR HENRY, *General Introduction to Domesday Book*. 2 vols. London, 1833.
ELLIS, T. P., and LLOYD, J. See *Mabinogion*.
L'Empereris de Romme. Ed. G. Paris and U. Robert. In: *Miracles de Nostre Dame*, vol. iv. SATF, 1879.
ENTWISTLE, W. J., *European Balladry*. Oxford, 1939.
—— 'Sir Aldingar and the Date of English Ballads. *Saga-Book of the Viking Society for Northern Research*, vol. xiii, pt. ii (1948).
Erex Saga (Norse translation of Chrétien de Troyes's *Erec*). Ed. G. Cederschiöld. Copenhagen, 1880.
(The) Erl of Tolous. Ed. G. Lüdtke. Berlin, 1881.
ESPINOSA, A. M. (ed.), *Cuentos Populares Españoles*. 3 vols. Stanford University, California, 1923–6.

Florence de Rome. Ed. A. Wallensköld. 2 vols. SATF, 1907–9.
Florence of Rome. Ed. W. Viëtor and A. Knobbe. Marburg, 1899.
FLORENT, *Vita Rusticulæ sive Marciæ abbatissæ Arelatensis*. Ed. B. Krusch, Mon. Germ. Hist., Scriptores Rerum Merovingiarum, vol. iv (1902).

FÖRSTEMANN, E., *Altdeutsches Namenbuch*, vol. i, 2nd ed. Bonn, 1900.

FOERSTER, W. See CHRÉTIEN DE TROYES.

FORSSNER, T., *Continental-Germanic Personal Names in England*. Upsala, 1916.

Fredegarii et Aliorum Chronica. Ed. B. Krusch, Mon. Germ. Hist., Scriptores Rerum Merovingiarum, vol. ii (1888).

FREEMAN, E. A., *The Norman Conquest*. 6 vols. Oxford, 1870–9.

FRINGS, T., 'Der Eingang von Morant und Galie'. *Teuthonista*, vol. iii (1926–7).

FRITZ, R., *Ueber Verfasser und Quellen der altfranzösischen Estoire de Seint Aedward le Rei*. Heidelberg dissertation, 1910.

FRUTOLF, *Chronicon Universale* (formerly ascribed to Ekkehard of Aura). Ed. G. H. Pertz, Mon. Germ. Hist., Scriptores, vol. vi (1844).

GAUTIER, L., *Les Épopées françaises*. 4 vols. Paris, 1878–92.

GAUTIER DE COINCY, *De l'Empereri Qui Garda sa Chastéé par moult Temptacions*. Ed. M. Méon. In: *Nouveau Recueil de Fabliaux et contes*, vol. ii. Paris, 1823.

GAYÁNGOS, PASCUAL DE. See *Historia de Enrrique fi de Oliua* and *Gran Conquista de Ultramar*.

GERBERT DE MONTREUIL, *Le Roman de la Violette*. Ed. D. L. Buffum. SATF, 1928.

GERING, H. See SIJMONS, B., ETC.

GEROULD, G. H., *The Ballad of Tradition*. Oxford, 1932.

GOLTHER, W., 'Lohengrin'. *Romanische Forschungen*, vol. v (1890).

GRABER, G., 'Hildegard von Stein'. In: *Festschrift für Eugen Mogk*. Halle, 1924.

(*La*) *Gran Conquista de Ultramar*. Ed. Pascual de Gayángos. Madrid, 1858.

GRIMM, J., *Deutsche Sagen*. 2 vols. Berlin, 1816–18.

GRIMM, W., *Die deutsche Heldensage*. Göttingen, 1829.

GRUNDTVIG, S., OLRIK, A., and NIELSEN, H. GRÜNER, (eds.), *Danmarks gamle Folkeviser*. 11 vols. Copenhagen, 1853–1948.

GUESSARD, F. See *Macaire*.

HÄPKE, R., *Brügges Entwicklung zum mittelalterlichen Weltmarkt*. Berlin, 1908.

HAGEN, F. H. VON DER, *Gesammtabenteuer*. 3 vols. Stuttgart, 1850.

—— 'Die Schwanensage'. *Abhandlungen der königlichen Akademie der Wissenschaften zu Berlin*, 1846.

HALLIWELL, J. O. See *Sir Tryamoure*.

HAMMERSHAIMB, V. U. (ed.), *Færøsk Anthologi*. 2 vols. Copenhagen, 1891.

—— *Sjúrðar Kvæði*. Copenhagen, 1851.

HARTLAND, E. S. (ed.), *English Fairy and Folk-Tales*. London, n.d.

HAUPT, W., 'Zur niederdeutschen Dietrichsage'. *Palaestra*, vol. cxxix. Berlin, 1914.

HEINZEL, R., 'Über die ostgothische Heldensage'. *Sitzungsberichte der philologisch-historischen Classe der Kaiserlichen Akademie der Wissenschaften*, vol. cxix. Vienna, 1889.

HELINANDUS, *Chronicon*. Migne, vol. ccxii.

HEMPEL, H., *Nibelungenstudien*. Heidelberg, 1926.

HENDREN, J. W., *A Study of Ballad Rhythm*. Princeton, 1936.

HENRY OF HUNTINGDON, *Historia Anglorum*. Ed. T. Arnold. Rolls, 1879.

HENRY OF SILEGRAVE, *Chronicon*. Ed. C. Hook. Caxton Society, 1849.

HERRMANN, P., *Die dänische Geschichte des Saxo Grammaticus*, vol. ii: *Erläuterungen*. Leipzig, 1922.

HERTZ, H. See SCHONDOCH.

HIBBARD, LAURA A., 'Athelston. A Westminster Legend'. *PMLA*, vol. xxxvi (1921).

—— *Mediæval Romance in England*. New York, 1924.

HIGDEN, RANULPH, *Polychronicon*. Ed. C. Babington and J. R. Lumby. 9 vols. Rolls, 1865–86.

HILKA, A., 'Zum Crescentiastoff'. *Archiv*, vol. cxxxiii (1915).

—— *See also* JOHANNES OF HAUTE-SEILLE.

HIPPEAU, C. (ed.), *La Chanson du Chevalier au Cygne*. Paris, 1874.

Historia de Enrrique fi de Oliua. Ed. Pascual de Gayángos for the Sociedad de Bibliófilos Españoles. Madrid, 1871.

HODGART, M. J. C., *The Ballads*. London, 1950.

HOLDER, A. See SAXO GRAMMATICUS.

HOOK, C. See HENRY OF SILEGRAVE.

HORNBY, R. See KNUDSEN, G., ETC.

HUCHOWN, *The Pistill of Swete Susan*. Ed. F. J. Amours. In: *Scottish Alliterative Poems*. Scottish Text Society, 1892–7.

HUET, G., 'Sur Quelques Formes de la Légende du Chevalier au Cygne'. *Romania*, vol. xxxiv (1905).

—— See also *Doon de la Roche*.

HUSTVEDT, S. B., *Ballad Books and Ballad Men*. Harvard, 1930.

JACOBSEN, J. P., OLRIK, J., and PAULLI, R., (eds.), *Danske Folkebøger*, vol. iv. Copenhagen, 1919.

JAMES, M. R., *Descriptive Catalogue of the Manuscripts in the Library of Corpus Christi College, Cambridge*. 2 vols. Cambridge, 1912.

—— *The Drawings of Matthew Paris*. Publications of the Walpole Society, vol. xiv. Oxford, 1926.

—— *La Estoire de Seint Aedward le Rei* (facsimile). Roxburghe Club, 1920.

—— *Lists of Manuscripts formerly in Peterborough Abbey Library*. Oxford, 1926.

—— and JENKINS, C., *Descriptive Catalogue of the Manuscripts in the Library of Lambeth Palace*. 5 pts. Cambridge, 1930–2.

JAMESON, R. D., *Three Lectures on Chinese Folklore*. North China Union Language School. Peking, 1932.

JEANROY, A., *Les Origines de la poésie lyrique en France*. 3rd ed. Paris, 1925.

JENKINS, C., *The Monastic Chronicler and the Early School of St. Albans*. London, 1922. See also JAMES, M. R., and JENKINS, C.

JIRICZEK, O. L., *Deutsche Heldensagen*. Strassburg, 1898.

JØRGENSEN, ELLEN (ed.), *Annales Danici Medii Ævi*. Copenhagen, 1920.

JOHANNES OF HAUTE-SEILLE (Alta Silva), *Dolopathos*. Ed. A. Hilka, Sammlung Mittellateinischer Texte, No. 5. Heidelberg, 1913.

JÓNSSON, F., *Den oldnorske og oldislandske Litteraturs Historie*. 2nd ed. 3 vols. Copenhagen, 1920–4.

—— (ed.), *Rímnasafn*. 2 vols. Copenhagen, 1905–22.

JORDAN, L., 'Zum altfranzösischen Joufrois'. *ZfrPh*, vol. xl (1920).

—— 'Zur Entwicklung des gottesgerichtlichen Zweikampfs in Frankreich'. *ZfrPh*, vol. xxix (1905).

JORDANES, *The Gothic History of Jordanes*, translated by C. C. Mierow. Princeton, 1915.

Joufrois. Ed. W. O. Streng-Renkonen, *Annales Universitatis Aboensis*, Ser. B, vol. xii (1930). Turku, Finland.

JUAN MANUEL, DON, *El Libro de los Enxiemplos del Conde Lucanor et de Patronio*. Ed. H. Knust and A. Birch-Hirschfeld. Leipzig, 1900.

Kaiserchronik, eines Regensburger geistlichen. Ed. E. Schröder, Mon. Germ. Hist., Deutsche Chroniken, vol. i (1892).

KALISCH, E. (ed.), *'Morant und Galie nach der Cölner Handschrift'*. *Rheinische Beiträge und Hülfsbücher zur germanischen Philologie und Volkskunde*, vol. ii. Bonn and Leipzig, 1921.

KALKAR, O., *Ordbog til det ældre danske Sprog*. 5 vols. Copenhagen, 1881–1918.

KALUZA, M. See *Libeaus Desconus*.

KARL, L., 'Florence de Rome et la Vie de Deux Saints de Hongrie'. *Revue des Langues Romanes*, vol. lii (1909).

Karl Meinet. Ed. A. von Keller, *Bibliothek des Literarischen Vereins in Stuttgart*, vol. xlv (1858).

Karlamagnus Saga. Ed. C. R. Unger. Christiania, 1860.

KELLER, A. VON. See *Karl Meinet*.

KENTENICH, G., *Die Genovefalegende*. Trier, 1927.

KER, W. P., 'On the Danish Ballads', I–II. In: *Collected Essays*, vol. ii. London, 1925.

—— 'On the History of the Ballads'. *Proceedings of the British Academy*, vol. iv (1909–10).

KESSLER, L. *Der Prosaroman vom Kaiser Oktavian*. Frankfurt-am-Main dissertation, Limburg-an-der-Lahn, 1930.

KLEMMING, G. E. See *Namnlös och Valentin* and *Själens Tröst*.

KNOBBE, A. See *Florence of Rome*.

KNUDSEN, G., KRISTENSEN, M., and HORNBY, R., *Danmarks gamle Personnavne*. 3 vols. Copenhagen, 1936–48.

KNUST, H. See JUAN MANUEL, DON.

KOEHLER, R., 'Die deutschen Volksbücher von der Pfalzgräfin Genovefa und von der Herzogin Hirlanda'. *ZfdPh*, vol. v (1874).
—— 'Saint Tryphine et Hirlande'. *Revue Celtique*, vol. i (1870–2).
KRAPPE, A. H., '*Florent et Octavien*'. *Romania*, vol. lxv (1939).
—— 'The Offa-Constance Legend'. *Anglia*, vol. lxi (1937).
—— '*Valentine and Orson*'. *Modern Language Notes*, vol. xlvii (1932).
—— 'Une Version norroise de la Reine Sibille'. *Romania*, vol. lvi (1930).
KRISTENSEN, M. *See* KNUDSEN, G., ETC.
KROGMANN, W., 'Die Grundform der Schwanenrittersage'. *Niederdeutsche Zeitschrift für Volkskunde*, vol. viii (1930). *Schriften der Bremer wissenschaftlichen Gesellschaft*, Ser. E.
—— 'Die Schwanenrittersage'. *Archiv*, vol. clxxi (1937).
KRÜGER, A. G., *Die Quellen der Schwanritterdichtungen*. Gifhorn (Hanover), 1936.
KRUSCH, B. *See* FLORENT and *Fredegarii et Aliorum Chronica*.
KURZE, F. *See* REGINO.

LANDSTAD, M. B. (ed.), *Norske Folkeviser*. Christiania, 1853.
LANGLOIS, E., *Table des noms propres dans les chansons de geste*. Paris, 1904.
LARSEN, H., 'Olive and Landres'. *JEGP*, vol. xl (1941).
LARSEN, S. (ed.), *Fire danske Viser*. Copenhagen, 1923.
LE BRAZ, A. (ed.), *Cognomerus et Sainte Tryphine*. *Annales de Bretagne*, vols. 20 and 21 (1904–5, 1905–6).
—— *Sainte Tryphine et Saint Mélar*. In: 'Les Saints bretons d'après la tradition populaire'. *Annales de Bretagne*, vol. x (1894–5), pp. 54 ff.
LEACH, H. G., *Angevin Britain and Scandinavia*. Harvard Studies in Comparative Literature, vol. vi (1921).
Libeaus Desconus. Ed. M. Kaluza. Leipzig, 1890.
LIESTØL, K., *Draumkvæde. A Norwegian Visionary Poem from the Middle Ages*. Studia Norvegica, ethnologica et folkloristica, No. 3. Oslo, 1946.
—— 'Det norrøne folkeviseumrådet'. *Maal og Minne*, 1937.
—— *Scottish and Norwegian Ballads*. Studia Norvegica, ethnologica et folkloristica, No. 1. Oslo, 1946.
—— 'Dei tvo systar'. *Maal og Minne*, 1909.
—— and MOE, M., (eds.), *Norske Folkeviser fra Middelalderen*. Christiania, 1924.
—— —— *Norske Folkevisor*. 3 vols. Christiania, 1920–4.
LIND, E. H., *Norsk-Isländska Dopnamn*. Upsala, 1905–15.
LLOYD, J. *See Mabinogion*.
LOOMIS, C. GRANT, 'King Arthur and the Saints'. *Speculum*, vol. viii (1933).
LOOMIS, R. S., *Arthurian Legend and Chrétien de Troyes*. New York, 1949.
—— *Celtic Myth and Arthurian Romance*. New York, 1927.

LUARD, H. R. (ed.), *Annales Monastici*. 5 vols. Rolls, 1864–9.
—— *Lives of Edward the Confessor*. Rolls, 1858.
—— *See also* MATTHEW PARIS *and* ROGER OF WENDOVER.
LÜDTKE, G. See *(The) Erl of Tolous*.
LUMBY, J. R. *See* HIGDEN, RANULPH.
LUZEL, F. M. (ed.), *Sainte Tryphine et le Roi Arthur*. Quimparlé, Paris and Nantes, 1863.

(The) Mabinogion, translated by T. P. Ellis and J. Lloyd. 2 vols. Oxford, 1929.
Macaire. Ed. F. Guessard. Paris, 1866.
MATRAS, C. (ed.), *Svabos færøske Visehaandskrifter*. Copenhagen, 1939.
MATTHEW PARIS, *Chronica Majora*. Ed. H. R. Luard. 7 vols. Rolls, 1872–83.
—— *Historia Anglorum sive Historia Minor*. Ed. Sir F. Madden. 3 vols. Rolls, 1866–9.
MEIER, J., 'Das Tanzlied der Tänzer von Kölbigk'. *Schweizerisches Archiv für Volkskunde*, vol. xxxiii (1934).
MENÉNDEZ PIDAL, R. (ed.), *Primera Crónica General de España*. Madrid, 1906.
MENÉNDEZ Y PELAYO, M. (ed.), *Romances Viejos Castellanos*. 3 vols. Madrid, 1912–23.
MENTZ, R., *Die Träume in den altfranzösischen Karls- und Artus-Epen*. Marburg, 1888.
MÉON, M. *See* GAUTIER DE COINCY.
MEYER, P. See *Doon de la Roche*.
MIEROW, C. C. *See* JORDANES.
MIGNE, J. P. (ed). *Patrologiæ Cursus Completus*. Paris, 1844 ff.
Miracles de Nostre Dame. Ed. G. Paris and U. Robert. 8 vols. SATF, 1876–93.
(Le) Mistère du Viel Testament, vol. v. Ed. Baron James de Rothschild. SATF, 1885.
MÖLLER, W., 'Die Sage vom Schwanritter'. *Germania*, vol. i (1856).
Morant and Galia. See KALISCH, E.
Mort Artu. Ed. J. D. Bruce. Halle, 1910.
MUSSAFIA, A., 'Eine altspanische Prosadarstellung der Crescentiasage'. *Sitzungsberichte der philologisch-historischen Classe der Kaiserlichen Akademie der Wissenschaften*, vol. liii. Vienna, 1867.
—— 'Über eine italienische metrische Darstellung der Crescentiasage'. Ibid., vol. li. Vienna, 1865.

Namnlös och Valentin. Ed. G. E. Klemming. Stockholm, 1846.
—— Ed. W. Wolf. Upsala, 1934.
NIELSEN, H. GRÜNER, 'De færøske Kvadmelodiers Tonalitet i Middelalderen'. *Færoensia* (ed. C. Matras), vol. i. Copenhagen, 1945.
—— (ed.), *Danske Folkeviser*. 2 vols. Copenhagen, 1925–7.
—— *See also* GRUNDTVIG, S., ETC.

NIELSEN, O., *Olddanske Personnavne*. Copenhagen, 1883.

NIGER, RALPH. *See* RALPH NIGER.

NOREEN, A., 'Geschichte der nordischen Sprachen'. In: Paul's *Grundriss*, &c., pt. iv (1913).

NYROP, C., *Storia dell' Epopea Francese*. Turin, 1888.

Octavian (English poem). Ed. G. Sarrazin. Heilbronn, 1885.

——— (French poem). Ed. K. Vollmöller. Heilbronn, 1883.

OLRIK, A., *The Heroic Legends of Denmark*, translated by L. M. Hollander. New York, 1919.

——— 'Riboldsvisen'. *Danske Studier*, 1906.

———*See also* GRUNDTVIG, S., ETC.

OLRIK, J. *See* JACOBSEN, J. P., ETC.

PARIS, G., 'Les Danseurs maudits'. *Journal des Savants*, 1899.

——— *Histoire poétique de Charlemagne*. 2nd ed. Paris, 1905.

——— 'La Karlamagnus-Saga'. *Bibliothèque de l'École des Chartes*, 5th Ser., vol. v (1864).

——— 'Le Roman du Comte de Toulouse'. *Annales du Midi*, vol. xii (1900).

——— See also *Miracles de Nostre Dame*.

PARIS, MATTHEW. *See* MATTHEW PARIS.

PAUL, H., *Grundriss der germanischen Philologie*. 3rd ed. 18 pts. Strassburg, 1913–16; Berlin and Leipzig, 1925–43.

PAUL THE DEACON, *De Gestis Langobardorum*. Migne, vol. xcv.

PAULLI, R. *See* JACOBSEN, J. P., ETC.

PÉREZ DE HITA, G., *Guerras Civiles de Granada*, pt. i. Ed. P. Blanchard-Demouge. Madrid, 1913.

PERTZ, G. H., *See* ADALBERT, *Additamentum*, &c., *Annales Palidenses*, and FRUTOLF.

PETIT DE JULLEVILLE, L., *Les Mystères*. 2 vols. Paris, 1880.

PEY, A. See *Doon de Mayence*.

PHILIPPE DE BEAUMANOIR, *Œuvres poétiques*, vol. i. Ed. H. Suchier. SATF, 1884.

PILGER, R., 'Die Dramatisierungen der Susanna im 16. Jahrhundert'. *ZfdPh*, vol. xi (1880).

POISSON, G., 'L'Origine celtique de la légende de Lohengrin'. *Revue Celtique*, vol. xxxiv (1913).

POLÍVKA, G. *See* BOLTE, J., and POLÍVKA, G.

RAJNA, P., *Le Origini dell' Epopea Francese*. Florence, 1884.

——— See also *Reali di Francia*.

RALPH DE DICETO, *Abbreviationes Chronicorum*. Ed. W. Stubbs. Rolls, 1876.

RALPH NIGER, *Chronica*. Ed. R. Anstruther. Caxton Society, 1851.

(*I*) *Reali di Francia*. Ed. P. Rajna and G. Vandelli. 3 vols. Bologna, 1872–1900.

RECKE, E. VON DER (ed.), *Danmarks Fornviser*. 4 vols. Copenhagen, 1927–9.

REGINO, *Chronicon*. Migne, vol. cxxxii. Also ed. F. Kurze, Scriptores Rer. Germ. in Usum Scholarum, 1890.

REIFFENBERG, BARON DE (ed.), *Le Chevalier au Cygne*. Brussels, 1846.

RENART, JEAN, *Guillaume de Dole*. Ed. G. Servois. SATF, 1893.

RENAUD DE BEAUJEU, *Le Bel Inconnu*. Ed. G. P. Williams. Paris, 1929.

RICHARD OF CIRENCESTER, *Speculum Historiale*. Ed. J. E. B. Mayor. 2 vols. Rolls, 1863–9.

ROBERT, U. See *Miracles de Nostre Dame*.

ROGER OF WENDOVER, *Flores Historiarum*. Ed. H. R. Luard. 3 vols. Rolls, 1890.

ROSS, H., *Norsk Ordbog*. Christiania, 1895.

ROTHSCHILD, BARON JAMES DE. See *(Le) Mistère du Viel Testament*.

(The) Roxburghe Ballads. Ed. C. Hindley. 2 vols. London, 1873–4.

RUBIÓ, J., 'Les Versions Catalanes de la Llegenda del bon Comte de Barcelona i l'Emperadriu d'Alemanya'. *Estudis Universitaris Catalans*, vol. xvii (1932).

RUBOW, P. V. (ed.), *Anders Sørensen Vedels Folkevisebog*. Copenhagen, 1926–7.

Sainte Tryphine. See LE BRAZ, A., *and* LUZEL, F. M.

SARRAZIN, G. See *Octavian*.

SAUERLAND, E., *Ganelon und sein Geschlecht*. Marburg, 1886.

SAXO GRAMMATICUS, *Gesta Danorum*. Ed. A. Holder. Strassburg, 1886.

SCHEEL, W. *See* WICKRAM, G.

SCHEFFER-BOICHORST, P. *See* ALBERIC OF TROIS-FONTAINES.

SCHELER, A., 'Fragments uniques d'un Roman du XIIIe siècle sur la Reine Sebile'. *Bulletins de l'Académie Royale de Belgique*, 2nd Ser., vol. xxxix (1875).

SCHELUDKO, D., 'Versuch neuer Interpretation des Wolfdietrich-Stoffes'. *ZfdPh*, vol. lv (1930).

SCHLAUCH, MARGARET, *Chaucer's Constance and Accused Queens*. New York, 1927.

—— 'The Man of Law's Tale'. In: *Sources and Analogues of Chaucer's Canterbury Tales*, ed. W. F. Bryan and Germaine Dempster. University of Chicago Press, 1941.

—— 'Saints Tryphine and Hirlanda'. *Speculum*, vol. x (1935).

SCHNEIDER, H., See *Wolfdietrich*.

SCHNÜRER, G., *Die Verfasser der sogenannten Fredegar-Chronik*. Freiburg, 1900.

SCHONDOCH, *Gedichte*. Ed. H. Hertz, *Germanistische Abhandlungen*, vol. xxx. Breslau, 1908.

SCHRÖDER, E., 'Die Tänzer von Kölbigk'. *Zeitschrift für Kirchengeschichte*, vol. xvii (1896–7).

—— 'Das Tanzlied von Kölbigk'. *Nachrichten von der Gesellschaft der Wissenschaften zu Göttingen*. Philologisch-historische Klasse, 1933.

—— See also *Kaiserchronik*.

SCHÜDDEKOPF, C., 'Eine unbekannte Erzählung Wimpfelings'. *Zeitschrift für vergleichende Literaturgeschichte*, New Ser., vol. iv (1891).

SCOTT, SIR WALTER, *Minstrelsy of the Scottish Border*. Ed. T. Henderson. London, 1931.

(*Der*) *Seelen Trost*. See *Själens Tröst*.

SEELMANN, W. See *Valentin und Namelos*.

SIEFKEN, O., *Das geduldige Weib in der englischen Literatur*, I: *Der Konstanzetypus*. Leipzig dissertation, Rathenow, 1903.

SIJMONS, B., and GERING, H., *Kommentar zu den Liedern der Edda*. 2 vols. (= *Die Lieder der Edda*, vol. III. i-ii.) Halle, 1927–31.

Sir Torrent of Portyngale. Ed. E. Adam. EETS, 1887.

Sir Tryamoure. Ed. J. O. Halliwell. Percy Society, 1846.

Själens Tröst (Swedish translation of *Der Seelen Trost*). Ed. G. E. Klemming. Stockholm, 1871–3.

SMITH, WINIFRED, 'Elements of Comedy in the English and Scottish Ballads'. *Vassar Mediæval Studies*, ed. Christabel F. Fiske. Yale, 1923.

SMYSER, H. M., 'The Middle English and Old Norse Story of Olive'. *PMLA*, vol. lvi (1941).

—— 'Olive Again'. *Modern Language Notes*, vol. lxi (1946).

SÖDERWALL, K. F., *Ordbok öfver svenska Medeltids-Språket*. Lund, 1884–1918.

STEENSTRUP, J., 'De danske Folkevisers ældste Tid og Visernes Herkomst'. *Historisk Tidsskrift* (published by the Danish Historical Society), 9th Ser., vol. i (1918–20).

STEFANOVIĆ, S., 'Das angelsächsische Gedicht "Die Klage der Frau"'. *Anglia*, vol. xxxii (1909).

—— 'Die Crescentia-Florence-Sage'. *Romanistische Forschungen*, vol. xxix (1911).

—— 'Ein Beitrag zur angelsächsischen Offa-Sage.' *Anglia*, vol. xxxv (1912).

STEINBERGER, H., *Untersuchungen zur Entstehung der Sage von Hirlanda von Bretagne*. Munich dissertation, 1913.

STEINDORFF, E., *Jahrbücher des deutschen Reichs unter Heinrich III*, vol. i. Leipzig, 1874.

STRENG-RENKONEN, W. O. See *Joufrois*.

STREVE, P., *Die Octavian-Sage*. Erlangen dissertation, 1884.

SUCHIER, H. See PHILIPPE DE BEAUMANOIR.

SUHM, P. F., *Historie af Danmark*, vols. iii, vii, and viii. Copenhagen, 1787, 1800, and 1806.

Susanna. Ein oberengadinisches Drama des XVI. Jahrhunderts. Ed. J. Ulrich. Frauenfeld, 1888.

SVABO. See MATRAS, C.

TAYLOR, A., '*Edward*' *and* '*Sven i Rosengård*'. Chicago, 1931.

TEUBERT, S., *Crescentia-Studien*. Halle dissertation, 1916.

Þiðriks Saga af Bern. Ed. H. Bertelsen. 2 vols. Copenhagen, 1905–11.

THOMAS, A., 'Le Roman de Goufier de Lastours'. *Romania*, vol. xxxiv (1905).

THOMPSON, S., *Motif-Index of Folk-Literature*. FF Communications, Nos. 106-9 and 116-17. Helsinki, 1932-6.

—— See also AARNE, A., and THOMPSON, S.

THOMS, W. J. (ed.), *Early English Prose Romances*. 2nd ed. 3 vols. London, 1858.

THORÉN, I., *Studier över Själens Tröst*. Stockholm, 1942.

ÞORÓLFSSON, B. K., *Rímur fyrir 1600*. Copenhagen, 1934.

THUREN, H., *Folkesangen paa Færøerne*. Copenhagen, 1908.

TORP, A., *Nynorsk etymologisk Ordbok*. Christiania, 1919.

Tryphine. See LE BRAZ, A., *and* LUZEL, F. M.

TWYSDEN, R. (ed.), *Historiæ Anglicanæ Scriptores X*. 2 vols. London, 1652.

ULRICH, J. See *Susanna*.

UNGER, C. R. See *Karlamagnus Saga*.

Valentin und Namelos. Ed. W. Seelmann. Leipzig, 1884.

Valentine and Nameless. See *Valentin und Namelos* and *Namnlös och Valentin*.

Valentine and Orson. Ed. A. Dickson. EETS, 1937.

VANDELLI, G. See *Reali di Francia*.

VEDEL, ANDERS SØRENSEN. *See* RUBOW, P. V.

VERRIER, P., 'Bele Aiglentine et Petite Christine'. *Romania*, vol. lxiii (1937).

—— 'Den firliniede Folkevisestrofe'. *Danske Studier*, 1937.

—— 'La Plus Vieille Citation de Carole'. *Romania*, vol. lviii (1932).

—— *Le Vers Français*. 3 vols. Paris, 1931-2.

VIËTOR, W. See *Florence of Rome*.

VINCENT OF BEAUVAIS, *Speculum Historiale*. Douai, 1624.

Vitæ Sancti Heinrici Additamentum. See *Additamentum*, &c.

VOLLMÖLLER, K. See *Octavian*.

VRIES, J. DE, *Altnordische Literaturgeschichte*. 2 vols. In: Paul's *Grundriss*, &c., pts. 15-16 (1941-2).

WAITZ, G., 'Zur Kritik dänischer Geschichtsquellen'. *NAGG*, vol. xii (1887).

WALLENSKÖLD, A., 'Le Conte de la Femme Chaste Convoitée par son Beau-Frère. *Acta Societatis Scientiarum Fennicæ*, vol. xxxiv, No. 1 (1907).

—— L'Origine et l'Évolution du Conte de la Femme Chaste Convoitée par son Beau-Frère'. *Neuphilologische Mitteilungen*, vol. xiv (1912).

—— See also *Florence de Rome*.

WECKERLIN, J. B. (ed.), *Chansons Populaires du Pays de France*. 2 vols. Paris, 1903.

WEILAND, L. *See* EIKE OF REPGOW.

WELLS, E. K., *The Ballad Tree*. New York, 1950.

WELLS, J. E., *A Manual of the Writings in Middle English*. Yale, 1916.

WHARTON, H. (ed.), *Anglia Sacra*. 2 vols. London, 1691.

WICKRAM, G., *Werke*, vol. i. Ed. J. Bolte and W. Scheel, *Bibliothek des Literarischen Vereins in Stuttgart*, vol. ccxxii (1901).

Widsith. Ed. R. W. Chambers. Cambridge, 1912.

WILLIAM OF MALMESBURY, *De Gestis Regum Anglorum*. Ed. W. Stubbs. 2 vols. Rolls, 1887–9.

WILLIAMS, G. P. *See* RENAUD DE BEAUJEU.

WILSON, R. M., *Lost Literature in Old and Middle English*. Leeds Studies in English, vol. ii (1933).

WOLF, W. See *Namnlös och Valentin*.

Wolfdietrich. Ed. H. Schneider, Altdeutsche Textbibliothek, No. 28. Halle, 1931.

WRIGHT, C. E., *The Cultivation of Saga in Anglo-Saxon England*. Edinburgh, 1939.

YEARSLEY, M., *The Folklore of Fairy-Tale*. London, 1924.

ZENKER, R., *Forschungen zur Artusepik*. Halle, 1921.

INDEX

Absence of husband at war, chase, or the like, 12, 16, 37, 38, 39, 40, 47, 48, 110–11, 121, 135, 161–2.

Accusation motif, 103, 113, 115, 116, 121; *see also* Murder, accusation of.

Accusers, two, 128, 138, 139, 141, 155; three, 138, 141; four, 140.

Adalbert, 97, 98.

Adalulf, 101.

Additamentum, Vitæ Sancti Heinrici, 97.

Adelring, 12, 13, 164.

Ailred of Rievaulx, 25 n. 2.

Aimoinus the Monk, 101, 102, 103.

Alberic of Trois-Fontaines, 122 n. 3, 132 n. 2.

Albinhamad, 140.

Aldingar, *see* Rodingar and *Sir Aldingar*.

Alexander, Emperor of Constantinople, 41.

Alice, second wife of Henry I of England, 159, 162.

Annales Fuldenses, 99 n. 1.

Annales Hildesheimenses, 95 n. 3.

Annales Palidenses, 97.

Annales Ryenses, 72.

Annales Slesuicenses, 60.

Apollonius of Tyre, 120 n. 3.

Arabian Nights, 120.

Arbuthnot, family of, 11, 18.

Ardus, King of Aragon, 39.

Arles chronicle, 130, 131, 132.

Arthurian legend, 52, 140–1.

Artus, Duke of Brittany, 151.

Athelston, 34 n. 1, 35 n. 4.

Attila (Atli), 44, 47, 59, 60, 162.

Aubedo, 101 n. 1, 104 n. 1.

Aubri (Aubry), 122, 123.

Balder, 71–72.

Ballads, definition of, 2; origin of, 3–9; ballad areas, 3; relation to romance, 1, 48–50, 110–11, 120–1, 133–4, 155–8; *see also* British, French, Scandinavian ballads, &c.

Bandello, 135, 157.

Barcelona, the count of, 127, 128, 129, 131.

Barnard, Earl of Toulouse, 38.

Battle, trial by, *see* Combat, judicial.

Beatrix version of Swan Knight story, 144 n. 1, 147.

Beauvais, Vincent of, 19–20, 119, 132 n. 2.

Belch, Sir Toby, 115.

Bel Inconnu, Le, 51 n. 3.

Belyssant, 41, 42, 99 n. 4.

Bergen, 85, 86, 87.

Bermer the Giant (Rise), 50.

Bernard, Abbot of St. Malo, 152.

Bernard, Count of Barcelona, 127, 131.

Berthe au grand pied, 163 n. 1.

Berting, 50–51.

Beuter, 129, 131, 136.

Bikki, 45, 46, 47 n. 1.

Birck, Johannes, 119–20.

Biterolf, 71.

Bjarni Erlingsson, 36–37, 87.

Blanchefleur, 122; see also *Floire et Blanchefleur*.

Blendemayn, 42.

Blöte, J. F. D., 145–6.

Bovis, M. J., 130.

Brabant, Geneviève of, 125–6, 151, 152.

Brahe, Karen, *see* Karen Brahe Folio.

Brandt, C. J., 47 n. 4, 49 n. 2.

British ballads, early evidence of, 5, 7–8; relation to Scandinavian ballads, 1, 84; British versions of Gunhild ballad, 1, 10–11, 14, 15, 16, 17–18, 29–32, 51–53, 55, 89, 92, 93, 94, 108, 109–10, 116, 142, 155–8, 161, 164; texts, 167–77; see also (*The*) *Earl of Westmoreland*, *Hind Horn*, *King Estmere*, *Sir Aldingar*, and *Sir Hugh le Blond*.

Broderus, 47.

Brompton, John, *see* John Brompton.

Brothers-in-law, 119, 139, 153.

Bruges, 96, 97, 106–7.

Bugge, S., 51, 52 n. 4, 53 n. 4, 62 n. 1, 75, 80, 81.

PRINTED IN
GREAT BRITAIN
AT THE
UNIVERSITY PRESS
OXFORD
BY
CHARLES BATEY
PRINTER
TO THE
UNIVERSITY